HP

D1777906

# 999 CSI

GW 6289006 9

# 999 CSI

## BLOOD, THREATS AND FEARS

LARRY HENDERSON
with KRIS HOLLINGTON

THISTLE
PUBLISHING

Copyright © Larry Henderson & Kris Hollington 2015

First published in 2015 by:

Thistle Publishing
36 Great Smith Street
London
SW1P 3BU

www.thistlepublishing.co.uk

ISBN-13: 9781910670804

"The criminal must never know what you know,
Mr Henderson."
Prime Minister Margaret Thatcher, June 17, 1985

# NOTE TO THE READER

I t is important to ensure that the secrets and histories of some of the individuals encountered through my work (witnesses, police officers engaged in sensitive work and informers, all of whom have good reason to fear retribution) are not set out in a manner that would enable people to recognize them. To be true to both requirements, the authors have, with the exception of names that are in the public domain, protected the identities of these people by changing names and altering some background details. The reader should be left in no doubt that every case is real, however. Those cases which are a matter of public record are reported in their original detail.

# RUDE AWAKENING

"**M**R HENDERSON!"

I jolted; I'd been deeply asleep and suffered that momentary confusion that comes with not waking in one's own bed.

"Would you mind answering the question?"

Um. I was in a stuffy classroom. Late summer light fighting to get through dirty windows. Eleven men were looking at me, most smiling, enjoying my dreamy confusion. And the speaker... The speaker was Detective Sergeant Jim Murray.

"Are you with us Mr Henderson?"

It was the afternoon of Monday August 31, 1971 and my first day of six months of lectures and training at the Metropolitan Police Detective Training School in crime scene examination, the first step on my way to becoming a fully-fledged Scenes of Crime Officer (SOCO).

I was in my early twenties and had quickly become bored with my job as a research chemist, so when I spotted the Metropolitan Police job advert in the Daily Telegraph for SOCOs, I thought 'that sounds interesting'. I was one of twelve successful applicants out of the 890 who applied.

I had arrived in London at 6.30am, commuting after a weekend spent with wife Jennifer and our two Labradors in a dormer bungalow in Eaglescliffe between Stockton on Tees and Yarm. The train journey was such that I had to start the commute the previous night at 10pm.

My plan was to stay with my uncle in Twickenham during the week and travel home at weekends, until Jennifer managed to sell the bungalow and we could move to the Big Smoke. Jennifer had also chucked in her job as House Craft Adviser for the Electricity Board. She gave talks on the radio, judged cookery competitions alongside celebrities and dispensed expert advice on cooking and general household affairs.

"Perhaps I've been boring you Mr Henderson."

"No, no, well, right, er, ok."

Now I'm for it. What was the last thing we were talking about? Animal versus human blood. I squinted at the black board. Blood types. A, B, O, Cellulose. Still dazed I volunteered a hesitant "Rabbits?"

This got a roar of laughter from my classmates and, with that, Sergeant Murray declared it was time for tea.

"But not you Henderson," he declared sternly. "If you wouldn't mind staying behind."

Better tell Jennifer to hold the sale, I thought glumly, expecting to be sent packing at the close of business. But, amazingly, the sergeant gave me a chance to explain about the long commute and, as time went on and he saw how keen I was, he went easy on me on Mondays, especially after Jennifer sent me back down to London armed with bags of her finest baking for the class and our instructors.

Day two started with the arrest of one of the students. Two men, dressed in drab raincoats, walked through the door and nicked the man right before our eyes for passing cheques with no money in the bank to cover them. "Obtaining a pecuniary advantage," they said. This was followed the next day by a second student being arrested for the same offence. Grassed up by his mate, no doubt. So we were down to ten.

"Anyone else got any criminal offences they'd like to confess to?" Sergeant Murray asked. "I suggest you either own up now or go on the run."

Fortunately, the ten of us who remained were all law-abiding civilians. Although most of us came from scientific backgrounds, our group also included two special-police constables and a former Coroner's officer. I was there because I thought that life as a Scenes Of Crime Officer sounded like an interesting career with prospects.

How naive I was.

In fact, I was so naïve I was actually unpleasantly surprised when we were told we would have to go to the mortuary to view a post mortem, as the dead would crop up frequently during our careers.

The teacher in this case was the famous pathologist Professor Keith Simpson, a founder member and President of the Association of Forensic Science, who was renowned for his post-mortems on high profile murder cases, including the 1949 Acid Bath Murders committed by John George Haigh (solved thanks to Simpson's spotting of a tiny human gallstone lying among some debris) as well as that of George Cornell, shot dead by Ronnie

Kray in 1966. His achievements were many and great but as much as I appreciated the pedigree of our teacher, as I walked into Southwark Mortuary, my trepidation was only increased as the Prof began chatting about the things we would see as if he were planning to cook a meal. Folding back skin? Cutting through bone? Removing and then slicing the brain?

"We have a dead white male in his thirties, hit by a train," Professor Simpson said as we entered the mortuary and saw the body, naked, lying on a white marble slab with guttering and plugholes. The body's foot was mangled but I could see little else to signify a man-meets-train situation. I had become momentarily absorbed by my first sight of a dead body; my professional interest had kicked in but, suddenly I realized I was at the front, and now I was becoming aware of a smell. Like... well like something had died and been left lying out in the sun for a few days, mixed with hospital disinfectant and various other mysterious chemicals that made the air turn so thick I felt like I had to swallow to breathe. And then the prof picked up a circular saw, fired it up and started to cut away at the man's head, removing the top of the skull to reveal the brain and-

I woke up sitting on a bench in the Southwark sun, Sergeant Murray by my side.

"You okay Larry?"

"Yeah. Did I pass out then?"

"We managed to catch you in time, lucky you fell back and not forwards otherwise you would have landed right in-"

"Yes, yes, thank you," I said quickly.

After the ordeal was complete, the class was given the afternoon off and we ended up in the Barley Mow pub in Horseferry Road, which, ironically enough, was just opposite Westminster mortuary.

The rest of the course was a little more in line with what I was expecting. For three months we learned about forensic evidence, its retrieval as well as packaging and preserving the integrity of our exhibits. Practical demonstrations featured such oddities as cutting a safe open with a thermic lance. And just as I was thinking, 'Who robs safes these days?' we have the Great Hatton Garden Robbery of April 2015, where criminals drilled into the mother of all safes, escaping with the contents of about seventy safety deposit boxes.

We also went on field trips, including a visit to the Woolwich Arsenal, which was truly awesome in terms of showing us the power of dynamite, gelignite, and cordite (which really goes off with a bang). We were shown how to break open a safe, using condoms to insert explosives into the locking mechanisms. I still dozed off from time-to-time on Monday afternoons but everyone let me be and my compatriots let me copy their notes. An end-of-term exam (we all passed) was immediately followed by three months of Fingerprint Studies.

In 1967 Met Police Commissioner Sir John Waldron decided that using civilians trained in all aspects of crime scene examination would be a lot cheaper than using specialized police officers. Needless to say, the highly specialized Fingerprint Department, which was run by police officers and staffed by civilians, were bitterly opposed to the idea of civilian SOCOs, who could step in and take their jobs away from them. We were not welcomed with open arms.

Nonetheless, we spent the next three months learning to classify, index and identify fingerprints, as well as how to take photos using a Polaroid camera to show where finger-marks had been found at a crime scene. Mondays rose to an all-time soporific high. We dusted and dusted and dusted, and learned how chemicals could be used to bring out marks on paper and other items and all the things you couldn't fingerprint (like a house brick, for example). These days, thanks to lasers and superglues (among other scientific innovations), no surface is off limits when it comes to fingerprint examination.

We attended fake burglaries and were marked on the number of exhibits we found and how well we examined them (one had to resist the temptation to declare *everything* an exhibit to cover all bases). An old rusty car, beyond drivability, parked in the school's recreational yard served as an 'abandoned vehicle' to test our outdoor dusting skills. At the end of three months I knew my whorls from my loops and had by then, thank goodness, relocated to Surbiton in Surrey.

The next part of training was with the Forensic Laboratory Liaison Police Sergeants (known as Lab Sergeants), who dealt with serious crimes such as murder, rape and armed robbery. There were eight such sergeants with two per area of London, which was divided North, South, East and West.

The Lab Sergeants were supported by four other Lab Sergeants, who worked from the reception counter of the Forensic Science Laboratory located in Lambeth. It was the Area Lab Sergeant's role to examine the crime scene for forensic evidence, and submit the relevant exhibits for analysis or examination to the laboratory. They did not examine scenes for fingerprints, as they were not trained to do so. So, once again, they weren't very fond of us SOCOs, who were being recruited to examine all types of crime scenes and eventually act as liaison receptionists at the Laboratory.

I began my on-the-job training with shots fired during the armed robbery of a cash transit in Croydon. I crawled up and down a busy high road looking for shotgun cartridges cases and bullet fragments, with no success.

My next case was the sudden death of little old lady in bed at her home. The Lab Sergeant, chatting after the body was taken to the mortuary asked: "Did you notice anything significant at the scene?"

"No, it looked like natural causes to me."

"Exactly, her teeth were still in the glass on the bed-side table!"

That didn't seem suitably scientific to me but the body was going to go through a post mortem and, as part of my training, I was expected to attend. It was necessary that I made it through at least one PM without passing out. I spent most of it switching my gaze between the ceiling and a clipboard, writing up the 'exhibits' as they were taken: blood, urine, brain tissue, slices of liver, and stomach contents. She hadn't had much for dinner, the poor old soul.

The following day I was in the canteen at Wimbledon police station when a constable entered and told me Lab Sergeant Keith needed me to join him at a suspicious death. I looked forlornly at my un-drunk cuppa and sighed. I really was going to have to get used to looking at dead bodies and attending post mortems.

A male body was in the middle of a field, naked, his clothes strewn all around him. Keith ran through the basics of an external scene. He showed me a path to the body and said we should examine this first, that way we'd keep contamination to a minimum, allowing access to the body without destroying evidence. I was really intrigued by this case, a real puzzler. It was midwinter, so no one in their right mind would want to undress in a field. Keith had me come up with a few crack-brained theories, including sexual assault, before he finally explained the cause.

"Paradoxical undressing."

"Para-who?"

"Paradoxical undressing occurs during the final stages of hypothermia, which is exacerbated by alcohol. I can smell the booze from here."

There are a couple of theories as to why this occurs. One is cold-induced malfunction of the brain's hypothalamus, which regulates body temperature. The other is that the muscles that contract peripheral blood vessels become exhausted and relax, leading to a sudden surge of blood (and heat) to the extremities, which tricks the sufferer into thinking that they're overheating to an extraordinary degree. Of course, the removal of clothes only serves to speed up their death.

Another symptom of hypothermia is terminal burrowing, also known as hide-and-die, which is when someone hides in a closed space, such as a wardrobe or in a corner. It is most common in cases where the temperature falls at a slow rate. I've seen this a few times spread out over my career, especially among the elderly in winter who cannot afford to heat their homes, who are usually found curled up behind the settee.

It is incredibly disturbing that this can happen in the UK in the modern age. This person, who has contributed to the well-being of our country, dies alone and in distress, all for the sake of a little heat, which was right at their fingertips but just beyond their price range.

You can't but help think of your own grandparents and the first time I saw this kind of case, I called them that same night just to say 'Hullo.'

Once training was complete, the ten fledgling Scenes of Crime Officers assembled in a briefing room at New Scotland Yard, waiting nervously to find out which police stations they were going to be posted to. The postings were not permanent, but would nonetheless last about three years before we'd be 'rotated,' so we'd end up sampling the different crime flavours each part of London had to offer. Whitechapel was rife with gas meter burglaries while suburbia suffered the attention of discerning burglars who were after televisions; the West End was home to pickpockets while cat burglars prowled the streets of Knightsbridge.

I found myself at the front yet again and was the first to face this terrifying game of roulette.

"Mr. Henderson, you are posted to Alpha Lima, Royal "A" District."

The word 'royal' got my attention, so I'd been spared Leman Street in Whitechapel then? My heart soared with hope.

"Gerald Road, Belgravia. You will report on Monday to the Uniform Chief Superintendent, who will introduce you to Detective Inspector Elsdon, head of CID (Criminal Investigation Department)."

Belgravia! Home to lords, ladies, celebrities and the richest people in the land, and the smartest and most scandalous of criminals.

"You can pick up your mini-van tomorrow morning from the basement here at the Yard. You will find your equipment at Arbour Square stores in Stepney. Good luck Mr Henderson."

Someone standing just behind me muttered: "Lucky git."

I had to agree.

# PART ONE

March 1972 – April 1975
Gerald Road Police Station, Belgravia,
London SW1

Station Code "AL" Royal A District
Sub division "AH" Hyde Park.

# THE UNKNOWN BABY

The phone rang. My heart leapt. It was 10pm on a Saturday. There was only one reason why the phone would ring at that time.

"You're the on-call SOCO?"

"Yes."

"This is the duty officer from Gerald Road. There's been an incident at Victoria Coach Station and we need you to attend."

My home was in Surrey and I explained I was without a car, and it might take me a while to get to the Yard where my mini-van and forensic gear was stashed.

"No problem, I'll send a fast car. Be ready."

I barely had time to explain to Jennifer and get my coat on when a blue Rover P6 screeched to a halt outside. We were burning rubber before I'd managed to close the rear passenger door, falling into the seat.

The speed was insane but I managed to tear my eyes from the road just long enough to ask them about the case in hand.

"What's the incident?"

"A concealed birth in the ladies' toilets - the baby died."

"What! Isn't that a job for a Laboratory Liaison Sergeant?"

"Normally yes, but he's busy with a murder, so the Duty Inspector asked for you."

I'd only been on the job a couple of weeks. I wasn't ready for this. My mouth was suddenly too dry for me to ask anything else.

Sick with anxiety, I asked myself over and over: How was I going to cope with a dead baby, and possibly its mum too?

I was ejected at the Yard; the car was gone before I had time to say 'Thanks guys'.

Arriving at the coach station five minutes later in my olive-green mini-van, I found the duty officer, an inspector, and was amazed to find myself behaving like a seasoned professional.

"Is it confirmed as a dead baby?" I asked.

"Yes."

"Any sign of the mother?"

"No."

"Have all the cubicles been searched?"

"Yes."

"OK, what would you like me to do?"

"Package up the baby for the mortuary and PM (post-mortem) and examine the cubicles."

"Which police constable is exhibiting the baby, or would you prefer to be down as the finder? Probably easier if we use the constable for continuity," I added, answering my own question. I rattled the words off as if I was an experienced examiner, but I was trembling inside.

"OK, fine," the inspector said, "I'll leave you to it. When you're finished let the WPC (Woman Police Constable) know so the toilets can be reopened to the public. After that, can you take the baby to the Westminster Mortuary?"

I quavered a little at the mention of the word 'mortuary'.

"OK, but I'll need the constable with me to maintain continuity as he can identify the baby tomorrow for the Pathologist".

Who is this other person, I wondered, saying all this stuff so confidently?

\* \* \*

I had arrived at Belgravia Station in Gerald Road, a three-storey white building with stone archway entrance and blue Police Lamp as a quiet, unassuming, newly-wed ex-research chemist from the north east of England. I had thought a career in forensic science sounded intriguing, with a great deal of varied and challenging work but I had no idea about the macho world I was about to step into, nor just how challenging the work would be from Day One.

All the houses were bright white with smart and shiny black doors. I could hear an opera singer going through her scales. A blue plaque told me that Sir Noel Coward lived here from 1930 to 1956. Not a typical street for a police station, to say the least. Taking the plunge, I stepped through the archway and then through double-leaf doors and turned right to the front counter. A uniform sergeant was sitting behind a desk. With white, collar-length hair and a large white, well-trimmed beard, he looked extremely distinguished. He escorted me up two flights to the uniform Chief Superintendent's Office. The Chief Super bade me welcome, and explained that he would give me the chance to organize a talk to the station personnel advising them what it was I did. Next stop was the Detective Inspector's office.

"Here's the new SOCO for you Inspector," the sergeant said. "I'll leave you to it."

I'm not a bit of kit I thought, but there it was. I realized the first hurdle would be establishing some kind of identity and trust with my colleagues. At the moment I was an unknown quantity - a civilian to boot.

Detective Inspector Elsdon was a rotund, white-haired figure who must have just scraped through the minimum acceptable height qualification to make it into the Force. I noted the glass of milk on his desk (he suffered from ulcers, not a man to stress out if you could avoid it). After a short conversation, I was introduced to the CID guys, and presented with my own tiny little desk in the corner of the office. I felt like a pet rabbit sitting in my hutch.

I was called to action a moment later.

"OK SOCs, we have a burglary to go to," said a voice behind me. This man introduced himself as Andy, a DC (Detective Constable) in his late twenties.

"It's your first day SOCs, so don't go berserk. It's an office burglary in Knightsbridge not the crime of the century."

"I'll just pop to the toilet before we head off, OK?"

The toilets were on the same floor as the CID office. I bolted the door, trousers down, sat up straight and jumped in surprise when a copy of the Daily Telegraph was shoved underneath the cubicle door. This would have been disconcerting enough on its own, but the paper was on fire. The flames were high and there was nowhere to run, especially as, um, things were underway, so to speak. I multi-tasked and stamped on the flames until they were out and walked back into the CID office as if nothing had happened. This was my introduction into that oh-so-special, so-called 'police humour'. The arsonist's identity was never revealed (and I never made inquiries).

After a terrifying jaunt around the enormous Park Lane roundabout with Andy yelling at me to ignore the Mad-Max-style traffic and get moving, we arrived at the Knightsbridge offices. My first crime scene. The burglar or burglars had approached via a metal fire escape at the rear and climbed through a third floor toilet window, probably left open overnight, as there were no signs of a forced entry.

Desk drawers had been emptied onto the floor and filing cabinets had been prized open with (probably) a screwdriver, which had also left striation marks (scratches) on the metallic surface of the cash box. Forensically, there were instrument marks to be cast and retained using a rubber solution called 'Silcoset'. Two compounds are mixed together and pasted over the area of interest. Once it's set into a rigid rubber mould, the cast is removed and the scratches can then be compared under a microscope with a suspected tool. Striation marks are specific to the wear and tear on the screwdriver blade, knife or jemmy. The screwdriver used here had a nine-millimetre blade and there were deep scratches on the edge of a cash box where it had been forced open. The point of entry was my main focus, to be examined for shoe marks, fibres, blood and finger marks. Cash boxes, items taken from desk drawers were all of interest. I was hoping to find a couple of finger marks. This meant taking fingerprints of staff who'd touched the items. Elimination prints are important otherwise the Fingerprint Department would spend needless time searching legitimate finger marks against known criminals. I had a rush of panic at all the things I needed to do. I wanted to take my time. I could have spent the whole day examining every item.

"How long do you think you will be SOCs?" Andy said restlessly, looking at his watch.

"I will need another hour to cast the instrument marks, take a Polaroid photograph of the position of the finger marks at the point of entry, and elimination prints are needed of some members of staff."

"OK take possession of the cash box that was forced, it will save taking a cast of the instrument marks."

Of course, the cash box was now unusable.

"I will take the elimination prints," Andy said, "And then we'll be ready to go, as I have another appointment."

I was delighted to find a couple of unknown prints and although this wasn't exactly the examination of the century, I was satisfied I hadn't missed any crucial evidence. Alas, the great Knightsbridge burglary was never solved.

I left New Scotland Yard at 6pm, having parked my minivan, and congratulated myself on getting through the day without any cock-ups. I rushed home and excitedly related the day's events to Jennifer.

I worked forty-one hours per week including lunch breaks and I was expected to work every other weekend covering the whole District: Cannon Row, Rochester Row, Gerald Road, and Hyde Park. My counterpart, Mick at Rochester Row, covered the other two weekends. There were three times as many burglaries reported at Rochester Row compared to Gerald Road and Saturdays were therefore four times busier than my weekdays. After a week of attending non-stop burglaries I felt like I was getting a feel for the job, until, that is, I got the call that brought me to Victoria Coach Station late on a Saturday night.

\*\*\*

Never had a public toilet been loaded with such foreboding. I entered, followed by the constable who found the baby.

It was just as you would expect. Cubicles, sinks. Tidier and better-smelling than the gents.

Except this one had a dead baby in it.

"It's in there," the constable said, directing me to a middle cubicle.

The door was open. The baby was inside a white plastic bag, left lying on the cubicle floor.

"Ok, wait there," I replied. I knelt down, opened the bag and lifted out the baby. It sounds terrible, but it felt like I was picking up a cold chicken off the supermarket shelf. It was a boy. He was very cold; rigor mortis had set in. I placed the tiny creature in a large brown paper sack, folded the sack top over, placed two labels signed by the constable over the fold and used sticky tape to secure them. I attached an exhibit label to the sack, known as a 420A label. I would sign this label after the constable, as it has to be signed in chronological order by everyone who handles the exhibit. This was to preserve the integrity of the 'exhibit' (I'm sorry but it's the police term), so when the pathologist examined the baby, he would be satisfied the body was in precisely the same state in which it was discovered. This done, I labelled the sack: *Unknown Baby, ex GB/1, Victoria Coach Station, police station code AL* with the date. I also dated and signed the 420A label.

I appeared calm and collected but I was constantly asking myself: "What do I do next?"

I searched the cubicle for traces of blood, and examined the metal sanitary towel container in which the cleaner had found the baby. Then I looked at all the other cubicles, peering into each sanitary towel container and lifting toilet seats, expecting to find the 'after-birth' (I wasn't even sure what that might be). Nothing. I checked the gents but they were clean, evidentially speaking.

Hold on! What about fingerprints? This was a serious crime, potentially a murder, and therefore a specialized fingerprint officer would have to examine the cubicle. I told the Duty Officer to get onto the Yard for the on-call fingerprint officer.

He arrived in less than twenty minutes and immediately started to throw his weight about.

"I should have been called sooner, this is a serious crime!"

"I had to carry out the forensic examination before you started covering everything in aluminium powder."

He wasn't happy.

"Why are you dealing with such a serious crime?" he demanded.

I had no other answer except for the fact I was the on-call SOCO, experienced or not and I'd been trained to do the job. His questions and apparent dismay at my presence did make me think twice, however and then it hit me that I hadn't labelled the brown paper sack into which I'd placed the plastic bag that had contained the baby. It would have to be examined for fingerprints. I left the fingerprint guy to it (he started moaning to the duty officer about my presence before I was out of earshot) and walked back as quickly as I dared to the mini-van where I placed the necessary fingerprint labels on the sack.

Eventually, about three hours after I'd arrived, I left for Rochester Row to pick up the key for the mortuary. George, the police constable who'd been guarding the scene came with me. As we talked, it emerged that George was also a newbie; he'd only been in the job for three weeks.

"So have you been in the mortuary yet?" I asked.

Young George shook his head, turning pale.

It was about 2am when we arrived at Horseferry Road mortuary, which was a short distance from the Houses of Parliament. Our grim errand was given a haunted air by the quiet streets and the unlit mortuary building. I cradled the brown paper sack while George put the key in the lock of the side door, normally used by undertakers, and turned the handle. The door creaked like it belonged to Dracula's castle. George was visibly trembling by the time it was open and, as my hands were full, it was down to George to find a light switch. He stretched out his arm, palm open, looking for a switch and laid it directly on the cold face of a dead woman an undertaker had dropped off earlier. George screamed and ran out of the building, leaving me literally holding the baby, in total darkness. I couldn't find a light switch, so I carefully laid the sack out of the way, next to the trolley with the dead lady and legged it after George. He wasn't outside, the poor fellow must have kept going back to the nick, so I drove back to 'Roch,' with the key and handed it back to the front desk sergeant.

"Everything OK Larry?"

"Yeah Sarge, no problems," I replied casually.

I got back home by about 3.30am. I needed to be back at work in a few hours and it occurred to me that this wasn't the best rota/covering system, and it took several years for the standby rota to be replaced by a full night duty system with two SOCOs available for serious incidents anywhere in London.

The mother of the baby was never identified. We assumed she'd given birth before travelling to Victoria

Coach Station and had hid the dead baby in the sanitary towel box, before boarding a coach to wherever. It was a heartbreaking experience and I think it was too much for George to bear. He never reappeared; he quit the Force and I'm pretty certain he never looked back.

# THE RUSSIAN PRINCE

I n those early days every job was an education, and I often found myself face-to-face with the great and the good; people I would have never dreamed of meeting.

For some reason, the weekend call outs always seemed to provide the most challenging jobs. Rochester Row CID called me at 11.30pm one Saturday evening. A burglar had stolen jewellery and watches of incalculable value from the home of a Russian prince who claimed to be descended from Tsar Nicholas II. He was deeply upset and wanted to have his staff clean up the place before he went to bed (the burglar had been of the smash-your-way-in-and-ransack-the place variety), and this was why I had been summoned.

The Prince was a very distinguished-looking gentleman. He was in his sixties with long white hair and a drooping white moustache. His clothes were made to measure and were probably worth more than my house, with his Cuban-heeled soft brown leather ankle boots probably costing more than I made in a year. I started my examination with the thick and heavy front door, which had been ruthlessly jemmied and we chatted for about thirty minutes while I worked.

"They were heirlooms," the prince mourned. "My last remaining connection to my family, to my homeland."

This was the height of the Cold War, and Communism was still going strong in Russia, so returning home was clearly impossible for the Prince. He grew more and more upset as he started to realize that he would probably never see his treasures again.

Once I'd finished, I explained to the Prince that I needed to take his fingerprints and those of his male friend who had accompanied him to the opera that evening, as well as those of his staff (who were also out at the time of the burglary) for the purposes of elimination. This didn't need to be done now, as it was so late, and I said I'd return the following morning at 11am, so he could get some rest and alert his friend and his staff.

I arrived at Gerald Road on Sunday at 9am to find my phone ringing. It was the DI (Detective Inspector) from Rochester Row.

"Larry thanks for coming out last night. Can you give me a lift to the prince's home? I need to show my face as it's such a high-value burglary."

I didn't know whom I was talking to so, for the first time I spoke the legendary phrase: "No problem Guv."

Everyone said 'Guv.' It was easier than trying to remember people's names (I had met the DI before but couldn't remember his name), unless you were talking to a woman of course, but in those days one rarely met a 'Ma'am'.

I addressed the constables and sergeants by their first names; inspectors and above were all 'Guv.' I used police lingo as much as possible, as it helped me assimilate into the world of the police. There was a lot of suspicion about civilians doing police work and I overheard the expression: "Bloody civvies!" many times.

The DI and I arrived at precisely 11am and were greeted by the housekeeper. Calm and order had returned to the house and the Prince walked into the lounge and greeted me with a big "Hi Larry!" followed by an enthusiastic handshake. I introduced the DI, clearly bemused by the Prince's bonhomie towards myself, and headed for the kitchen to take the elimination fingerprints. The Prince joined me shortly afterwards. I explained that I was using a chemical process to take his prints. I had a pad impregnated with a chemical that reacted with an elimination fingerprint form. The chemical turned purple on the treated gloss paper and the fingerprint developed before your eyes. It was much cleaner than the ink and brass plate used at the station for prisoners.

Hands cleaned up, I then explained that the finger marks I had found would be compared with the elimination fingerprints. Any unidentified marks would then be searched against the fingerprints of all the convicted criminals in the country. I looked at the Prince, who was just a shade taller than myself, and said

"Sir, we will do everything possible to recover your beloved possessions. Hopefully the finger marks I have found will assist the detectives in their investigation."

The Prince looked at me for a moment. "Excuse me Larry, I will be back momentarily."

He returned clutching a bunch of keys. The DI watched in amazement as the Prince presented me with the keys and a photograph.

"Larry, these are the keys to my villa in Morocco. The address is on the back of the photograph. Please take your wife there next week, I will inform my staff and they will take care of you."

I took the keys and photograph, which was of one of the most beautiful buildings I'd ever seen in my life.

"Sir, that is extremely generous gesture of you," I said, "But sadly I can't accept as at the moment as I don't have any holiday time to take."

Even if I could have accepted I wouldn't have been able to afford the flights to Morocco. I handed back the keys and we drove back to "Roch" where the DI just couldn't wait to tell the CID guys how I'd just been offered the keys to Moroccan palace. This caused quite a stir and helped break a little more ice in terms of their acceptance. This was a key moment for me; as a young naive scientist, with perhaps not the greatest skills, I had managed to become friends with a Russian Prince and impress a group of hardened CID detectives. This was progress indeed.

# BOMBS AND BANK JOBS

I was alone in a deserted Victoria train station, save for a nervous-looking duty police officer crouched some yards distant. In front of me were three red phone booths, possibly booby-trapped by IRA terrorists and it was down to yours truly to give them the forensic once-over. The IRA had used an authentication code when they called it in, so we knew that this was not a hoax (the call had been traced to one of these booths).

A few minutes earlier, I'd battled my way through the thousands of noisy and frustrated commuters being herded away from the station before being waved straight through the cordon by constables whose expressions said: "I'm glad I'm not you."

I pulled on the heavy, cast-iron door to the first booth. It didn't move. I started to panic; this was perhaps a sign that the door had been booby-trapped. I took a closer look, saw nothing suspicious, so pulled harder and it popped open. I stepped inside, let the door close behind me, and started my examination, gingerly picking up the directories, and flicking through them. I took a number of fingerprints, and moved onto the second booth. I had just started dusting the phone when it started to ring.

I froze and looked at the handset.

A phone's ring has never sounded so loud or terrifying as it did at that moment. I felt my bowels wobble as the Duty Officer screamed: "Get the fuck out of there! RUN!"

I instantly took to my toes and quickly caught up with the duty officer. We stopped at what we supposed was a safe distance; both of us clutching at our chests, hearts pounding like pneumatic drills.

When the phone stopped ringing and failed to explode, I returned to finish the examination of the telephone booths. The device was found under a platform seat and diffused by the Bomb Squad and soon, all returned to normal - until the next time the IRA called. All we could do, like everyone else, was to hope we weren't in the wrong place at the wrong time.

I was in the wrong place at least once a day. The IRA had recently developed sophisticated letter bomb devices and so one of my regular - and perhaps most 'specialized' – daily jobs was a round robin run in my mini-van, picking up suspicious envelopes and packages and transporting them to the Bomb Squad to be X-rayed. I usually had a detective with me (who had drawn the short straw). An officer once remarked that if one of the letters had a bomb in it then the bumpy roads of central London would soon let us know. Fortunately, that never happened, but out of the hundreds that were transported in my mini-van, there were a few that were live and primed.

On one occasion an American financier living in Eaton Square called the police about a potential letter bomb. I went with DC 'Dinger' Bell. Dinger was from a small village near Newcastle. He was in his early 30s, good-looking, if slightly overweight, dark-haired and blue-eyed and occasionally smoked a pipe.

The plan was to pick up the envelope for examination but we couldn't get away - the guy could talk the legs of a table. Coffee turned to whiskey as the day progressed and he told a story that would have had Mario Puzo reaching for his typewriter. To cut to the chase, the financier's criminal brother had hired a mafia hit man to kill him, and the financier believed he was heading for London. The letter was all part of a campaign to frighten him into handing over half his fortune, and the financier produced a three-page document from his brother that explained how he would be killed. It was grim and gruesome stuff. Dinger advised the financier to speak to his embassy in Grosvenor Square and report the threats to the FBI. If the threat were genuine then they would liaise with Scotland Yard.

Three hours later, our schedule obliterated, we left the apartment. Three months later, Dinger called me over to show me a report from the FBI. They'd arrested a hit man in New York with papers in his possession identifying our financier.

10am and I was at my desk, planning my morning visits when Dave, a stick-thin CID detective slammed down his phone and yelled across the room at me: "Larry, quick, we need your mini-van! It's the only car outside the nick. There's an armed robbery in progress at Barclays Bank in Knightsbridge, shots fired."

Myself, Dave, Andy and Graham ran down the stairs together. Andy and Graham jumped into the back of the mini-van and Dave sat in the front with me. I floored it, although the little van wasn't best pleased to find itself fully loaded, and the engine groaned until we hit the downward slope towards Knightsbridge.

Suddenly, Dave said: "Pull in Larry, we're gonna get there too soon. They have guns, we don't. We arrive now they might shoot their way out. People could get hurt. Turn off the engine".

We sat there for five minutes before Dave gave us the go ahead to proceed. We arrived amidst chaos, with panda cars mounted on the pavement outside the bank. Inside, one woman was hysterical, a guy was lying on the floor from a suspected heart attack, waiting for an ambulance, and the girl cashiers were in tears after being terrorized by the robbers – there were no floor-to-ceiling screens in 1972.

My heart was pounding at the trauma the gang had left in their wake but all the same I was excited to be part of the investigatory team. The robbers had fired their sawn-off shotguns into the ceiling - an extremely effective way of frightening customers and staff.

As the heart attack victim was removed, the crying mum calmed down and the cashiers given hot, sweat tea, I got started and set about fingerprinting the front door, worrying all the while that with all these people around and emergency service personnel coming in and out of the door, scene preservation was going to be a nightmare. That would be my excuse to the DFO (Divisional Fingerprint Officer) when he finally rolled up from his base at Rochester Row.

Politics were always present when the DFO was about. It's not an exaggeration to say he hated SOCOs. He was very clear about this, believing it was easier to train fingerprint personnel in forensics than recruit a hundred new SOCOs and, despite having lost that argument, he did all he could to sabotage the work of SOCOs (without damaging evidence, it must be said). He would always arrive before Mick, my fellow SOCO, or myself, to pick the crop of the burglaries reported from the previous evening. In these early days he was able to examine a scene a lot faster than Mick and I, although in fairness we were examining a scene for both forensic evidence and finger marks. The DFO also deliberately visited scenes Mick and I had already examined and 'found' finger marks we had 'missed', taking his 'evidence' to our Detective Inspectors (these were most likely our fingerprints that we'd left while handling objects at the scene).

So, Mick and I fought back. We explained to our governors that we had the ability to examine a scene for both fingerprint *and* forensic evidence. We made a point of saying how the DFO, untrained in forensics would accidentally lose or destroy evidence he didn't even know existed. Those CID guys we worked with every day cottoned on quickly. They preferred the continuity of having a dedicated scene examiner for their office and so supported

Mick and I by specifically requesting our attendance. After all, we could examine a wide variety of exhibits for corroborative evidence, such as tools, shoes, blood, hair, fibre and paint samples, all of which had the potential to send a suspect down for a long stretch.

So I told the DFO the fingerprinting was already done when he arrived, by which time I was balanced atop a wobbly step ladder with my head in the high ceiling, shining my seek and search lamp into the dark ceiling cavity, collecting lead shot and wadding from the cartridges from both blast areas. This would be good evidence if a shotgun and/or ammunition were recovered later - but no such luck. The robbers were never caught.

Not long after this a call came in that an armed robbery was taking place in the jewellers that resides in The Grosvenor Hotel, Park Lane. I was just around the corner, on my usual burglary run, DC "Dinger" Bell beside me, when the shout came. I paid special attention to the phrase "suspects on premises," but this time Dinger Bell ran headlong into the hotel, ahead of me (I'm not that stupid) and dashed into the jewellery shop to find embarrassed staff saying: "Sorry we set the alarm off by mistake."

I immediately turned back to re-park my minivan, as I'd abandoned it on the hotel steps. As I approached the minivan, the Area Crime car came hurtling up the slip road and I stopped in front of them. "Don't worry lads, false alarm," I said as the officers jumped out. A second later I found myself spread-eagled on the car's bonnet, shouting: "Lads I am Gerald Road's SOCO!" The Area Crime car was from Paddington and not knowing me from Adam, they'd taken no chances. After a highly amused Dinger Bell had told them to release me, I was dusted down and sent on my way, more than a little shaken, with apologies ringing in my ears.

I was rapidly learning that no two days were the same and some incidents were so unique they could simply never be repeated, as in the case of Flasher Willy.

# FLASHER WILLY

"**G**et your gear Larry, you're needed in the Park."

"What's up?"

"You'll be looking for shoe prints and semen."

I gulped. So far, the majority of my crime scene examinations had involved burglaries or stolen motor vehicles.

"A woman has just been flashed in Hyde Park. The flasher came at her from inside a hollow tree, opened his rain coat, exposing his erect member."

With allegations of indecent assault or rape, the rule is you take everything for examination to identify bodily fluids such as saliva and semen. Clothing and bedding are obvious exhibits followed by an examination of the victim by a Divisional Surgeon who takes intimate samples such as vaginal swabs, which I would then submit to the Forensic Science Laboratory in Lambeth for examination. When searching for traces of semen on clothing, bedding, mattresses etc., an ultra violet light is used as semen fluoresces. I suspected that a hollow tree would prove to be challenging environment in which to work. The incident had taken place just thirty minutes earlier, so the scene would at least be fresh.

I spotted the tree, a mature oak with a girth of ten feet, from quite some distance as a uniform constable was standing in front of it, on guard. Unfortunately he didn't have a clue about crime scene preservation as he was standing just inches from the entrance to the hollow trunk, so there was little chance of finding shoe marks in the soil around the tree. The entrance to the hollow came from a split in the trunk, which was about two feet wide. I peered through and saw that the split led to a hollow about seven feet high before the trunk became solid again. It was a flasher's dream lair. I shone my seek-and-search light around the interior. This was easier said than done; the light was intensely bright but the battery weighed twenty-eight pounds. I found some sweet and ice-cream wrappers were on the ground inside the hollow and I placed these items inside a clear plastic bag. The base of the hollow was solid and no shoe prints could be recovered, but I took a sample of the dirt, which could be compared to dirt on a suspect's shoes. There was no sign of any semen (the woman, who was a schoolteacher, had clearly stated that the man's penis was not 'at rest' and therefore it had seemed unlikely that I would find some).

Two days later, the same victim was flashed at again in exactly the same place by the same raincoat-clad flasher. Screaming, she eventually attracted the attention of a policeman passing in a panda car, and he drove around with her, searching for the culprit among the walkers, sunbathers and tourists. They had reached the far west of the park, by Kensington Gardens, when the woman screamed: "There he is! Over there, by the bushes!"

The guy was duly nicked and protested his innocence in no uncertain way as he was carted off to a cell in Hyde Park police station. He continued yelling as he was ordered to undress, so his grey raincoat, grey trousers and brown leather shoes could be taken as exhibits. He made it plain to us that he was an innocent man, and an influential and high-ranking civil servant, to boot.

An identity parade was organized for the next day with the guy still in the cell and still vigorously denying the offence. The victim came out of a side room, having been briefed by the duty officer that if she saw the flasher, she was to tap him twice on the shoulder. She looked at the ten reasonable lookalikes and with no hesitation walked straight up to our civil servant and smacked him in the face.

Clutching his nose, he bawled: "You stupid idiot, it's not me!"

The suspect's leather shoes revealed nothing forensically. The soles were leather and fairly new with no visible dirt. The duty officer was extremely experienced and, out of both suspect's and victim's earshot, said his gut was telling him that the guy was innocent. He became so convinced that he even organized special branch surveillance, in that he placed a constable up in the branches of the hollow tree for three days in two-hour shifts.

On the third day, a guy in his fifties, dressed in a grey raincoat, grey trousers and brown shoes stepped into the hollow. The police officer spotted a woman in her sixties walking along the pathway, approaching the tree. Nothing happened. Five minutes later, a woman in her twenties strolled along the same path and, just as she drew alongside the tree, out he popped, raincoat open wide, a big smile on his face. The woman screamed and the constable fell out of the tree.

This, naturally, was not the constable's intention and it took him a few moments to recover, during which time the flasher, clearly fleet of foot, had taken off at a clip across the park, heading towards the Serpentine, which is where the constable caught up with him and launched a death-defying full-stretch rugby tackle, grabbing the flasher around the knees, bringing them both crashing to the ground, at which point the poor constable found his face pressed into the flasher's groin which, due to the nature of the flasher's attire, was completely exposed.

Goodness knows what the victim made of it all. It certainly took a few cups of hot sweet tea back at the station before her cup and saucer stopped rattling.

The flasher looked identical to the civil servant and for a moment I thought the first victim's identification had been right all along, but closer inspection revealed otherwise. The most obvious difference was that apart from the flasher's grey 'trousers' (which turned out to be more like socks, as there was nothing above the knees, each leg was tied under the knee with pieces of string) he was completely naked under the raincoat.

The flasher was convicted and the civil servant received a written apology from both police and victim.

# A KIND OF MAGIC

managed to settle in after two months at Gerald Road and most lunchtimes I could be found playing cards with DI Elsdon and Dinger Bell, along with three or four other CID officers in the police canteen. I'd given my talk to the station about what I was able to do and so everyone knew who I was and what I was able to bring to an investigation. More and more uniform officers were getting in touch about relatively minor crimes (minor to CID, that is) they were investigating.

A significant part of my talk was given over to the ways one could set traps where repetitive thefts occurred from lockers, desks, changing rooms and communal areas of commercial premises. The easiest way was to use Fuchsine powder, prepared by the Forensic Science Laboratory. Fuchsine is a purple powder, which stains on contact with moisture, including human sweat, so hands and clothes appear beetroot-coloured. The lab prepares the powder by adding specs of fluorescent chemicals to the Fuchsine to render that particular mixture unique, which prevents the defence that the stain could have come from an innocent source.

The minor crimes unit asked me if I could help with a case where cash was being stolen from staff lockers in a hospital. I was keen to have a go, as this would be my first attempt using a chemical marker trap. So I stained a number of £5 notes, along with a few coins, which I placed inside a purse with receipts and a train ticket, and a photograph of a child (me, aged five). The purse was placed in a locker of a trustworthy member of staff recommended by a senior manager who would check the trap several times a day. A plainclothes police officer was positioned close by. The purse was stolen the next day, but unfortunately the theft had taken place during in a two-hour window when the staff member had been unable to check the locker.

There were no signs of the Fuchsine in or around the locker, so I concluded that the purse had not been opened in the locker room. Work rotas were checked and we checked the hands of all members of staff on that shift. No signs of the powder or fluorescent specs, but there were two porters who'd gone off duty.

Bob, the plainclothes constable, radioed the Q-car, (an unmarked car crewed by a Detective Sergeant (DS), temporary detective constable (TDC), and uniform constable driver). Their brief was to nick, nick, nick as many suspects as possible each week and there was intense rivalry between Q-car crews. The Q-car arrived and we piled in. The police driver could have given Jackie Stewart a run for his money, for in no time we were at the high-rise block in Tottenham where the suspects lived.

Dave, a dark-haired six-foot tall sergeant, knocked gently on the door of the fifth-floor flat. The rest of us stood to one side, out of immediate view. Almost immediately, the door was opened to reveal a man with a huge beer belly. Moments later we were standing in his lounge where the skipper asked: "Could I look at your hands please?"

The guy immediately held out his hands. I reached for my ultra-violet light and the guy flinched. I have to admit, in those days, the UV light looked like a giant death-ray gun (they're the size of pencils now) but once he was reassured I scanned them looking for the fluorescent specs. Nothing!

John the TDC was told to stay with our new acquaintance to prevent a warning phone call, and we left to visit the next address, which was on the seventh floor of the building. The guy was a short thin lad in his twenties, who was very quick and confident with his answers.

Dave asked very politely for the lad to show us his hands. First glance and my heart sank. Nothing! Absolutely bloody nothing! We were all sure this was the guy who had stolen the purse. I went back over his hands with the UV light and, hold on, there was a small fluorescent spec, and another spec of purple on his index finger literally developing in front of me as his hands released a nervous sweat. I asked him to turn out his pockets and there was a purple stain on the lining. Dave cautioned him, then asked where he had been after he left work, as there was no purse or money to be found in the flat. Eventually the guy admitted to having a drink with our first suspect in a pub around the corner. The constable was left with the arrested suspect as we ran to the pub.

The landlord opened the till. There were two purple-tinged £5 notes inside and purple stains on the landlord's fingers.

The thief later admitted this offence along with other thefts from his work colleagues. I would like to report he was adequately punished but unfortunately he got away with a slapped wrist and three months' probation.

I was still buzzing with excitement when I caught the late train home to Surbiton. My first attempt at the chemical trap had been a resounding success and I couldn't wait to tell Jennifer but, walking in at midnight, I found both her and the dogs fast asleep.

# A SCANDAL IN BELGRAVIA

arly on the evening of November 7, 1974, 39-year-old Richard Bingham, the 7th Earl of Lucan, popularly known as Lord or 'Lucky' Lucan, telephoned the Clermont Club to reserve a restaurant table. Lord Lucan's wife, Veronica Mary Duncan, Countess of Lucan, was at home at 46 Lower Belgrave Street, as was the nanny to their three children, Sandra Rivett. The countess had separated from her husband and had recently won custody of the children after a difficult legal battle.

Countess Lucan and Rivett were the same height, five-foot-two, although Rivett, a 29-year-old redhead, had a slightly larger build. It was Thursday, which was normally Sandra's night off, but she'd changed the night to Wednesday.

Lord Lucan, an aristocrat and former member of the Coldstream Guards, lived for the gaming tables but his luck had finally run out and, with family, household expenses and legal bills, he was living on overdrafts. He stopped by the Clermont at about 8.45pm and asked the doorman if any of his gambling friends were there. They were not and he said he would return later.

At 8.40pm Rivett went downstairs to make some tea – something the countess normally did. After Rivett had been gone an unusually long time, over half an hour, Lady Lucan went to find her. As she made her way downstairs, Lord Lucan attacked her, hitting Lady Lucan several times before trying to strangle her. The countess reached between her husband's legs and squeezed as hard as she could. Lord Lucan released her and suddenly gave up on the idea of killing his wife. He said they should talk and attend to the countess's injuries. As they went upstairs he confessed to killing the nanny. She was dead in the basement, battered to death with a blunt instrument.

While Lord Lucan was in the bathroom, Lady Lucan fled the house and ran to the nearby Plumbers Arms Pub, where she cried: 'Help me, help me, help me, I've just escaped being murdered! He's in the house. He's murdered my nanny.'

At 11pm, disturbed and unkempt, Lord Lucan arrived at the house of some friends in Uckfield. He left at 1am. Three days later his car was found abandoned in the coastal town of Newhaven.

\*\*\*

Belgravia Nick was almost within sight of the Lucan home, just at the opposite end of Chester Square. DI Elsdon had by this time retired after twenty-five years' service, determined not to let the ulcer get the better of him. He was replaced by Detective Chief Inspector Dave 'Buster' Geering, who took on the Lucan case, along with Chief Superintendent Roy Ranson.

Like DI Elsdon, 'Buster' Geering was a smidgen below average height and a more than smidgen over average girth. He spoke the Queen's English like a royal and always arrived at work immaculately dressed in a navy pinstripe suit, with striped shirt and Detective Training School Instructors' tie (navy blue with red diagonal stripes). Before taking his seat, he would remove his jacket to reveal bright red braces and shirt-sleeve holders.

Two or three times a week he would ask: "Larry old boy, could you give me a lift at three o'clock?"

"No problem Guv," I would reply. I'd drive him to the West End, the pair of us chatting all the way until he quietly commanded, "Just drop me he here old fruit," pointing to a corner. It was never the same corner. As soon as I stopped, he slipped gracefully out and vanished into the crowds. I had no idea what he was up to but it was nothing to do with me and so I never troubled him with questions.

One day I received an urgent call from Buster. He was at the Old Bailey, giving evidence in a case where a soldier was being tried for rape. He asked if I remembered the case.

"Yes Guv," I replied. "I had to write up a statement about some of the exhibits a few days ago."

"Good. We've broken for lunch and I'm due back in at 2pm. I can see I'm going to be asked why, as Investigating Officer, I didn't submit the rubbish bin to the forensic lab for analysis of the contents."

The incident happened about ten months previously. The private, on leave and staying in a Victoria hotel, had picked up a girl from a pub and they'd ended up back at his hotel room. The girl tried to call an end to the night but the private refused to let her out of the room and raped her repeatedly over a two-day period. As she was not allowed out of the room, she had to use the rubbish bin as a toilet. The arrest came after the hotelier heard 'distressing sounds' coming from the room and called the police who crashed through the door and arrested the guy.

Part of a defending barrister's strategy is to show that an officer is inept or has deliberately withheld evidence, so I could quite understand the Guvnor's concern.

"Guv, that's no problem. We didn't submit the contents for analysis as the bin only contained urine from both of them and you can't group pee to a particular person like blood. Urine is just a bin in its own right; the body dumps all the rubbish into it. We've submitted the bedding along with the victim's and assailant's clothing for examination for semen and blood staining, both of which can be linked to a person."

At this time blood and semen was not as specific as it is now, thanks to DNA, but we could then, given the right circumstances, narrow it down to 1 in a million (i.e. only 56 people in a population of 56 million were likely to produce the same result).

"Thanks old fruit," Buster said, much relieved. "Gold watch later?"

"Of course," I replied. This was one of Buster's many upmarket catchphrases (gold watch = scotch).

Unfortunately for me, the Forensic Science Laboratory Liaison Sergeants closed the door on my involvement regarding scene examination of the Lucan home, so I was only able to contribute to follow-up enquiries as and when Buster asked. Graham, our DS, was assigned to protect Lady Lucan and walked around the office with a 38 Smith & Wesson revolver hanging out of his back pocket and, when I saw them together, with the gun clearly visible, the whole thing had a feel of the Wild West. This was intensified by the constant presence of the press who approached as soon I stepped out of the nick, opening their jackets to reveal fat brown envelopes filled with cash, whispering: "So where are you going today? Any breaks?"

The identity of the killer was never really in doubt. The pathologist was, as one might expect, my 'tutor', Professor Keith Simpson who didn't take long to diagnose blunt trauma as the cause of death, with the lead piping as the murder weapon. On 19 June 1975, an inquest jury took just thirty minutes to pronounce Lord Lucan as the murderer. Lucan was the last person ever to be declared a murderer this way, as the law was changed with the introduction of the Criminal Law Act 1977.

The location of the killer, however, plagued Buster for the rest of his career. The first theory was that Lucan had "done the honourable thing" and "fallen on his own sword," a view publicly repeated by many of Lucan's friends, including John Aspinall (who owned the Clermont and was one of 'Lucky's' gambling buddies), who believed Lucan's body was "250 feet under the Channel". Buster changed his view, along with Ranson, thinking that it was more likely that Lord Lucan had managed to escape to southern Africa.

# THE THREE CARBUNCLES

The Lucan case was an extraordinary investigation but, thanks to its many unique inhabitants and buildings, Belgravia had more than its fair share of extraordinary crimes – even the minor crimes were a cut above the everyday incidents that dominated other areas.

Opposite Gerald Road, on the other side of Ebury Street is Chester Square, filled with multi-million pound residences of an extremely salubrious nature. The first house on the right was the London home of the actor Tony Curtis, who I regularly saw having lunch in Massimo's, an Italian restaurant on the corner of Gerald Road.

One particular morning in July the talk in the canteen was that Rod Stewart, the rock singer, had bought Tony Curtis's house and was having the place fitted with plush pink carpet. The carpet fitter, for some unknown reason, had unrolled a large section of the carpet outside, behind his van but on the road. A panda car heading for the nick had driven straight over it and there were black tyre marks the whole length of the carpet. There was loud laughter in the canteen as an enthusiastic traffic warden finished relating the story. When I finished my bacon roll I walked over to Chester Square and sure enough the carpet fitter was re-rolling the ruined carpet to go back in the van.

Apart from the rich and famous, Belgravia is awash with embassies, from Austria to Turkey, from Lesotho to Trinidad and Tobago, and from Finland to Malaysia. I ended up visiting most of them and we had good relationships with many of the people working there. Andy liked to stop by at the Turkish Embassy because he was a fan of their coffee, but it wasn't quite my cup of tea, if you see what I mean.

As part of my orientation upon joining Gerald Road, I was given a course on how to address all the different ambassadors, to shake the hand of the Chinese but with a light grip and pump, but without looking into their eyes (considered rude) and if you're meeting someone for the first time then you might sometimes give them a round of applause. If you're meeting Tibetans, then stick out your tongue to show you harbour no ill thoughts; Ukrainians like three kisses on the right cheek followed by a hug; for Indians press one's hands together and wish them 'Namaste' and 'Sawadee' if you're in Thailand.

Needless to say, all this was impossible to remember and I usually relied upon addressing ambassadors as "Your Excellency," and then held out my hand for a shake and this usually did the trick. I was once caught out after being called to investigate a burglary at an African embassy when His Excellency ignored my outstretched hand, placed his right hand behind his back, picked up my briefcase with the other hand and placed it on his desk. I had a horrible feeling I'd just committed some mortal sin but luckily this turned out to be a sign of respect. In the end, experience was my only guide.

One of my favourite buildings in Belgravia, a short distance from the Bolivian Embassy, is St. Peter's Church, built between 1824 and 1827. It stands at the eastern end of Eaton Square and is practically cathedral-sized. The Grade II* listed building has been described by *The Times* newspaper as 'one of the most beautiful churches in London.'

I was called to help after a thief had repeatedly targeted St Peter's, taking petty cash, silver candlesticks and anything else he could get his hands on. The staff who ran a day nursery in the church basement had the feeling that he'd been regularly sussing out the place while they were at work, having heard noises and also having 'felt' someone's presence.

We'd been called to the church six times in just two weeks. Increased police patrols had failed to spot, let alone catch the villain, which led to me to suggest installing an alarm with a movement sensor that would send an alert to police radios.

I had a few teething troubles setting up the alarm (this was new-fangled technology back then), so I had to return to the church to for a tinker one afternoon. I was nearing the St Peter's when I suddenly noticed a character across the road from me, heading for the church. I caught his eye and he stared back. He looked as guilty as hell and my gut told me that this was our guy. Obviously, his gut was telling him that I was police, for he took off down the road and was beyond my chasing capabilities. I did notice one thing about him, however. He had three large carbuncles on his balding head and when I described him to the station collator (a police officer who collected and recorded intelligence for the station area) he searched his index cards and came up with a name.

Five days later the alarm went off at around 1am. The nearest patrol car responded and this time the guy was nicked red-handed. He was the man I'd seen, Mr Three Carbuncles. Suddenly my name was top of the pops at Gerald Road Police Station with uniform and CID officers alike.

# THE SILVER FOX

**B**elgravia was an incredible place to work as a Scenes of Crime Officer. While my counterparts out in the sticks were dealing with burglaries, Friday night assaults and stolen motor vehicles, I was shaking the hands of Ambassadors, movie stars and MPs.

Of course, while I might have been thrilled to meet Rex Harrison and Michael Heseltine, they weren't in the best mood to handle a star-struck SOCO and the best I could usually hope for was something like: "It was nice to meet you, but I hope we don't meet again".

Part of the reason so many wealthy people got burgled was because so many of them stashed a great deal of cash at home - the oldest form of tax evasion. Heseltine and Harrison hadn't hidden any cash but nonetheless the burglar had escaped with many valuable items. Heseltine and Harrison both lived in Wilton Crescent and, I suspected, had been burgled by the same person. I was pretty certain it was the same person as both burglaries had featured an extremely clever and unusual method of entry - sorry no clues, I don't want to give budding burglars ideas.

We never caught that particular burglar, and it seemed as though the professional burglars of Belgravia were a crafty bunch and well-versed in law evasion. One such pro, nicknamed 'The Silver Fox,' for his fine head of grey hair, had been described by witnesses as a smartly-dressed individual who wore a navy-coloured pin stripe suit, white shirt, white spotted blue tie and black leather shoes.

One day, the Silver Fox entered a large Victorian apartment complex just off Belgrave Square, walking in as a resident walked out of the security door. Once inside, he chose an apartment at the top of the building - less likely to be disturbed - and picked the lock using a set of 'twirlers' or 'jigglers' (lock picks) then hunted for jewellery and cash that he could easily conceal in his pockets.

The owner of the apartment, a woman in her fifties, arrived home to find The Silver Fox in her bedroom, carefully vetting her jewellery. Without waiting for a scream, he scampered straight past her and out of the apartment, down three flights of stairs and away. She followed him, yelling: "Stop thief!" and chased him out onto the pavement in front of the building as he emptied his pockets of the stolen bounty. He vanished around a corner in a flash and the lady gave up the chase, knowing she was never going to catch up with him, let alone overpower him.

Unfortunately for the Silver Fox, he ran straight into a police officer on guard duty outside a nearby embassy. They had a tumble on the pavement during which the Silver Fox shouted: "I'm trying to catch a bus!"

The constable was having none of it and kept him pinned to the floor until assistance arrived. It was in the middle of summer, but the Silver Fox had a pair of black leather gloves in his jacket pocket.

I was briefed to examine the scene in the knowledge he was almost certainly wearing gloves at the time of the burglary. It was early days in glove mark recognition but I found a couple of glove marks on the front door and collected a print in the usual way, by dusting the surface with aluminium powder, and lifting the enhanced glove mark with a low adhesive tape which was rolled onto an oblong piece of clear celluloid about six inches by four inches. The exhibit, as it was now was identified with exhibit number, station code, address of premises and date was then placed in a brown envelope for submission for comparison with the gloves of the Silver Fox. The Fingerprint Department said the results would be ready in about four weeks. Not terribly useful to CID who wanted to lock the man away sooner rather than later.

The Silver Fox stuck to his story during the interview: "I was running for a bus when that copper attacked me for no reason."

The next morning the TDC's (Temporary Detective Constables) were sent out into Victoria Station to find ten well-dressed men who were aged about fifty with silver or greying hair. It was impressive how these willing identity "paraders" were always found, although Victoria railway station was an excellent pond in which to fish.

Parade duly assembled, the burglary victim ready after Dinger had instructed: "Please tap the shoulder of the person you recognize as the burglar in your flat yesterday." The cell door opened, and the burglary suspect walked into the charge room where ten law-abiding citizens were waiting to do their public duty and stand in line with a villain.

Except the Silver Fox had transformed overnight into a black panther. His solicitor had visited him in the cells the previous evening and, realizing his silver hair would be his downfall, passed him a bottle of black hair dye. After a quick rinse in the toilet bowl, he was good to go.

The ID parade was cancelled and the Black Panther was bailed to return to the nick in six weeks' time, in the hope the glove marks I found would be positive. Alas, the Fingerprint Department decided there was insufficient detail in the glove marks to make a reliable comparison.

# EDUCATING ENOCH POWELL

**T**he modestly dressed middle-aged man who one day walked into Gerald Road Nick and enquired of the desk sergeant: "I believe you are looking for me?" was short and round-bellied. The desk sergeant thought this must be something minor; perhaps the gentleman was a witness.

"Name please?"

"Maurice Johnson."

"Occupation?"

"Burglar."

Maurice, it turned out, was the UK's most wanted burglar. He was responsible for the theft of £5million in jewellery and cash and had been on the "most wanted" list for two years.

Belgravia attracted the richest people in the land and these in turn attracted the country's 'best' burglars. I was called to the home of Enoch Powell, MBE, the controversial Conservative Member of Parliament who lived in South Eaton Place, one road across from our police station. This particular burglar had simply crashed his way through the front door.

Mr Powell was charming and highly intelligent, as one might expect. He followed me around as I started my examination and, when I took his prints for the usual purposes of elimination, he said: "Tell me, how were fingerprints 'discovered'?"

The skin has two layers, the epidermis, the outer layer of epithelial scales, and an inner layer of dense connective tissue known as the dermis. Mostly, the skin is stickier on the posterior area of the body but this is reversed on the hands and feet. The outer surface of the skin of the hands and feet is - unlike the skin on the rest of the body - arranged in a series of grooves which are known as furrows and ridges which are supposed to help us grip onto things. Our fingerprints are created by the patterns of these ridges, which - although lying parallel to one another - twist and turn and start and stop in patterns that are unique to each individual. Our fingerprint pattern forms in the foetus and remains the same throughout our lives and beyond death - until decomposition has taken hold. Sweat glands on the summits of each of the ridges cause us to leave latent fingerprints wherever we go.

As a conclusive identification tool, we've relied on the fingerprint system for over a century. The Fingerprint Bureau at New Scotland Yard was established in July 1901, in the wake of the publication in 1900 of *Classification and Uses of Fingerprints* by British civil servant Sir Edward Henry. When he became Inspector General of Police for the Bengal Province of India, Sir Henry noticed that fingerprints and handprints were used for identification purposes by the colonial authorities (the idea came from fellow civil servant Sir William Herschel). After he returned to the UK and was appointed Commissioner of the Metropolitan Police, Sir Henry came up with the classification system for fingerprints in 1899.

In terms of the type of pattern about 60-65% of the population have loops, 30-35% have whorls and around 5% have arches. These formed Henry's first classification, which allowed the grouping of categories to save searching time. Under the Henry Classification System, each finger was also assigned a number (right thumb = 1; left little finger = 10). Each finger with a whorl pattern was then assigned a numerical value. If they were whorled, fingers 1 and 2 each had a value of 16, fingers 3 and 4 = 8; fingers 5 and 6 = 4; fingers 7 and 8 = 2; fingers 9 and 10 = 1. Fingers with a non-whorl pattern (an arch or loop for example) were given a value of zero. The sum of the even finger values was then calculated and placed over the sum of the odd finger values in a fraction format and 1 was added to each sum of the whorls, meaning that the maximum obtainable score on either side of the fraction = 32. A person with a 32/32 classification has patterns such as whorls on all fingers and thumbs, while someone with 1/1 has no whorl patterns.

Identification of an individual fingerprint was like plotting a route on a map. By moving from a ridge ending at the end of a line to another identifiable feature such as a 'lake' (where a ridge diverts left and right – bifurcates - and meets back up again forming an ellipsis or 'lake') and so on in sequence, the fingerprint could be identified as belonging to a particular person. (This classification system made for fairly easy searching of the database, until the advent of automated computer systems, which began to take effect in the UK from 1984.)

Mr Powell thanked me for an interesting interlude, offered me a cup of tea, which his private secretary quickly produced. I wanted to ask him about his infamous "Rivers of Blood" speech, given a few years earlier in 1968, that criticized Commonwealth immigration and anti-discrimination legislation, leading to his sacking from the Shadow Cabinet by Conservative party leader Edward Heath, but he was called away - and I had other burglaries to attend to.

A serial burglar was plaguing Belgravia. Their MO (modus operandi) was to kick in the front or basement door and ransack the home for jewellery and cash. There was no sophistication and the burglar left his fingerprints at almost every scene, so much so that I soon got to know them by heart. My record discovery time was about two minutes into a scene examination, in which I found a right thumb mark with a whorl pattern that matched the burglar's. The final number of fingerprint identifications from burglary scenes was certainly in the fifties. And then they stopped - or at least this MO stopped.

About eighteen months after these prints stopped appearing, Graham (Lady Lucan's bodyguard) came up to me a said: "Larry I have somebody in the DCI's office I want you to meet."

In the corner of the room, sitting on a chair, was a shabbily dressed round-faced guy. He smiled as we approached.

"Larry, meet Maurice Johnson, our door-kicking burglar."

"Him? Are you sure?" I said, quickly adding, "Let me see your fingers." I quickly examined them and saw it was indeed he.

"Why didn't you wear gloves?" I asked.

"I'm allergic," he replied in a soft voice with just a hint of the East End.

I was astounded. "What, woollen gloves, rubber gloves?"

"No, all gloves; my hands just swell up and a rash develops."

I found this incredible but clearly he wasn't stupid. He'd committed fifty-plus burglaries and netted more than £5million in jewellery and cash. I wondered how on earth this man had managed to force all those doors, but Maurice assured us he was as strong as any man and could open Fort Knox with a steel toecap boot.

"So how was he captured?" I asked Graham as we handed Maurice over to the duty sergeant for processing.

"Just walked in and confessed."

Most odd, I thought. But then no property was ever recovered, Maurice was sentenced to three years in prison and was out after two with a clean slate.

Having said that, if his fellow prisoners ever found about his exploits, his life would have become a misery, as they wouldn't hesitate to try and get their hands on his fortune, even if he no longer had it.

# THE POISONED REDHEAD

Ian, the senior Detective Sergeant emerged from the DI's office and called me over for a chat at his desk.

"A rich redhead in her late twenties has alleged that she's being poisoned by her husband. He stands to inherit her family fortune, so we have motive but how would I know if someone is being poisoned?"

"Samples of head hair and nail cuttings," I replied. "The hair needs to be pulled out by the root, mind you. A urine sample might tell you something, it's indicative of the previous 48 hours. Head hair and nails show up if something's been administered long-term."

"Can you do it?"

"Yeah, I suppose so," I said, without really knowing what the procedures were.

An appointment was made for the woman to return to the station the next day with a urine sample, and I was to take the samples of head hair, and finger nails for analysis at the Metropolitan Police's Forensic Laboratory.

To our amazement, she waltzed into the CID office the following morning carrying a two-pint jar full to the brim with bright orange urine.

I took it gingerly and with Ian, went down to the Divisional Surgeon's room, where I found two specimen bottles that would take about twenty centilitres each, more than sufficient for analysis.

"Why is it bright orange?' Ian asked. "And so cloudy."

I had no idea. Nor did I know why she'd thought to bring such a large sample. I carefully decanted the urine and poured the rest down the toilet. I winced when I did this as it stank. Was that significant? Bracing myself, I took a big sniff. There was a hint of something, was it garlic?

We returned to the potential victim and I handed her a pair of fingernail clippers.

"Would you cut your fingernails please?"

I picked up the nail samples with a pair of tweezers and placed them in a small specimen jar. Fingernails packaged, sealed and exhibited, I turned to the issue of the head hair sample. I explained that I needed to pull the hairs out by the root and I would be wearing a rubber glove simply to get a better grip of the hair. I pulled what I thought was a few strands of hair and, bloody hell, a whole clump came out leaving a bald patch the size of a couple of fifty-pence pieces.

I exchanged a significant look with Ian; hair loss is a symptom of arsenic poisoning. We sent the hair and nails off to the lab, impressing the urgency and the results came back showing a high concentration of arsenic that had been administered over some months.

We brought the lady in and gave her the bad news. Even though she had suspected, she was shocked and started to weep in front of us. It was then that it occurred to me that this could be a case of accidental self-poisoning. Napoleon Bonaparte and George III had both been poisoned by accidentally administered arsenic (wigs contained up to 300 times the 'safe' amount). I left the room and called a toxicologist who advised me that some pesticides contain arsenic that, although banned in this country were used widely in other parts of the world.

"Anywhere in particular?" I asked.

"East Asia," he replied. "China, places like that."

I returned to the interview room.

"Have you been to East Asia recently," I asked the red-headed lady. "Somewhere like China?"

"No, no I haven't."

"Anyone you know?"

"No. The only things I have that are related to China are some herbal supplements."

Aha! A quick test revealed these so-called herbal health supplements were loaded with forty times more arsenic than what was considered safe. The fact that she was a heavy smoker only compounded the problem, as arsenic is also used in tobacco farming.

The redhead was delighted to know her husband was innocent but was now mortified that she'd suspected him. I explained that her paranoia was another symptom of arsenic poisoning and this would ease as the arsenic left her system.

She left, relieved and determined to get well.

"Was that true Larry?" Ian asked as we watched her leave. "The paranoia thing?"

"To be honest, I'm not totally sure," I replied with a sigh, "But she has a long road to recovery ahead of her and she's going to need all the support she can get."

# THE HAY PROBLEM

"**L**arry, we've been asked to go up to the barracks. Ready to go in ten?"

The speaker was Gerwyn, a Welsh DI with a huge black, droopy moustache.

"Sure Guv, do I need any equipment?"

I always asked because not everything fitted in the mini-van, especially if passengers were involved, and they often were. I'd sometimes carry one or two officers in the back to the police station if we were short of police vehicles.

The 'barracks' was the world famous Household Cavalry Mounted Regiment, garrisoned at the Hyde Park Barracks in Knightsbridge. These were the Queen's official bodyguards, of black bearskin hat fame. Gerald Road CID had a good relationship with the HCMR and we were due to join them the following night for a social do at their Warrant Officers' mess, which consisted of a buffet-style meal and drinks.

I assumed we'd been called to help with something related to the social event but it soon became clear that something serious was afoot. I'd been to the barracks a few times before as part of an investigation into thefts of ceremonial swords and bearskins from lockers. These could easily fetch £800 apiece and there were plenty of wealthy American tourists prepared to pay what was an extraordinary amount of cash in those days.

The Senior Warrant Officer, Don York met us at the barracks gate, and escorted us past the horse yard. I was always surprised to see just how much stable hay had blown into the barrack building and was simply left piled up in stairwells and along the ground floor corridors.

"I have to warn you gentlemen," Don said gravely, as we rode up in the lift to the fifth floor of the thirty-three-floor building, "That you are about to see a deeply disturbing sight. I have kept quiet as I didn't want anyone finding out before we've been able to talk to the family and give them some idea of what exactly happened."

We arrived at the open door of a small bedsit. Inside was a single bed, a freestanding wardrobe, desk and TV. This was the cell-like home of the guys you see bouncing up and down, sat on their magnificent horses, clanging away in their shining regalia.

Behind the bedsit door was a 6"4' guard in full uniform, boots and all, hanging from a short rope. His boots were only half an inch from the floor.

The barracks doctor had already pronounced him dead.

Both Gerwyn and I were stunned into silence.

When I did finally find my voice, I spoke in a whisper. "Need to call a photographer Guv, before we cut him down."

"OK Larry, can you organize it while I speak with Don?"

This experience made a deep impression on me. Only the best of the best were able to join the Household Cavalry, seen by many as a plumb job, a stepping-stone on a glittering career. Indeed, everything about this young man screamed perfection. He was even clean-shaven, for god's sake. He'd been alive that morning, had shaved, showered and dressed and gone about his day, walking and talking, breathing, just like the rest of us, but something had made his life so unbearable that he could not stand to spend another moment alive.

I later heard that there was bullying at barracks and Don swore he would root it out but alas, this is easier said than done and, over the years, I heard of two more suicides.

The following evening, I was with Jennifer at the Barracks buffet when Don came up to us and started to thank me for my help. I stopped him and quickly tried to think of something to change the subject to anything superficial, and then I thought of their hay problem and Don, realizing, took the baton. I simply wasn't ready to discuss that tragic death in front of Jennifer.

# MOUNTBATTEN'S NEIGHBOURS

Our daily sudden intrusion into people's lives meant that I soon learned that everyone really is different - but at the same time, we're all extremely similar. In other words, we all (generally speaking) want the same things (a home, family, wealth, sex and so on) but we all have quite different ideas about how, who, when and why.

A prime example of this occurred after I was called to a burglary that had taken place in a ground floor flat of a mews house, which was next door to the London residence of Earl Mountbatten.

Earl Mountbatten was a prime target for assassination by the IRA and so Special Branch were kept informed as we made sure that the burglary wasn't some kind of a set up in order for terrorists to enter or bomb the Earl's house.

I went with Dinger Bell and we arrived at 10am to find that the entrance door had been forced open with a jemmy, although the lock was only a rim lock, so any heavy booted villain could have gained access. It was open so, after knocking and shouting "Police!" a few times and getting no response, we entered. The front door led to a long corridor with rooms off to the right. Sitting room first, dining room, kitchen and at the bottom of the corridor was the bedroom. No one was in the first three rooms, and we started to wonder whether something fishy was going on until finally, we reached the bedroom door. Dinger knocked, shouted "Police!" and opened.

"No one there," I said craning to see over Dinger's shoulder. But I'd spoken too soon. The duvet moved. Someone was underneath. Dinger repeated the knock and "Police!" and this time a woman's head appeared.

"Good Morning, I am Detective Constable Bell from Gerald Road Police station. You reported a burglary?"

"Yes, Yes," replied the woman, who was dark-haired and in her early thirties.

Then a guy's head appeared from under the same duvet. He smiled, wished us good morning and disappeared again.

"Um," Dinger said, "Alright if we look around? We'd like to examine the door."

"Yes, yes, thank you."

Dinger Bell went to speak with the neighbours while I examined the door. I took samples of wood and paint from the doorframe and a Silcoset cast of the jemmy mark. Dinger returned a short time later to report that the Earl was not currently in residence.

My examinations completed, we walked back down the corridor to the bedroom. Dinger knocked on the door and opened it without waiting for a reply, saying "We're all done, I'd get that lock seen to if I-" he stopped in shock.

The dark haired woman was on her back, still covered by the duvet, which writhed and bucked over her like a live thing, while her head bounced off the headboard.

"Thank you officer!" she gasped, and her gentleman friend didn't even break his stride.

We both walked down the corridor in a state of mutual disorientation and, as we emerged into the sunlight, Dinger said: "I don't know about you Larry but I suddenly feel like a stiff one," and we strolled to the Star Tavern, which was just at the end of the mews and which had just opened. We took our seats at the bar and ordered drinks.

"The only loud bangs Lord Mountbatten's going to hear," I muttered, as the scotch arrived, "Is the sound of next door's headboard."

# STAIRWAYS TO HEAVEN

The Profumo Affair began on 14 December 1962 when journalists picked up on the story that War Secretary John Profumo had slept with a prostitute by the name of Christine Keeler. At first, Profumo publicly denied any close relationship but was eventually forced to admit he'd been lying and resigned the following year. The scandal nearly crippled Harold Macmillan's Conservative government and contributed to their defeat in the general election of October 1964.

Keeler's pimp, Stephen Ward, was charged with living off immoral earnings and was being tried at the Old Bailey when he committed suicide – although some conspiracy theorists have speculated that MI5 silenced him so he wouldn't reveal any more ministerial dalliances. Ward was found guilty while still in a coma – he died three days later.

When a barrister, examining Keeler's friend and fellow prostitute, Mandy Rice-Davis, made the point that Lord Astor (one of the alleged high-profile clients) denied the affair, Mandy answered with: "He would, wouldn't he?" (often misquoted as "Well, he would, wouldn't he?"

or "Well he would say that, wouldn't he?"). This phrase has since been established in legal circles as MRDA (Mandy Rice-Davies Applies).

Christine and Mandy were both regular visitors to Gerald Road police station. No, it's not what you're thinking, they both made various allegations of burglaries at their homes (possibly by the press) and of harassment by journalists who made their lives a misery by following them in the hope of finding "more dirt".

I visited Mandy's home in Ennismore Garden Mews, Knightsbridge, after it had been broken into. It was in a row of tiny terraced houses, and after opening the front door you were confronted with a white builder's ladder, positioned close to a ninety-degree angle. This stairway to heaven was the only way to access Mandy's bedroom and I was surprised that Lord Astor and possibly Profumo did not argue in their defence that such a ladder was beyond the climbing capabilities of most politicians, let alone Lords.

Heights, as it turned out, were an occupational hazard in my line of work, as many burglars like to enter properties via the roof. Late one afternoon, I was on the roof of the Grosvenor Hotel in Buckingham Palace Road, ten very tall floors above street level, overlooking Victoria Station. A particularly adventurous cat burglar had targeted the room of a wealthy individual by leaping to and from a fire escape. It was a death-defying leap. One slip and you were dead.

Dinger Bell was checking the burglar's suspected route while I examined some shoe marks in the dirt on the flat roof. These must be the burglar's, I thought, slowly walking backwards as I examined each footmark in turn. Shoeprints can be as unique as fingerprints, if you're able to get a good cast and/or photograph of the print and I was totally absorbed, hoping to find a suitable sample.

"LARRY!"

The yell had come from Dinger who quickly grabbed my arm and pulled me forward.

"Christ Larry, another foot and it would have been all over for you."

I turned to look and had indeed been just one step from death; I'd nearly backed myself over the edge.

I'm not the sweary type but when it sunk in that Dinger had literally just saved my life, I let out a series of expletives and spent the rest of the week buying the detective all the drinks he could manage.

Once I'd calmed down, facing the other way, I started to label the marks for the photographer. "Better advise the photographer to face this way while taking the pictures," I told Dinger.

Once our work was done we left the hotel and, as it was the end of the day, we went for a drink in the Shakespeare, one of our regular haunts. Drinking after work was a habit. Our local was the Duke of Wellington, affectionately known as 'The Duke of Boots,' and George Best was a regular when he played for Fulham. On Friday afternoons at around 4pm, one of the DI's would pull out a bottle of gold watch and the whole office would have a glass. This proved to be a highly effective way of debriefing the week's events, planning the next week, as well as giving the team time to relax together and bury any hatchets that may have been thrown during the week. The scotch would, naturally, be followed by a drink in the Duke of Boots and then, if we were feeling in the party mood, a pub-crawl would ensue, which usually involved the Shakespeare.

While Colin the landlord poured our drinks, he mentioned he had a problem. He was convinced that one of his many staff (it was a large and busy pub) was nicking cash from the tills. I thought about suggesting one of my fuchsine traps, but they could be messy, so I suggested marking some money with a UV pen and then, with another three or four detectives, keep watch. My plan was quickly agreed (what detective in his right mind doesn't want to stake out a pub?) and so I marked my initials on the notes with a fluorescent pen and the next night we returned for a drink. We arrived in twos without acknowledging each other. Two sat at the bar, another two where they could easily see the tills, and the third pair were on the opposite side of the bar. If someone spotted the thief, the signal was to go to the toilet. Dinger spotted the guy first and after about an hour or so we observed 'under ringing' at least five times. It was a busy pub, so it was easy for Dinger to speak to Colin without any suspicion. Just before last orders Colin asked to see the thief in his office. The guy was asked to turn out his pockets and I examined the notes he placed on Colin's desk. Two of my UV notes were there. He had been under-ringing the rounds and taking out the equivalent in notes over the course of the evening. He was sacked on the spot. No charges were brought against him but it served as a warning to the rest of the staff. More importantly for us, we had a very grateful pub manager who stood us a great many rounds that probably (I can't quite remember) involved a lock-in and I have no idea what time I finally managed to stagger through my front door.

# FOR THE LOVE OF MAUD

Although the hours were long (made worse by my commute), the police way of life suited Jennifer and I. We shared friends and I loved my job and loved working in Belgravia (despite the long commute) where, like much of London, rich and poor lived side-by-side. This love of the job sometimes inspired me to break what Dinger Bell told me was Golden Rule No. 1: "Do not get involved with the victims."

Golden Rule No. 2 was: "Always leave them smiling." Sometimes, Golden Rule No. 1 was broken in favour of Golden Rule No. 2.

The Peabody buildings off Pimlico Road were built for the poor, a Victorian enterprise financed by George Peabody, the American-British entrepreneur and philanthropist. This area was Belgravia's equivalent of the East End, with gas and electricity meter burglaries being the most frequent crimes. The local 'tea-leafs' would work out when the meters were fullest and generally, a quick kick against a feeble rim lock was enough to gain access to the tenement property. After that it was simple enough to crack open the gas and electricity meters that were in the cupboard under the stairs, or just above the front door. Another method of entry involved pushing back the thumb catch in the middle of a sash window using a strong knife slid between the window frames.

One such burglary involved Maud, a dear old soul in her seventies. I visited her at 5pm to find that both of her service meters had been broken open. I carried out a routine examination, which revealed finger marks on the coin boxes of the meters; that was something at least. I closed the window and locked it, hoping Maud would be spared any more visits from the local villains. Sadly, two weeks later I was back again, and this time the thugs had used brute force to snap the brass window catch. I again found finger marks on the cash boxes.

Maud was really upset. "The catch is broken," she said "And I've no one to fix it."

"You could call someone to come and beef up your security," I said, offering her a couple of recommendations of places to try.

Maud shook her head. "I'm stoney," she said, clearly ashamed to have to admit she was hovering just below the poverty line.

I found a screw and managed, after a great deal of muffled cursing and a little spilt blood, to get it through the wood, securing the two sides of the window together. Good enough for now - although I'd managed to chip off quite a bit of paint in the process.

The next morning on my burglary round, I detoured to a hardware shop just off Regent Street. I bought the latest thumb-style catch for the sash windows, returned to see Maud and fitted the new lock, removed the screw and touched up the paint and left, having achieved Golden Rule Two.

I was in quite a reflective mood that day, as my next stop was the Forensic Science Laboratory's canteen, where I met with twenty other SOCOs and sat together nervously, hugging mugs of tea, waiting to hear where our new three-year postings were going to be.

I didn't want to leave Belgravia. I counted Dinger Bell and Buster as close friends and now I was going to lose them. The only way to keep friends in the police is to keep working with them because everyone is so damn busy and working such long hours. I was also worried about my next posting; I didn't fancy Brixton, or the East End, both had especially bad reputations for ridiculous amounts of burglaries and thefts, as well as for violent crimes.

I stood up when my time came and approached the desk behind which the Chief Super from the Fingerprint Department was sitting, riffling through our files.

"Mr Henderson, you have a home posting, you will be going to Zulu Tango, Sutton."

I again heard the words "Lucky bastard," muttered this time by a tall sepulchral like man who had been unfortunate enough to be awarded Brixton. He didn't know the half of it. I had moved house ten months earlier and now resided in West Ewell, ten minutes' drive away from Sutton. Compared to the ninety-minute train and bus journey to the Yard, I couldn't complain.

But I was sad to leave Belgravia (at my leaving drinks, which were held in the office, Buster presented me with a Parker pen) and, walking through Victoria Station, with the thought that on Monday I would be working at Sutton Police Station, I couldn't help look back at my three-and-a-half years at Gerald Road. I'd met film stars and politicians, royalty and state representatives which along with the relevant investigations, had proven to be more than an education but as the train swept me away from central London, I saw the tenement flats of Pimlico and my thoughts turned to Maud and my job. I was here to make a difference; this job was all about helping people like Maud, those who couldn't always help themselves and thanks to those finger marks, the thieves were brought to justice. At the time, I couldn't think of any other case that had brought me greater satisfaction.

# PART TWO

April 1974 – March 1976
Sutton Police Station, Carshalton Rd, Sutton SM1 4RF

Station Code ZT
Sub-station Wallington ZW

# BURGLAR-DETECTING RADAR

**M**y new DCI was John O'Connor, who went on to become Commander of the Flying Squad and, after his retirement, a regular TV News pundit. Straight to the point and loaded with common sense, you knew where you stood with John.

I was responsible for Sutton and the sub-division of Wallington, (ZW). As usual, burglary incidents ruled the day, with the odd stolen car thrown in every now and again. There were no fancy MOs; just broken rear windows, back doors smashed in with a spade found in the garden shed, and so on.

I saw something a bit different when I was called to the house of Chelsea striker Ian Hutchinson, famous for his ability to confuse defenders with long throw-ins that were more like corners. His home was alarmed with contact points on the doors and pressure pads under the carpets, although the windows were not alarmed. The burglar had cleverly removed a small pane of glass to open a window, and once inside, he only stepped on the furniture. He entered each ground floor room the same way and escaped with a number of valuables. You didn't have to be Hercule Poirot to realize the burglar had some inside knowledge. I recovered glove marks from the small windowpanes but they were unidentifiable, so I wasn't much help and the burglar was never caught.

There was little time to reflect on one particular burglary case at this time; it was June 1976, the height of that famous long, hot summer, and so people slept with their bedroom windows open at night. This was great news for burglars and for one glove-wearing cat burglar in particular who had little trouble finding the ladders residents left lying around in their gardens. He crept through bedrooms while people slept, taking jewellery and cash. He was confident enough to search the whole house before leaving via a ground floor window.

I soon noticed that the burglaries all had one factor in common: all of the victims' houses backed onto the same golf course. I got hold of some night vision binoculars and special patrols were put in place to try and catch him in the act but they came up with nothing.

I then came up with the idea of 'preparing' a house for burglary as bait, as long as we could find a cooperative owner, and lie in wait. The consensus was that "*Agent Provocateur*" (i.e., when police officers instigate a situation which leads a person to commit a crime), would provide our cat burglar with a possible defence. I argued that at least the burglar would be caught and we would put an end to the spree, which by then totalled thirteen victims. It was not to be, but the Technical Support Department offered me a "man-seeking radar" so we could monitor certain parts of the golf course. I plotted the burglaries, and along with the DI, we chose two areas that we thought were likely to be targeted.

The bulky ex-military radar equipment required a special operator. It worked like sonar on a submarine, so the operative needed to be skilled in interpreting the noise coming back through headphones. A crackling noise could be a fox, or other small mammal such as a mouse, or a human being.

The first night we got nothing, only a few false alarms. We speculated that the burglar had perhaps seen the installation, which we'd concealed in some bushes at the rear of a row of back gardens that backed onto the golf course. Nothing again on the second night but on the third night, a new noise was heard and this time, the operative gave us the nod and lead us to a particular house. The Area Crime car was sent and reinforcements followed, all on "silent approach".

The burglar's MO was to climb into a back bedroom facing the golf course, so officers surrounded the rear of the house and sat down to wait. A ladder was already up against the bedroom window and, hey ho, three minutes later a rear ground floor window was opened and the burglar climbed out into the arms of a sixteen-stone, six-foot-two uniform constable.

This was a real team effort and I was proud to have been part of it, my first success in suburbia. But if I imagined I would settle down into any kind of suburban routine of one burglary case after another, my illusions were quickly shattered by the many weird, wonderful and nasty characters that I now know exist in every part of the UK.

# THE SUSPICIONS OF
# MR HENDERSON

J ane, a woman living on her own in Carshalton had made an allegation that was officially recorded as burglary, but was in reality something else entirely but, as we didn't have a category for ghosts, burglary it was.

Jane, who was in her forties and seemed quite sane and sensible, told me, "I wake up in the middle of the night and my room has gone really cold. Then, when I get up in the morning, I find marks on the screen of my television, similar to a hand mark."

"Anything stolen?" I asked.

"No, nothing."

I was a Scenes of Crime Officer, not an exorcist, I thought but, I was here now and the woman was understandably upset at the idea of somebody or something wandering around her house at night. I started with the TV. The mark was from a greasy or extremely sweaty human palm. Such marks can be identified the same way as a fingerprint. Ok, so this was no ghost (although who was to say ghosts can't leave such an impression?) but with no other evidence the detectives were at a bit of loss.

I was called back twice more, as Jane kept finding the mark on the television each morning, despite wiping it clean each day, and this was always preceded by the cold blast of air.

It was during my third examination that I noticed the loft hatch, which was in the bedroom, was ever so slightly out of place. I lightly dusted the white painted hatch and there were some unidentifiable finger-type marks around the edges. Well, better take a look up in the attic. Obviously, being of scientific stock, I don't tend to believe ghost stories (although I did once run out of my local cinema during a screening of an X-rated Boris Karloff movie when I was fourteen years old) but, as I gently lifted the hatch, I felt more than a little apprehensive. I carefully lifted my head into the darkness, switched on my torch and peered around. The loft continued for the entire the length of the terrace of the four cottages with no separating walls. I shone my torch up and saw a rope had been tied to a roof timber above the hatch but did not think this in itself was suspicious. However, if someone was opening that hatch at night, then the cold air would soon become noticeable (it was February). I informed the officer in charge, a young sergeant called John who, luckily for Jane, had boundless enthusiasm for his job.

"So, the question remains," he said, "Who or what is descending that rope, and how do we catch them? Any ideas?"

"Not really," I said. "Apart from a panic button in the bedroom." The idea was put to Jane but she was understandably not happy with the prospect of confronting a stranger in her bedroom and hitting a panic button, which would only alert the police station.

"Fair enough," John said. "I'll sit in the bedroom myself."

Jane made arrangements to sleep at a friend's house for a couple of nights. The plan was that she would arrive home as usual around 6pm, and follow her normal routine until around 10pm. Then she would quietly leave by the back door to go to her friend's home. John went in by the back door accompanied by a uniform constable. They made the bed to look like Jane was in it by using a couple of pillows from the second bedroom, turned all the lights out and sat on the floor in a corner of the lounge.

At 3am they heard a stair creak, and both sergeant and constable prepared themselves for the confrontation by taking their truncheons out of their back pockets. The constable moved to the light switch and, as a shadow entered the lounge, the light went on. There was a guy in his late twenties dressed in black, wearing a balaclava, which totally covered his face, except for two eyeholes.

"'Allo mate, can we help you?" John asked cheerfully.

The man jumped out of his skin, and John quickly got the truth out of him before he had time to calm down and think up a lie.

The owner and landlord of the terrace of the four cottages wanted to sell to a developer, but Jane had refused to move for as long as her tenancy agreement said she could stay. The landlord was in a hurry, he urgently needed the money, so had paid this young man to frighten Jane so that she would move out 'voluntarily'.

When we talked to Jane, she admitted she was in dispute with her landlord.

"Why didn't you mention this earlier?" I asked.

"I didn't think it was important," she said. "But it worked, I was about to give in. Calling the police was the last resort and I'm just glad you didn't tell me I was crazy."

The young 'ghoul' received a custodial sentence as he was on probation for theft and the landlord was charged with a conspiracy offence and received a slapped wrist. Jane won a stay of execution but, deciding she didn't want to remain in her home with such an angry landlord, found a new place to live a short time later so, in a way the landlord's ploy worked.

# BETHANY AND THE BANK ROBBERS

C hanging attitudes to authority, the growth of motorways and the arrival of cheap, fast cars, helped robbers stay ahead of the law. 'Crossing the pavement'
became the crime of choice for a generation of post-war,
mostly white, working-class criminals who introduced
the sawn-off shotgun to Britain. In 1972, the annual total
of armed robberies in the Metropolitan district was 380.
By 1978, it had risen to 734 and by 1982 it more than doubled to 1,772 (that's five a day) - a 366 per cent increase in
a decade.

The core of British criminality has long resided
within the Bermondsey Triangle (so-called because of
the high incidence of unexplained losses of goods and
people that cross its borders), which runs from London
Bridge, to Peckham and back up the Old Kent Road
into Bermondsey. The hardened bank robbers of south
London often decided to target the softer areas (as they
saw it) of Surrey. One particular gang decided to pick on
the Abbey National Building Society (known as Santander
today) in Cheam, which stood on a corner of a busy cross
roads: London Road and Sutton Common Road. It was

the perfect location for a robbery as the getaway driver had several avenues of escape.

I arrived fifteen minutes after the bandits had left and was pleased to see a uniform constable was already standing outside the entrance door to the building society, preserving the external scene. I was then dismayed to see him wait until a member of the public attempted to open the door before he stepped in to stop them. I had a gentle word with him advising that I would examine the outside of the premises as quickly as possible but in the meantime he should keep the public's sticky fingers well away from the door. I was constantly surprised by the lack of police constables' knowledge with regard to crime scene preservation.

The staff had coped well, and despite the threats made by the two be-stockinged, sawn-off shotgun-carrying robbers, they'd handed over notes that were clipped to an alarm. As soon as the clip snapped, the alarm had been raised at the police station, hence my quick arrival. The robbers had escaped with around £20,000 so they were happy, and no shots were fired.

I searched for anything that could have been dropped in the blaggers' haste to jump into their getaway car. Then I fingerprinted the entrance door and lifted a number of finger marks. I completed the examination of the interior and then informed the manageress that if she wanted to re-open for business she could do so. There was a queue forming outside so, displaying a stiff upper lip, she opened up immediately.

There was nothing particularly remarkable about this case. It was just another bank robbery; no one hurt, gang gone, investigation started and evidence collected. The reason I'm telling you this story at all is thanks to a four-year-old girl called Bethany.

I was still in the bank, sitting at a desk behind the counter completing my notes when a mum, accompanied by her demure four-year-old daughter with red hair in short ringlets, approached the cashier.

Despite her experience only an hour earlier, the bespectacled cashier, who was in her mid-thirties, asked the mum in an upbeat voice how she could be of assistance. The mum explained that her daughter Bethany had been working all week with the builders at home who were constructing an extension. Mum went on to say Bethany had been paid for washing up the builders' teacups morning and afternoon, and now she wanted to open a savings account to deposit her wages.

The mild-mannered cashier looked at Bethany and said: "Of course, I'll get that all arranged for you," before adding, by way of making conversation, "So why aren't you working today, young lady?"

Bethany's reaction was quite remarkable. Her timidity suddenly vanished, to be replaced by a look of disgust. She leant forward, placing her hands on her hips and yelled: "How do you expect me to work when they don't deliver the fucking bricks!?"

Clearly she was imitating some behaviour seen at home, no doubt Mum's frustration at her builder's delays. Almost everyone in the bank started to giggle uncontrollably while Mum, red-faced, just wanted the floor to swallow her up.

# A DEATH IN THE FAMILY

I was booked to play in a badminton tournament at my club in New Malden, a longstanding commitment that I'd trained hard for, and Jennifer was right behind me, even coming to some matches to cheer me on. This was getting harder for her, however, as she was eight months pregnant by the time of the tournament. Jennifer was also under considerable stress as her mother was seriously ill with cancer and, because she lived 300 miles away, doctors had advised Jennifer against travelling to see her until after the birth.

On the night of the tournament, I happened to be the on-call SOCO and had to work until 8pm. The majority of burglaries are discovered when people return from work, so it had been decided that an on-call SOCO should provide cover for six police stations up to 8pm every day. Time was tight, but I was not due on court for my mixed doubles match until 8.30pm and I was all set to leave by 7.55pm; my gear was tidied away, paperwork filed and mini-van safely berthed and booked into the station records.

I was marching out at 7.59pm when I heard "Larry!" come from the back of the nick.

'Keep going,' I told myself, but I knew better and turned around to see the sergeant approaching

"There's been a fatality on the railway line at West Croydon," he said. "The Duty Officer has asked that you attend."

I ran back to my desk to call to the club and asked if we could reschedule. Sadly not, the match had to be played tonight. I was gutted, mainly because I was about to let down my doubles partner (the organizers had arranged entrants by standard so a strong woman played with a weaker man, and vice versa and my partner from the "A" team, was easily county standard and perhaps even higher) but also because I'd worked so hard to reach a standard where we thought we had a chance of winning. Badminton and squash were passions of mine, a valuable way to let off work-related steam and I'd been determined to maintain this hobby despite my ever-increasing workload.

I arrived at West Croydon railway station and met up with the Duty Officer. He explained that a train had hit a white male, thought to be about thirty years old.

"This is one for the Accident Investigators Guv, why do you need me?"

"We need help removing the body and body parts from the line, and I thought you would have body bags and all the exhibits stuff."

Fair enough. The night was now doomed and, even worse I was now engaged in what proved to be an extremely grim and disturbing task. The man had been hit first by the southbound train, which pushed him into the northbound line where he was hit a second time. His torso and head lay to the right side of the northbound line. One leg was lying inside the line, completely crushed, while the other lay just outside the southbound line. I had come a long way since my fainting fit at the mortuary and could just about cope with gruesome cases like this but what made it worse than being in a mortuary was that you were so close to this person's life. You were witness to their last moments and our brains lead us to seek connections to other humans and one can't help but start to wonder, as I started to plan the removal of the remains, about this man's life, his family; what had driven him to throw himself under a train, or whether it was perhaps some bizarre accident.

At the time, the Americans already had zip-up body bags as seen on TV shows, but us Brits had a large white plastic sheet, eight-feet long and four-feet wide, upon which we laid the victim. First the hands were covered in plastic bags, which were closed with sticky tape (to preserve evidence/prevent contamination), then the head, and then the feet.

This done, the body was wrapped in the plastic sheet and the ends were bound closed with sticky tape. The end result looked like an enormous white plastic Christmas cracker. We repeated the same procedure for the severed legs. Although it was fairly obvious the legs were the victim's, I treated them as separate exhibits. Once this had all been completed, I advised the Duty Officer who then handed the incident over to the British Transport Police. I was in my van and just about to head off when the Transport Police DI came jogging over to me, making 'hang on a minute' hand signals.

'What now?' I wondered. I had found the procedure deeply upsetting and just wanted to get away.

"Any info Larry?"

"Yeah, the guy was pissed."

"How do you know that?"

"Well, he's legless, isn't he?"

My expression had remained deadpan throughout this short exchange but the DI understood my bad joke represented the cop coping mechanism in action.

'Oh no,' I thought, as I drove away, 'I'm developing cop humour.'

I drove back to the station and phoned the badminton club. They said the tournament was just coming to a close but, if I could make it by 10.30pm, our opponents were still willing to play. If not we would have to scratch it off as a loss.

Not wanting to disappoint my A-class partner, I made a beeline for the club, got changed and by 10.32pm and, after a two-minute warm-up, our shuttles were cocked and ready.

We won, and after a fast shower, I dashed home, arriving at 11.45pm but of course Jennifer was in bed and our two labs, as usual, raised neither eye nor brow. Honey, the older of the two, was even snoring.

Over the next couple of nights we won our matches and reached the semi-final, which was to be played on the

Friday night. Jennifer was going to come and cheer me on; it was a welcome escape from the boredom of pregnancy and the stress of her mother's illness. If we won, then the final was set for the Saturday, followed by presentations, buffet and a disco.

I was changed and ready to go in plenty of time. My partner, Liz, talked me through our tactics. We were all set when I felt a tap on my shoulder. It was the bar steward, "Phone call for you, well for your wife actually," he said.

Jennifer took the call and burst into tears. It was her Dad. Her Mum had died that evening, at the age of fifty-four, less than a month before her first grandson would be born. The match was abandoned and I drove Jennifer home, still sobbing.

If only I hadn't rushed around on Monday to get to the club, I thought. We would have cancelled and Jennifer and I would have been at home when the call came. I felt awful for her. She'd had to take the call at the club and then leave in tears in front of two hundred club members who were wondering what all the commotion was about. We arrived home and the two labs, seeing Jennifer upset, were all over her, their way of showing sympathy.

We're told we can have it all, the work, family and play, the so called life-balance, but it's just not like that in reality; when you try to do it all, sometimes it feels as though you end up letting everyone down.

# MACABRE (BANK HOLIDAY) MONDAY

The routine of suburbia: Up at 6am. Breakfast, kids up and dressed, to school, to work, lunch if there's time, then everyone back home by 7pm and in bed by 11pm.

Sometimes, the routine snaps. And that's when I arrive on the doorstep. Like this one. A nondescript semi-detached house in Wallington. A rolled-up carpet lay in the hallway. Items strewn about the kitchen. No sign of anyone. A possible burglary. The burglar may have been disturbed and left the carpet. You can't rule out anything. I've attended more than one burglary where owners have returned from holiday to find their patio doors have been nicked.

Neighbours had called the police because of screaming.

"So where's the screamer?" I said to the constable, adding with a chuckle, "I suppose you have checked the carpet in case the missus is in there?"

I had arrived just a couple of minutes after the police and the constable suddenly looked uncomfortable, as if a very unpleasant penny had just dropped.

We started to unroll the carpet and spotted a painted fingernail poking out one end. Suddenly, with the momentum of the unrolling and the weight of the contents, a woman's body spilled out and onto the floor. A carving knife was sticking out of her chest.

I travelled to a Mortuary in South London, where I joined John, the Detective Sergeant, to witness the post mortem. It was a Bank Holiday Monday, one of the most popular days for domestics, apart from Christmas Day, and we had to wait because there was a bit of a backlog and some of the staff were off enjoying the miserable bank holiday weather.

I remember it like it was yesterday because on this day, one of those so-called urban legends was born; it grew to the extent that Jethro, the Cornish comedian, told the story on mainstream television. This one, however, I swear is true because I was there.

We heard a bit of a commotion going on in the mortuary and shortly afterwards we were joined by the mortuary attendant, whose name was Hannibal (yes, it really was).

"What was all that noise about?" John asked. "Sounded like you had a rush on or something."

"Well," Hannibal said quietly, "Nothing much really."

He explained how a woman in her seventies had arrived at the mortuary to identify her husband who had dropped dead of a heart attack when he went to buy a newspaper. Hannibal escorted the lady into a viewing room where her husband lay on a trolley with a purple shroud covering him. When he folded back the shroud, the old soul gasped. Obviously very upset she said: "Yes, that's my Fred but he was wearing his favourite green suit this morning. That suit's brown. I don't understand. I know he would want to be buried in his favourite green suit".

Hannibal told the lady he would see to it and immediately wheeled the corpse out of the viewing room and back into an anteroom. He returned five minutes later with the shroud once again laid over the body. He rolled it back and the widow was as happy as she could be on such a day. Fred was now wearing his favourite green suit.

"Oh thank you. Fred will be pleased he's now in his favourite suit".

Hannibal admitted he'd dressed Fred in the wrong suit that belonged to another guy of the same size. He'd simply muddled them in his rush to get Fred ready for the viewing.

"But," I said, "How the hell did you undress and redress the corpse on your own in just five minutes? Surely that's impossible."

Hannibal looked at me deadpan and said: "I swapped the heads over."

Gobsmacked is a term that probably didn't do our expressions justice at that moment but I had to admit that Fred's wife was at least happy and, being old, hopefully never heard the story retold and put two and two together. Hannibal swapped the heads back and redressed Fred and the other man later that night, so all was right for the funerals.

Our murder victim's post mortem was straightforward enough. Cause of death: knife through the heart. Death was instantaneous. By the time I got back to Sutton nick the husband had turned himself in. The argument had started because the wife said she was leaving him and was taking the family dog, a black Alsatian called Jet, with her.

# THEY EAT HUMANS, DON'T THEY?

Surrey suburbia looks like a heavenly place to live, superficially. Quiet streets lined with mature trees that rustle in gentle breezes, detached houses with roomy gardens and garages, the sound of children playing. But of course, peep behind the curtains and it doesn't take long to find pain and heartbreak.

I was called to attend a suspicious death in the garage of a semi-detached house. A mother (and now widow) with two children, had found her husband lying against the wall, propped up with a large cushion and the top of his head blown off by a shotgun.

It looked to me as though he'd shot himself from below the chin, up into his head. The man's brains were splattered all around the garage. An unbelievably awful sight for his young widow.

The problem was that the double-barrelled shotgun was lying a couple of feet away from the body.

If this had been a suicide, I would've expected the gun to still be underneath the chin from where it was fired, or laid in a recognizable position on or close to the body as a result of the recoil. Of course, the position of the body propped against the wall, with no signs of any other trauma such as scratch marks, or bruises, suggested suicide. On top of this, his widow, although in shock, had managed to tell a constable that her husband was a prison officer and had been suffering from depression after failing to gain promotion. Fair enough, but as a prison officer, he may have made some particularly nasty enemies.

Once all the photographs had been taken I picked up the shotgun to render it safe as there was still a cartridge in the chamber. Blood had congealed around the gun barrel. The blood, would in due course, be grouped and compared with the victim's blood group but there was no question that, before it was sent off for analysis, the gun had to be made safe. The congealed blood made it very difficult to break open I was looking around the garden for a bin so I could point the gun into it in case it went off accidentally when I forced it open. It was at this point that I noticed the family's Jack Russell was about to enter the garage via the side door, which I'd noticed was open when I arrived. I put the gun down and hurried over to the dog to stop it contaminating the scene. As I picked it up I noticed pink-coloured pieces of brain tissue around his mouth.

I managed to stifle an "Argghh!"

After cleaning up the dog, I checked with the widow who confirmed that her husband had let the terrier out and into the garden at around 6.30am that morning.

Aha. So he had blown his brains out, then the dog had feasted on them, knocking the gun off the body in the process. Mystery solved, confirmed by our subsequent comparisons of the blood on the weapon and the victim, as well as the powder burns on the victim with the gunpowder in the cartridges. The dog's involvement was, thank goodness, not mentioned during the inquest. Official verdict: suicide.

# BEASTLY CASES

I was standing in a field, surrounded by about thirty donkeys. Of all the places I thought this job would take me, this seemed to me to be the most unlikely, even though Epsom was a 'horsey' town, with riding schools, pony clubs and sanctuaries. At first, I'd thought it was a wind-up. Apparently, a woman passing this field, which was off the Chessington road in West Ewell, had noticed a man stood on a box, wearing black Wellington boots, with his trousers around his ankles, having sex with a donkey.

When I'd finally been convinced that this was a genuine case (young police officers were sometimes sent on bizarre call-outs as part of their initiation), I called in a vet to help with the examinations.

I found a sturdy wooden box hidden under a hedge but, disappointingly, it was a dry sunny day, so no Wellington boot marks, although I did take a sample of the soil it was caked in.

I then turned my attention to the donkeys, wondering: 'Where does one start?' before thinking of the obvious answer. But we also needed some system for identifying them, so we didn't end up examining the same donkey twice.

Fortunately, Roy the vet had thought of this and had brought some dye, so, as we examined each donkey, we painted a number on their rump. It wasn't easy. The donkeys did *not* want to be examined and two hours later, were had only got as far as No. 10. During a break, perspiring heavily, I decided to walk around the field to see if I could spot any signs that singled one donkey out from the rest. I then saw a donkey with its ears down. I looked around the field, checking. All the others were ears-up. This donkey looked distressed to me. I called over Roy he agreed that this female donkey was indeed showing signs of distress.

Examination revealed she was bleeding. The vet confirmed that it seemed as though she'd been attacked. We were then obliged to check out the rest of the donkeys for injuries. By the time we got to the final donkey, No.32, we had to use a torch, as night had fallen. No other donkeys had been attacked. Swabs taken from the distressed donkey confirmed the presence of semen, so the offence of bestiality had indeed occurred (bestiality is a criminal offence and also counts as Animal Cruelty, as part of the Animal Welfare Act) but no further incidents were reported, and the offender was never apprehended.

This was not my only encounter with this most bizarre and cruel perversion. One weekday afternoon, I received a phone call from the Duty Officer asking if I could attend a vet's clinic to look at a dog that the owner felt had 'in some way,' been 'attacked,' a feeling confirmed by the vet who had suggested this was a 'forensic case.'

I arrived to find a very distressed six-year-old Labrador bitch called Candy (so-named because she had eaten a bag of sweets as a puppy). The vet, a man around my age called Geoff, talked to me privately before I met the owners: "Some person has interfered with this dog sexually," he said gravely.

Geoff took internal and external vaginal swabs and I took swabs of her back, neck, and hindquarters before then using tape to take samples of her fur, to search for human hair and clothing fibres. I spoke gently and quietly to Candy as I worked but she was terrified, totally traumatized. I could imagine this sweet creature, like all labs, wagging her tail as this new person had approached, pleased to say "hello".

The owners had to endure a soul-destroying few minutes as Geoff quietly explained what had happened to Candy. I chipped in towards the end, assuring them, as an owner of two Labradors myself, that I would do my utmost to assist in any way I could but, in reality I felt fairly helpless, especially after the vet explained that Candy's prospects weren't good.

"She has internal injuries," he said, "And she doesn't appear to be coming out of shock."

I was horrified at the implication. "It's only been a few hours since the incident," I said in desperation, "Perhaps give her the night?"

Geoff agreed the couple could take Candy home, after giving her a sedative, and they promised to return with her first thing in the morning.

I left with the samples and drove to Epsom nick where I booked them into the property system and placed the swabs in the surgeon's fridge. Time to head home. Except I couldn't. I'd never brought my work back with me but, our two labs, Honey and Tanya, were vulnerable to attack from this pervert. They were allowed the run of our large garden, which ran onto green belt land. I wanted to keep an eye on them without alerting Jennifer to the fact, so that she wouldn't be tormented with the fear of something that would *probably* never happen. When I did finally get home, Tanya and Honey greeted me, as usual, as if I'd not seen them for a year and I gave both of them a big hug and a kiss and, without thinking, ignored Jennifer. I casually mentioned I'd heard a report about a fox attacking a dog on the other side of town so we should keep an eye on Tanya and Honey while they were in the garden. Candy's likely fate played heavily on my mind, leaving me with no appetite for dinner, so I headed to bed.

I was out the next morning by 8am and, after checking all the overnight reports for similar incidents and finding none, I phoned Geoff. He told me that the couple had sat up all night with Candy but couldn't cope with seeing her in such a state. Guided by Geoff, they put her to sleep at 8.30am.

"Bastard! Bastard! Bastard!" I shouted, and then quickly apologized to Geoff, in case he thought I was referring to him. Later that day I stopped by the heartbroken couple's house and examined their garden but there was no evidence to collect. The swabs proved positive with a human blood grouping but this was little help to us then. Today we would have been able to get a DNA profile from the swabs and, if the culprit had ever been prosecuted for any other crime, then we'd have an excellent chance of identifying him. Sadly the bastard was never caught, although no further incidents were ever reported.

This case hit me hard. For the first time in my career I felt the emotional pain that comes from powerlessness in the face of cruelty and injustice. My rule up to this point had been "don't get involved" but Candy broke the dam. I couldn't get Candy's tortured expression or her broken body out of my mind. For months I obsessively checked the overnight reports for another incident and while I was at home I wouldn't let the labs out of my sight. This was the beginning of my self-conditioning, as I promised myself that I wouldn't ever let 'The Job' get the better of my emotions again.

# THE FLESH EATERS

Although suburbia couldn't compete with central London in terms of excitement, it did now and then throw up a real humdinger of a surprise, as well as the occasional danger. This particular day began with me mulling over the state of my enormous garden and how I should start planting some veg. Thoughts of lawns, orchards and a 200ft long veg patch were still circulating through my mind so I only half heard the desk sergeant telling me something as I walked in to the station.

"Come again?" I asked.

"Welcome to the land of the living, Larry. Lab Sergeant Ken is at a house in Carshalton. He's asked if you can join him. Apparently a chap was digging out some foundations for a garage and he's unearthed a dead body."

If the area lab sergeant needed me to attend, then that usually meant I'd be lifting and shifting. There was an interesting aspect to this case however, in that twelve months earlier a woman from the house opposite had gone missing. I knew the routines for exhumations, but this might be my first 'live' one.

I arrived at the scene to find Ken, whom I hadn't met before (he was covering for the regular Liaison Sergeant) having a cup of coffee.

"Right Larry, I have to shoot off to a post mortem, so if you could excavate the earth away from what *might* be the protruding um, head."

"Is it a head?" I queried.

"Not sure yet."

Wellies, overall, rubber gloves, trowel and I was ready. I descended into a clay pit about four-feet deep and four-feet wide, with a twelve-inch blackened mass protruding from the base of the vertical wall of the pit. After about two hours of hunched, back-breaking excavation, the black mass was sixteen inches long. It had no resemblance to a human skull or any other part of human anatomy, although I did think at one point it could be a femur bone. I picked up a spade and dug six inches into the vertical side just above this mass and took out a large slither of earth. Then, with a trowel, I carefully excavated around the blackened bone.

"Bloody hell," I said to myself. "That's a horse's snout!"

The Victorians buried horses where they fell. Mystery solved, I took off my rubber gloves and started to climb out of the pit, noticing that Ken had just returned. As I put one foot on the topsoil, I slipped and flew back into the 'grave'. I instinctively threw out my hands to break my fall. My right hand went straight through the horse's head, which felt like paper-mache.

"I would get washed up if I was you!" Ken exclaimed as I climbed out, successfully this time. "Could be anthrax in that horse, you know!"

I washed my hands under an outside garden tap at the rear of the semi before returning to the nick for a thorough scrub with hot water and disinfectant.

Three weeks later, I arrived home from a fairly typical day's work feeling under the weather. I had a temperature and felt queasy, so I passed on dinner, took two paracetamol and went to bed. It was spring; surely I couldn't have caught the flu?

After a rough night, I woke up and kissed Jennifer good morning. She gasped in horror, which, I'm glad to say was not her usual reaction.

"Something's really wrong with you Larry! Your head's swollen and you're covered in yellow sores!"

Could this be anthrax? I spent a pretty unpleasant and anxious couple of hours waiting for a doctor who immediately said: "Do you think you would be better off in hospital?"

I shouldn't have waited.

"Get me in there ASAP!"

An ambulance arrived minutes later and full barrier nursing procedures were instigated. For the next twenty-four hours I was prodded and poked, but the only treatment I received was two paracetamol and a large fan to keep me cool.

"Have you been around sheep recently?" the doctors asked.

"No but I put my hand through a dead horse's head three weeks ago."

"Have you been camping anywhere recently?"

"No but I did put my hand through a dead horse's head three weeks ago".

"Do you do a lot of gardening?"

"Not a lot but I like sitting in the garden at home, plus three weeks ago I PUT MY BLOODY HAND THROUGH A BLOODY HORSES HEAD!"

I was given two paracetamol.

The following morning a nurse arrived carrying a large kidney tray covered with a cloth.

"Turn over please Larry."

I saw, as I turned over, the biggest syringe with the longest, thickest needle known to man.

"Just a little scratch then we're done, ok?"

I had to laugh.

"Don't tense Larry, it only makes my job more difficult," she said, wielding the needle like Fatima Whitbread about to launch a gold-winning javelin throw.

I tensed. WHAM! XMAS!

I lay, rigid with pain, sicker than ever, as the nurse told me I'd feel better soon.

Maybe I would have if she hadn't then told me I was going to have to endure these injections twice a day for at least a week.

After my injection the doctor told me I'd contracted erysipelas, a terrible bacterial infection and the injections were superhuman doses of antibiotics to prevent something called necrotizing fasciitis, a rare flesh-eating bacteria syndrome. Princess Amelia, daughter of George III died of it, not that I knew that at the time, thank goodness. I stayed in hospital for two weeks, but it took six months of treatment and recovery (all the while suffering from the worst un-scratchable itching) before I could get back to work.

# A SUDDEN MOVE

Just before I returned to duty I requested a meeting with a newly-appointed Senior SOCO, Dougy Cresswell, who had received this appointment after retiring as a Detective Superintendent from the Forensic Science Laboratory. Working alongside Dougy was Detective Chief Superintendent 'Salty' Brine, a large, blustering man who had previously been the head of the Fingerprint Branch, CO3 (now SO3) before he'd also retired (so they got their police pensions plus the salary of their new civilian role). Career-wise, we were sworn enemies. As a SOCO, I was part of a movement that was attempting to usurp the once rock-solid position of the fingerprint branch.

I thought Dougy was ok at first but he was so smiley and so jokey that it couldn't be anything else but a façade, so it was clear he wasn't one to be trusted, a suspicion that was confirmed during this meeting. I explained to Dougy that I was now fully recovered and was looking forward to getting back into the harness, so to speak. We chatted a bit about the dead horse incident until I asked:

"On my return, should I report my illness as work-related?"

"No, no you can't relate your illness to work," Dougy replied.

"I think I can."

"No Larry, it's not reportable," he said, smiling as he spoke.

I accepted his instruction and left it at that, not knowing that I could have reported my illness as work-related and should have, as I would have been due some compensation, if I'd suffered any lasting effects or developed related illnesses further down the line. This incident, although minor, proved to be typical of the old guard's response to the SOCOs. If they could make life difficult for any SOCO, or if they could find a way to publicly disparage the SOCOs, then they would.

I returned to Sutton, got back into my routine and gently worked on getting my fitness levels back up to par. Christmas was approaching and with it, a promotion board. The promotion pyramid was now constructed so that there were fifteen Grade 1 SOCO's headed by two Senior SOCO's, and I applied for promotion to Grade 1 SOCO.

I was at the Christmas CID party when the new DCI, Mick O'Neil stood up and announced congratulations were in order as I had passed my promotion board. I nearly blew my Xmas budget by buying everyone drinks and waltzed home in celebratory delight. Two days later I received a brown envelope through the dispatch office: the official promotion board result. I smiled and opened it confidently and - FAILED.

"What!?" I kept repeating it in shock. "What!? What!?" Before realizing it I was knocking on the DCI's office door.

"Come in Larry," Mick said. "You look as though you have a problem."

"I've dipped the promotion board Guv', just received the official notification."

"I was definitely told by Dougy Cresswell you had passed. Leave it with me."

He checked and called me back in. "It's not good news. Can you go and see Dougy at two this afternoon?"

"OK Guv', thanks for trying." I slouched off, totally gutted.

Dougy was all apologies.

"Mick misunderstood what I said to him Larry. I told him you had a very good board and you would PROBABLY be promoted". This account was completely different to Mick O'Neil's account of the conversation, in which I was DEFINITELY promoted.

"What can I do to make this up to you?" Dougy asked. "I'm prepared to offer you a posting to any nick you fancy."

He smiled as he spoke and I knew he was lying. Besides, I wasn't about to try and oust some poor SOCO from his position so I could step in, and Dougy knew it. I told him I'd stay where I was and would reapply when the next promotion board came up. I wasn't about to give up. I walked out of his office without waiting for his reply.

Years later I was working with Don Bremner, from the Detective Training School, who had by that time become a Detective Chief Superintendent. We had a drink and

Don revealed that as long as Dougy and Salty Brine kept their jobs, they were never going to promote me, even if I cracked the Jack the Ripper case. I still don't know exactly how my promotion turned from a pass into a fail overnight but I had little time to reflect as I was suddenly posted to Wimbledon.

# PART THREE

March 1976 – March 1978
Wimbledon Police Station, 15 Queens
Rd, Wimbledon, SW19 8N

And

New Malden Police Station,
High Street, New Malden, KT3 4EU
Central Office V District
March 1978 – May 1980

# NOT A ZOMBIE

CID's Guvnor was DI Minors, who'd been a principal investigator in the Muriel McKay murder case of 1970. Brothers Arthur and Nizamodeen Hosein had kidnapped Mrs McKay, thinking she was Rupert Murdoch's wife, planning to put her up for ransom (she was actually the wife of one Murdoch's deputies). Her body was never found but it was suspected the Hosein brothers fed her to pigs at their Hertfordshire farm. It was one of the first murder trials to take place without a body and alerted the police to the fact that they didn't necessarily need a cadaver to prosecute someone for murder.

DI Minors was enthusiastic about the new SOCO system and we hit it off immediately, which made it easy for me to settle in quickly with the rest of the team. The key difference for me this time was that the CO3 Divisional Fingerprint Officer also worked from the CID office. His name was Paul, and although he was taciturn at first, we were both keen squash players and allowed us to break through the Fingerprint Branch/SOCO barrier.

Everything could have been perfect but, alas, my line manager, Malcolm, a SOCO Grade 1 based at Kingston

Police station, lived up to his overbearing reputation and never got off my back, even chastising me after I failed to sign out on the Duty Register when leaving the building. On this occasion I'd left the station at a sprint with Jim, the CID sergeant, as a robbery was taking place in a jeweller's shop on the Broadway, close to the police station.

Malcolm did his best to make my life a misery; he even forbade me from playing squash for the Metropolitan Police during working hours, even though police policy made provisions for training and competing during police hours, as long as you were representing the police.

Malcolm, who was not particularly tall, always wore a full-length black leather trench coat and, with his spectacles, looked like a Gestapo Officer. This didn't go unnoticed with the CID guys who named him 'Herr Flick,' after the character from the BBC TV sitcom '*Allo 'Allo!*

I got on better with the CID guys than with my own department. Police officers in the 1970s did not always appreciate the finer points of forensic evidence and crime scene preservation and, unlike Malcolm, who talked down to them, I'd chat to detectives and police officers of any rank and if anyone had 'cocked up' forensically, I always explained why, and the implications later down the line, particularly when it came to giving evidence at court. We developed a mutual respect for each other's roles and needs. After all, we all wanted the same thing: to bring criminals to justice.

My crime-filled career had started to have an impact on my home life. Our son was two-years-old and like all little boys, he had an irresistible urge to explore the world, indoors and out. I'd seen too many terrible accidents and incidents to let him do this and I became over protective. I argued with Jennifer, who was pregnant with son No.2, about what our son could and couldn't do.

I didn't tell Jennifer about many of the incidents I was called to; it wouldn't have been fair to burden her with the worst aspects of my job (I did moan about Malcolm, however, and Jennifer was a great help there). The only way to survive is to talk with your colleagues because they're the only ones who understand. They've been through it too. That's where police humour comes in; it helps us diffuse. It's either laugh or cry and no police officer I ever met ever shed a tear. But of course there are events where it's impossible to find anything to laugh at. I'd been called to a school to cut down a five-year-old girl who'd somehow managed to strangle herself on a roller towel and then had to watch her being cut up on the post mortem table. Then there were the mutilated bodies, tragedies involving children, nasty bastards who beat their wives to death and those who tortured animals. I'd tell some of the more entertaining and less unpleasant stories to dinner guests and they would usually say something like: "You must get used to it, so it doesn't disturb you."

Nope. Only a zombie can behave like that. I felt just as strongly as anyone else when I was called to an incident. I could feel how the job was changing me and shaping my personality and although this was mostly for the positive, there were parts of me I wasn't sure I liked. This over-protective dad routine was one of them, and it took a superhuman effort on my part not to overreact when we were crossing a road for example, or getting out of a car. I had dealt with a young child who'd climbed out of a car and had been wiped out by a lorry. I thought about that child (and the horror of what I'd seen) every time I was with the kids.

# DELAYED RESPONSE

I t was an all-too familiar situation. A young woman, Sue, aged 20, had been raped but had not reported the crime to the police because she felt 'dirty and humiliated' and, to be perfectly honest, the police didn't have the best reputation for dealing with rape victims or prosecuting rapists at this time - and it still seems as though problems remain at the time of writing.

It was only after a friend urged Sue to come forward with the words: "Suppose he does it to someone else?" that she arrived at Surbiton nick (which I happened to be covering, as the local SOCO was on leave) with a bag containing the clothes she'd been wearing on the night she was attacked.

It was too late for vaginal swabs and, as the clothes had been washed, there was no chance of finding semen and saliva. Although blood can still be detected after washing, examinations revealed there was no blood on Sue's clothing.

The rape had taken place in Sue's car. She had offered a lift to a guy she'd met while with a friend at a Wimbledon nightclub. Sue and this guy hit it off and so Sue's friend hitched a lift with another acquaintance and left Sue to drive the man home. Sue still lived with her parents, so they stopped for a 'kiss and cuddle' in a lay-by before she dropped him off.

The man, described as being in his late twenties with thick blonde hair and about 5"10' suddenly turned aggressive and raped Sue on the car's back seat before dragging her outside and throwing her to the ground, still semi-naked, where he urinated over her, laughing. He then walked away, laughing into the night.

Sue, who was obviously hugely traumatized, could only remember one other thing about the man: he was wearing a black-and-white dogtooth jacket.

I examined Sue's mini, sweeping the carpets, screening the seats for semen using a UV light, taping the rear and front seats and the roof lining for fibres as well as pubic and head hair. I then fingerprinted the whole vehicle but only found prints on the steering wheel, which turned out to be the victim's.

I did find some head hairs in the tapings from the roof lining above the rear seat, however. The rapist must have rubbed his head on the roof lining during the attack.

Detectives repeatedly visited the nightclub and mingled with the crowd looking for the man in the dogtooth jacket and, six weeks to the day after the rape, they got him: blonde hair, 5"10', a black-and-white dogtooth jacket. They brought him to Surbiton police station.

The first phone call I received that day was from Jack, a Detective Sergeant from Surbiton CID, who told me about the arrest. Yes! I was delighted. They were confident this was their man but they needed someone to come down to take head hair samples and package up his clothing.

"OK, I'll be with you in fifteen minutes."

As I put the phone down, Malcolm walked in.

I quickly explained the situation. Malcolm refused to let me go, citing concerns about cross-contamination because I'd examined the Mini.

"We'll have to send someone else," he said.

"Bollocks! That examination was six weeks ago! I'm wearing different clothing and I'll be wearing plastic gloves during the sampling. I want to do this Malcolm; this man is a bastard who deserves to go down and I don't want another SOCO pussyfooting around him. I am bloody well doing it!"

Malcolm looked at me for a moment; then nodded. "Ok Larry, go ahead."

I left, pleasantly surprised at Malcolm's reaction. I'd expected a fight.

I arrived at Surbiton Nick with a head-hair sampling kit, which consisted of two small plastic head hair combs, one fitted with cotton wool. There was a pair of plastic gloves in the kit but I preferred to use surgical rubber gloves as they provided a better grip. I reminded myself to exhibit the gloves as well, in view of Malcolm's concerns.

The suspect was moved to the Divisional Surgeon's examination room and I entered with a uniform officer behind me.

The alleged rapist was very polite, and calmly claimed that this was a case of mistaken identity as I pulled on my surgical gloves, letting them snap into place, seeing him wince apprehensively at the sight.

'Bollocks,' I thought. 'The CID lads are certain it's you. How many 5"10' men with thick blonde-hair and wearing a dogtooth jacket have been in that nightclub in recent weeks?"

"I'm a Scenes of Crime Officer," I said. "And I will be taking head hair samples from you, both combed and pulled. I understand that this has already been explained to you, and you have given permission for the samples to be taken. If you do not agree to have samples taken, or have decided to withdraw your consent, then this is the time to do it. If you do withdraw your consent, I will seek authority to have the samples taken by force. Do you understand?"

I received a mild-mannered response: "Yes officer."

Standing in front of him, I pulled the comb through his hair, collecting any fibres on the cotton wool that was laced through the comb's teeth.

I then turned to the uniform constable, Andy: "I'll be a while yet finishing the sampling and packaging," I said. "Why don't you go a grab a cup of tea? Our friend here is ok."

I turned to the alleged rapist, adding: "Aren't you?"

"Yes officer."

Andy, who was standing behind the suspect, signalled he'd wait outside the door. I nodded.

I ran the second comb through the man's hair; gathering blonde strands and placed it inside a second plastic bag.

"I'm going to pluck some hairs now," I said, moving around behind him.

Once I was behind him I grabbed a clump of hair and yanked his head back, so his neck was stretched over the top of the seat back, his mouth an 'O' of surprise, looking up at me. Leaning over the guy until my face was inches above his, I said:

"How would you like me to spit down your throat, so you felt the disgust of something unwanted inside of you. Or maybe I should piss over your face?"

As I finished speaking, I pulled out a large chunk of head hair and released my grip, placing the head hair samples in a third plastic bag.

I walked back around the front of our prisoner, who'd gone very pale and said nothing, as I signalled to Andy and left the room.

I was trembling afterwards. Anger, at the rapist, for that's what the samples proved him to be, and shock at my behaviour, but crimes where the strong abused and tortured the weak made my blood boil, especially when they thought they could get away with it.

On top of the matched hair samples, both Sue and her friend identified the man in separate ID parades, despite his assurance during police interview that he'd never met them before.

The decision was made to charge the guy with rape. It's a hard case to prove because even though we'd proven the man had lied about knowing the girls and even though we linked him to the car in which the rape took place, this by no means guaranteed a conviction. There was no physical evidence of rape; it was Sue's word against her attackers and everything would depend on the jury's acceptance of her testimony and how she would handle what was likely to be a lengthy and aggressive cross-examination in Crown Court.

Six months later, two days before the trial, Sue withdrew her testimony on the grounds she couldn't bear to face her rapist again, or face cross-examination, when she would be expected to relive every moment of the horror she had endured some months earlier.

The case was dropped.

The delayed reporting of (and responding to) rape cases was always incredibly frustrating and it often felt as though the legal system was on the side of the rapist, as proving a case was so difficult, even when you had all the evidence you could hope to collect.

It was December, Christmas party season, always a busy time. One particularly long day I had just returned my police mini-van to Wimbledon nick following a nasty GBH (grievous bodily harm); a pub fight in which, due to the abundance of broken glass had led to some life-changing injuries for some young people. I glanced at my watch; it was midnight. I was just on my way out and saying goodnight to the desk sergeant, when the station door banged open and an attractive 30-something brunette, wearing a full-length fur coat, collapsed into the reception. I ran around the desk to help and realized as I picked her up that, under the fur coat, she was naked. She was sobbing uncontrollably. Before I had a chance to ask if she was ok, she blurted out: "I've been raped!"

"Where did this happen?" the sergeant asked.

"Behind the Rapid Results College."

The sergeant and I exchanged a glance and for a second, just a fraction of a second, I think the same thought crossed our minds; this could be a wind-up. But of course this was for real and we quickly got into response mode. The victim, whose name was June, explained that she was walking home when she was attacked from behind and dragged to the ground where the attacker punched her in the face before raping her.

The sergeant took June into a side room and set about contacting her family.

I telephoned the night duty CID and the duty Divisional Surgeon. As I arrived at the scene the Area Car was also pulling up, with the CID car behind it. We soon found a pair of red, high-heeled shoes, then a pair of tights, a red dress, and white knickers and bra. They lay just ten feet from a public pavement.

First objective was photography; then I could take possession of the exhibits. Contact evidence was crucial. June's clothing would be submitted to the forensic science laboratory and they would look for traces of semen, fibres, blood and any other foreign material; any one of these items might be enough to put the rapist behind bars.

The Photographic Duty Officer advised me that it would be two, possibly three, hours before his photographer arrived. He was already busy photographing the scene of a fatal road accident in North London, some twenty-five miles away. Until the exhibits were photographed *in-situ* I couldn't do anything, other than protect them in case it rained or snowed. I covered the various items of clothing with plastic body sheets, and scoured the area for heavy stones to pin them down. I also extended the search, using my powerful lamp, but turned up nothing new. The Duty Officer ordered a constable to stand guard over the scene, to await the photographer, and also ensured that at the end of the night shift another officer would be tasked to guard the exhibits, and I would return at around 9am. It was now 3am, and there was no point in my hanging around, as the photographer said he was still at least two hours away. I made it home at 3.30am, after a total of 19 hours on duty.

Next morning I told Malcolm about the incident before returning to the scene. He immediately complained about my overtime and how much this had cost the department. He argued that I should have contacted the on-call Lab Sergeant and let him handle the case.

"It's not as if I could have ignored the situation," I said, "The victim was right in front of me. I was the nearest SOCO to the crime scene and was there in minutes. Once I'd assessed the scene, I needed to protect and preserve the evidence."

There should have been no argument about my actions but I still got one.

I packed the clothing and fur coat plus the personal samples as exhibits; then submitted them all to the laboratory. Sadly, despite our quick response and despite the fact that fibre evidence was recovered from the dress along with a blood grouping from the vaginal swab, the Rapid Results rapist was never found.

# A CONCHOIDAL CLUE

Anne was a rare thing - a female detective sergeant. She'd spent three years on the Flying Squad before being posted to Wimbledon. Needless to say, she was a shrewd cookie. We attended the scene of a burglary in a semi-detached house in the Merton area. To get in, the burglar had broken a window on the ground floor and released the window catch.

When I asked the homeowner what had been stolen, he listed televisions, jewellery, cash, various kitchen items and some soft furnishings. It was a huge list, like no other burglary I'd ever come across. It was as if the burglar was setting up house – not beyond the bounds of possibility, and one has to keep an open mind where criminals are concerned, but when I took a close look at the point of entry I smelt a rat. There wasn't much broken glass on the inside and the impact would have sent slithers of glass a considerable distance into the house. There was a double bed within three feet of the window, and I would have expected to find some glass fragments there (although the homeowner said he'd replaced the covers as the original bedding had been stolen).

I examined a piece of broken glass by looking at the conchoidal stress marks along the broken edge to determine which side of the windowpane had been broken. Thanks to marks left by dried rain I could tell which side was the glass's exterior. I was able to position one of the larger shards back into the window frame, which allowed me to identify a radial crack (which branches out from the point of impact). Stress marks in glass are shaped like scimitars, and the wide part of the 'blade' points to the side opposite to the impact. It was obvious to me that the pane had been broken from the inside, but I would need a scientist at the forensic laboratory to officially confirm this.

I finished my examination and had a quiet word with Anne about my suspicions. She then delved into the owner's background and managed to uncover the amazing fact that this man had made twenty different insurance claims over twenty years, and had always used, more or less, the same list of 'stolen' items. All of the claims had been paid.

He was convicted of fraud and received a short jail sentence. This case was used to help persuade insurance companies to maintain pooled databases, preventing a great deal of fraud. This was a 'small' job but remains a perfect demonstration of how forensics and good old-fashioned detective work goes hand-in-hand.

# FREE GEORGE DAVIS

**M**y only encounter with the All England Tennis Club came in January 1976, courtesy of armed robber George Davis. Davis had been sentenced to twenty years in prison in March 1975 for an armed payroll robbery from the London Electricity Board (LEB) offices in Ilford, which had taken place on 4 April 1974. Davis was the only one of the accused to go down and the evidence used to convict him was seen by many as sketchy. This had resulted in a radical 'Free George Davis' campaign to bring attention to Davis's case and, on19 August 1975, some of his supporters dug up the pitch at Headingley's cricket ground, preventing further play in the test match between England and Australia. This was accompanied by graffiti proclaiming:

> FREE GEORGE DAVIS
> JUSTICE FOR GEORGE DAVIS
> GEORGE DAVIS IS INNOCENT - SORRY IT
> HAD TO DONE (sic).

There was a missing 'BE' in that last sentence, but one has to suppose they were in a hurry. One of the protestors, a man called Peter Chappell was jailed for eighteen months.

And then it was Centre Court's turn. I was obliged to ring Malcolm to advise him that the court had been vandalized. Normally, I wouldn't have heard from him again but this time, because it was the All England Club, he rolled up at the scene within twenty minutes of my call. Also there was our new DCI, Bernie Davis (no relation), along with the Chief Super.

Slogans had been sprayed on the grass of Centre Court and over the large stadium clocks. As part of my examinations I was going to have to take a sample of the hallowed Wimbledon turf. Bernie asked if he could have it when I was done, to keep on his desk.

Once Malcolm had arrived and we had established exactly what I'd be doing, the Chief Super turned to me and said,

"Larry, try and get finished before the Press arrive."

So I cracked on, and asked the groundsman to dig up a small piece of the vandalized grass using his special turf lifter. Malcolm joined me and together we crouched down to view the vandalized turf, at which point I looked up to see a row of press photographers lined up in front of us. Before we had time to say: "Where the hell did they come from?" Malcolm and I were already on our way to becoming tomorrow's front-page news.

All I could do was apologize to the Chief Super the next day when he arrived at the station to find a slab of turf sitting on his DCI's desk, along with a collection of the newspaper front pages featuring his forensic officers.

George Davis was released from prison in 1976, using an unusual Royal Prerogative of Mercy (the Queen can grant pardons to convicted persons and has only done so four times since World War II), because of doubts over the evidence presented by the police (the Court of Appeal finally quashed the original conviction in 2011).

In 1978 Davis plead guilty to a role in an armed bank raid that took place on 23 September 1977 at the Bank of Cyprus in Finsbury Park, North London. Davis was arrested at the wheel of the getaway van with weapons beside him. Shots were fired in the raid and a security guard was beaten to the ground. Released in 1984, Davis was jailed again in 1987, this time after he pleaded guilty to attempting to steal mailbags.

Not guilty of the Ilford robbery? Maybe. Innocent? I think not.

# THE SAFE BLOWERS

I was standing in a peaceful part of Wimbledon Common and, in front of me, guarded by a woodentop (an unflattering term for a police constable) was an abandoned Milner Safe (Milners, founded in 1814, was one the oldest and best known safe makers in the UK).

The safe, about three-feet square, was locked and on its back so the door faced skywards. I examined the outside and powdered it for fingerprints but found nothing. It was too heavy to lift so the constable agreed to organize the safe's removal by crane and lorry to the police station.

The constable found me at my desk in the nick later that afternoon and told me the safe was now in the yard. It was still lying on its back and a curious bunch of detectives and constables had gathered around. Speculation was rife. Might there be thousands of pounds of cash inside? Deeds and documents? Gold and silver? Bonds?

I called in a specialized locksmith who searched his Milner templates to find this particular model's lock mechanism. He then measured out three drilling locations and got to work. About an hour later he announced it was ready to open.

The door was bloody heavy, and it took the two of us to pull it vertical as a circle of ten police officers craned over our shoulders. My eyes adjusted to the dark shadows and - empty. And... I could see the ground through the back, which had a bloody great hole cut into it. Total embarrassment as the detectives roared with laughter and promptly set about taking the Michael.

I glared at the constable who'd organized the safe's transportation to the nick.

"Didn't you check the back as it was being loaded onto the lorry?"

He shook his head. "Didn't think of it as it was a straight lift on and off."

Safe cracking was common in the days of cash and commodities. A typical method involved chisel and hammer. It's hard work but a safe is only a reinforced metal box, and the sides are folded over forming a seam around the safe. Using a chisel, it was possible to pry open a seam, then literally chop around the seam to either remove the back, or peel it back enough so that the contents could be removed. This takes a long time and is noisy - but not as noisy as the then dying art of safe blowing, which had the advantage in terms of speed.

Safe blowers were nicknamed 'petermen,' (a safe was known as a Peter, and some well-known petermen ended up in Scotland's Peterhead Prison, and the French word for 'explode' is 'peter', so take your pick as to the term's origin) and the normal technique was to push a condom into the safe's lock before injecting it with gelignite. A detonator was then pushed into the gelignite and connected to a battery with a switch mechanism. The skill was judging how much 'gellie' to push into the condom and how far away to stand to avoid injury (I can quite believe Michael Caine's iconic exclamation in *The Italian Job*, "You are only supposed to blow the bloody doors off!" is based on a true story).

Petermen started to die out with the development of sophisticated safes with anti-safe-blowing mechanisms. But one day I was called to a burglary scene at a Wimbledon Chase estate agents where someone had tried to access their brand spanking new walk-in safe. The door was normal-sized but, as you would expect, being made of metal, was extremely heavy (it was supported by a reinforced metal frame) and could (supposedly) only be opened with an eight-inch long key. No damage had been done to door or lock, which still worked perfectly. The only oddity I could find was a small black mark just above the keyhole.

"Was this here before?" I asked the estate agent.

He shook his head, so I took a swab of the mark for analysis, but I was fairly certain it was soot.

A week later the estate agents was burgled again. This time there was a bulge above the keyhole and the door, which was closed, could no longer be opened. I advised the staff to call a locksmith and then the CID office as soon as the locksmith arrived so I could be present when he got the door open. However, the locksmith didn't turn up until the following day, and I was on annual leave, so Malcolm got the call.

When the door finally swung open, it was revealed that the back of the keyhole was stuffed with explosive material, and a condom, also filled with explosive was lying on the strong room's floor. It was at that moment that one of the staff remembered that just the day before, the cleaner had found a "funny pen" on the office floor. She told them she'd left it in a drawer. I can only imagine the expression that crossed Malcolm's face when he opened the drawer and found the 'pen' was in fact a live detonator, primed and ready to explode. I guarantee that Malcolm's thought after he realized what he was looking at would have been, more or less: "Bomb Squad! Bomb Squad!"

The detonator was safely dismantled and the would-be safe blower, who had attempted his raid over several nights, cottoned on that he'd been rumbled and never returned.

Malcolm turned up at the station the next day and found me in the canteen, where he tried to give me a bollocking, arguing that I'd 'missed' the fact it was a safe blowing. Fortunately, like the detectives, I kept a written record of everything I did, along with the advice I'd given the estate agents, and had filed my report which stated: 'potential safe blowing, awaiting locksmith, caution advised.'

Malcolm had thought he'd caught me out and was so crestfallen he didn't even think to offer to buy me a cup of tea.

Malcolm was always out to impress his civilian bosses, and was big mates with senior SOCOs Dougy Cresswell and 'Salty' Brine. He came up with the idea of centralizing the

V District SOCO's at one station, New Malden, together with the fingerprint officer. His argument was that it would even out workloads, but in reality he wanted to keep a close eye on the SOCO/fingerprint teams in an attempt to cut down overtime and thereby improve his managerial reputation (which was poor). So I left Wimbledon for New Malden in March 1978, where I almost immediately had one of my most unique and spectacular successes.

# PURPLE RAIN

Johnson Matthey was a company that refined and recycled precious metals; they had a small refining complex in Surbiton that dealt in extremely valuable commodities like platinum.

A number of thefts had occurred from the men's locker rooms and Surbiton CID asked me if I could set up a trap to catch the villain. We found a trusted employee who left his wallet filled with money marked with lots of fuchsine in the changing room. I also added a small new device from the Dirty Tricks Department. It was a spring clip placed on the bottom of the wallet. If the wallet was removed the device sent out a radio signal to a receiver. With a couple of plainclothes constables installed in the company car park with the receiver, the trap was set.

Experience shows that if money is stolen it tends to go at clocking off time so the thief can escape quickly, before the theft is discovered. Sure enough, ten minutes before shift's-end, at 3.50pm, the radio beeped into life. The plainclothes lads made straight for the changing room but were momentarily stalled by a very efficient receptionist, who told them to sign in first, and wear a visitor's badge.

Jim, one of the constables, shoved his warrant card under her nose and they ran to the changing rooms.

Once in the changing room Jim and his colleague stopped in amazement. The workers at the metals plant had to shower in a communal area at the end of their shift; the platinum was seen as being so valuable that the water was filtered, so any grains could be recovered. A man was standing, naked, in the centre of a circle of his colleagues, also naked, in the showers.

He was purple from head to toe.

Every part of his body, and I mean every part, was stained bright purple from the fuchsine. The marked notes were found in his jacket. Result!

# UNANSWERED QUESTIONS

I f there's one thing I'd like people to know about my job, it's that real CSI is not like television. Investigations nearly always end up with loose ends and many unanswered questions.

Malcolm had ordered me to meet him at Kingston Hospital Mortuary at 10am, no other explanation. Malcolm was a competent scene examiner, but he had a habit of ordering me to accompany him if he was examining a serious crime scene or major post mortem, so could delegate any work he didn't fancy doing himself (and had someone to blame if anything went wrong).

I arrived before Malcolm and introduced myself to the pathologist, whom I hadn't met before; he wasn't a regular Home Office Pathologist, suggesting this case, whatever it was, had some unusual aspects.

Malcolm finally turned up with Pete, a Kingston CID officer who I knew very well. Pete explained he was investigating the suspicious death of a Nigerian male who'd been found dead, lying half-in and half-out of bed. The night before, his neighbours had heard an argument between the man and his wife, who was now missing.

As the PM got started, I wondered why I had to be there, as it didn't take two to observe. Looking at the body on the slab, there were no obvious signs of trauma, although the man's face was slightly distorted on one side. The pathologist said there were signs of a small amount of bleeding in the brain and he seemed to be heading towards a conclusion of natural causes due to a cerebral haemorrhage. Then he opened the stomach and poured the contents into a dish.

There's always a horrible smell, but when my nose caught the odour, I immediately said: "That's not the usual smell."

All of us took a sniff. Definitely something not right there, I thought saying out loud: "Perhaps he's been poisoned."

As a former analytical research chemist I'd worked on techniques to identify iron in sand down to one part in a million for an Argentinian glass-making plant. This is crucial in glass making, as iron colours the glass, not a good thing when you're trying to make something people can see through. As part of my research, I'd worked with potassium cyanide which had the distinctive smell of pear drops and that was what I was getting a whiff of now. Some of the man's stomach contents had spilled into his rib cage when the Pathologist had removed the stomach, so I put my head inside the ribs and took a long sniff.

"Definitely cyanide."

I'd come a long way since the days of passing out at post mortems.

My comment triggered what I can only describe as a technical, and somewhat political argument, at the end of which the pathologist stuck his neck out by stating his conclusion was 'natural causes'. Analysis of the stomach contents, blood and urine samples would provide the definitive answer, however, and Malcolm lumbered me with labelling the samples, blood, urine, stomach contents as well as samples from all the organs, hair samples and fingernail cuttings. Two sets of everything, with one set for the pathologist and one for the police investigation. 'This wasn't even supposed to be my case,' I moaned to myself as I set about my task. This was just typical of Malcolm; he was in charge and wanted to show his authority.

Once Malcolm had left I started to chat to the pathologist and asked him an obvious question.

"Is the distortion on our friend's face indicative of cyanide poisoning?"

"No, more likely the bleeding in the brain," he answered curtly.

Fair enough. I took the exhibits to Kingston nick, placed them in the fridge in the Divisional Surgeon's room, and left a message for Malcolm. He would submit the exhibits, just in case there was glory to be had. The Forensic Laboratory got back to us three weeks later. Traces of cyanide had been found. I was right! But the report concluded that there hadn't been enough cyanide in his body to cause death. Verdict: death by natural causes.

The wife was never found, despite numerous police appeals, made over several months. Had someone killed or abducted her? Was she on the run, having poisoned her husband? Surely, once her husband's death had been put down to natural causes, she would have come forward? Ah, those unanswered questions…

# A GOOD DAY

It was a sunny afternoon and, after a decent day's work, I strolled from the office to the local mechanic's garage, where I was due to pick up my car. I was thinking about a lovely couple in Esher I'd met that day. They'd been burgled and had had their world turned upside down. After examining their home and reassuring them that this was almost certainly a one-off, they offered me the use of a field they owned in the New Forest, where I could park my caravan at weekends, allowing my two Labradors the chance to run free.

I was brought back to the present moment by the sounds of dogs barking. I'd been so lost in thought that I hadn't noticed that a group of travellers had moved into a disused field, which was now filled with caravans and campfires. I was by this time halfway across a patch of open ground, a no-man's land between two small roads. The barking was getting louder and then I spotted a pack of dogs, clearly outraged by my presence, hurtling towards me, teeth bared. Wasting no time, I turned and ran but I was never going to beat a 35kg Alsatian travelling at 30mph, which caught up with me in seconds and leapt onto my back, while another two dogs, a pair of Jack Russells, snapped at my ankles. A fourth dog, a crossbreed as big as the Alsatian got in front of me, preventing any chance of my making some forward progress and jumped at my throat. I started to panic; if they got me to the ground, I was dead. My only chance proved to be a bramble hedge that ran alongside the path I was on, so I hurled myself into it. This surprised the Alsatian and it fell from my back, landing somewhere deep into the brambles, and as I rolled and crawled to the other side of the hedge I was able to kick the two Jack Russells off my right leg as they got tangled in the branches. Although the crossbreed was huge, with the head the size of a mastiff, it wasn't prepared to jump over the hedge and I didn't stop to look back at its huge dribbling jaws, as I half-ran, half-staggered away.

I somehow made it home, found my key and collapsed on the sofa, panting as the adrenaline started to leave my body. Jennifer had heard me come in and called hello before entering the lounge and asking "And how was your day, darl-".

The trouser legs of my grey pinstripe suit were in tatters from the thighs down; my jacket had split down the middle of the back and was hanging off my shoulders in opposite directions; the right-arm was a mess of rags. Blood was dribbling down my legs from bites and scratches and my hands were scratched, punctured and bleeding. My face was also scratched from the bramble hedge and clumps of hair were missing from my head.

I was in shock and actually tried to answer Jennifer's question. After a contemplative sigh, thinking about the couple from Esher, all I could think to say was: "Pretty good, actually."

Jennifer got the kettle on and waited until I'd started making sense before taking me to the hospital for a shot of tetanus.

The next morning, I took my savaged suit straight to the Duty Officer in Surbiton nick and explained what had happened and he agreed to visit the encampment and see what he could do. Surprise, surprise, the travellers collectively told the Duty Officer that they didn't own the dogs and that they just hung around the camp for whatever food they could find.

I met the Duty Officer in the station yard: "Sorry Larry," he said, "I tried, but my hands are tied, as no one 'owns' the dogs."

Now I knew how victims of crime felt when we were unable to help. All I could do was be thankful that I hadn't ended up on the mortuary slab.

# THE ELEVENTH HOUR

**M**y fellow SOCO Gerald arrived at the office look-ing particularly smart. Quite a change from the brown jacket with leather elbows he normally wore, with casual shirt and dark brown trousers. Len, the other SOCO, was not around and neither was Malcolm.

"What's going on this morning, are you due in court to give evidence?" I enquired. "And where's Len and Malcolm? It's not like them to be late in."

"Promotion Board this morning," Gerald said. "Len has gone there directly and I'm on at 11am," he added before quickly heading out of the door.

Promotion Board! Nobody told me! It was Malcolm's duty to advise me. The bastard!

All of that morning's jobs had been dumped on me and so I had five burglaries to deal with before I could start to do something about this travesty.

It was noon by the time I stormed into Wimbledon's CID office and found DCI Bernie Davis who listened as I fumed. He told me to get the appeal submission done right now, he would initial it and then to take it over to the Detective Super at Divisional Headquarters as it needed to go through official channels. I knocked out the appeal stating that my line manager had failed to tell me about the promotion board,.

I then went straight to the Divisional Detective Superintendent's office and explained the situation with a liberal amount of added "bastards," whenever Malcolm got a mention. I had a piece of luck as Buster Geering from Belgravia happened to be visiting and he leant me his influential support as I talked to the senior officers, who promised to sort this mess out and talk to Malcolm. In the meantime I had to get my appeal in that afternoon and hope the board would see me the following day. Candidates usually spent months preparing for promotion boards; if I was lucky I would have less than 24 hours.

The Chief Super and Super arrived in the SOCO office at 2pm precisely and said they'd been unable to find Malcolm, who was clearly hiding. The senior detectives were not impressed and signed my appeal and I managed to hand it in with a few minutes to spare. The next morning I received a phone call in the SOCO office informing me I had a Board at 4.30pm that same afternoon.

Malcolm was still nowhere to be seen so I went and found Bernie to thank him for his help before preparing for my board, trying to remember the last promotion board's questions, and then read the various monthly bulletins from the Forensic Science Laboratory followed by all the police notices for the past twelve months.

This done, I went home to change into a navy blue pinstriped suit, white shirt, and smart tie with diagonal red stripes on a navy background. Clean, polished black leather shoes and black socks and here we go!

The Board Secretary, a smartly dressed woman in her 30s, was sat outside the interrogation room, sorry, promotion board venue. After giving me enough time for my palms to get nice and sweaty she announced: "The Board is now ready for you."

The room was huge, with a very high ceiling. In front of me were three men sitting behind a trestle-style desk like the three wise monkeys.

No policemen amongst the interviewers; damn. They were the Head of Personnel department, someone from the Forensic Science Department at the Laboratory and Dougy Cresswell.

I was immediately asked about my appeal and the eleventh hour application. I held back from accusing Malcolm there and then and explained it was all in the appeal report I had submitted (chances were they'd already taken a look). Questions flowed and I handled them confidently to the point I had all three interrogators laughing. I left the room and drove back to New Malden nick, analyzing every question and answer, wondering how I'd done.

The procedure was that the morning after the board met, all twenty candidates were to line up in the corridor outside Dougy Cresswell and Salty Brine's office. Then, we would be called in separately and handed individual letters from Dougy. The brown envelopes contained our results and debrief. We'd been told not to divulge our results when we emerged from the office but the successful candidates couldn't hide their satisfied smiles. There were three positions to be filled and, by the time it was my turn, I reckoned there was one place left.

I knocked on the office door and walked into the lion's den. Salty Brine didn't look up from his desk and Dougy was his usual smarmy, smiley self. I knew that my chances were pretty much zero, but I held onto the fact I had performed well the previous day.

I was handed the brown envelope, and I looked at Dougy as I opened it. Then I looked down. 'I am sorry to advise you....'

I stopped there.

"Larry you had the best Board of all the candidates," Dougy said, "And if you hadn't arrived on appeal, you would have been promoted. As it stands, the Board recorded you as number four on the promotion list, so if another vacancy occurs in the next twelve months, you will be promoted."

"OK, thank you Mr Cresswell," I replied. As I stood up to leave, Salty Brine suddenly sprung into life.

"Larry over here!" he said, pointing to his desk. When I walked over he hit me with a tirade of criticism for blaming Malcolm for keeping the Board from me, and for criticizing a more senior officer. The more he ranted the redder his face grew, until he was practically spitting and snarling like a rabid dog. I wanted to tell him that Malcolm had hidden the fucking notice in his locked desk drawer for a month (I'd opened his drawer to find the notice after I'd realized the deception had taken place). He had done that even though he knew it was his responsibility to advise me on the Board, and how to present my application. I couldn't tell them that I'd opened a senior officer's locked desk drawer (even though it was to prove his underhanded behaviour); neither could I rant, rave and swear at this senior officer. Salty would have loved it if I had freaked out because then he could have hit me with disciplinary action. I had to keep calm.

"I stand by the report Guv. Malcolm was out of order, He has no idea of man management."

Salty ranted some more and as soon as I could, I interrupted and said: "May I leave Sir, as I have an appointment with Head of Documents regarding exhibits in a complex fraud case?"

He waved me to the office door. The last couple of guys left in the queue looked up as I stepped out and stomped past, my thumb pointing down.

"Don't let the bastards get you down Larry!" one of them called after me as I slammed the door on my way out.

Dougy Cresswell called the next morning.

"Larry you're being transferred, report to Fulham police station Monday morning."

There'd been no sign of Malcolm. What a surprise! He was obviously terrified what I was going to do to him when I got my hands on him. There was no way we could ever have a working relationship now, hence my transfer. I left the office and bought three bottles of Whiskey, one for Bernie Davis, one for the Super and one for the Chief Super. The Chief Super offered to speak to Dougy and get me promoted but I declined.

"Thanks Guv, it's hugely appreciated, but three guys have been promoted, so no changes will be made now. Anyway, I'm being transferred to Fulham on Monday."

"What! Nobody told me," the Chief Super said. "How dare they transfer one of my officers without telling me? I'll put a stop to this."

"To be honest guv, I'd prefer a transfer from the present SOCO team, if you see what I mean."

"Ok, I understand, good luck Larry. You will get there. Don't let them get to you."

I learnt later that the Chief Super did in fact call Dougy Cresswell and gave him a good roasting. Sadly, I think this only helped keep Salty Brine and Dougy Cresswell my bitter enemies. I'm sure they badmouthed me to the fingerprint department and anyone who listened, which was anyone who wasn't a police officer. Thankfully, my reputation amongst the cops was second to none, practically untouchable and that, in the end was what counted.

I arrived at Fulham police station at 8.30am on Monday only to be told by the CID clerk that Dougy and Salty had changed their minds and I was to head over to Battersea Police station instead.

Inner city policing, here I come.

# PART FOUR

**Battersea Police station
112-118 Battersea Bridge Road,
London, SW11 3AF
May 1980 – October 1984**

**Sub station Lavender Hill (WL)**

# BE CAREFUL OUT THERE!

After arriving at Battersea nick on my first day, I'd sneaked a quick look at the crime book, which listed the crimes for the past months. It ran to many pages: armed robbery, attempted murder, rape, burglaries and drugs possession by the score. Surrey wouldn't see this much action in a year.

Despite my reservations about the crime-ridden council estates, I nevertheless liked the area and its famous landmarks (the Dogs' Home, the Park, the iconic Power Station, and the picturesque Albert Bridge). Battersea society was a 50/50 mix of rich and poor with several huge council estates (the Doddington, Winstanley, Patmore and Surrey Lane, for example) surrounded by some of the wealthiest residential areas in London, known colloquially as South Chelsea. The area policed was from Nine Elms to Wandsworth Common, taking in Clapham Junction, always a hive of criminal activity.

Every kind of crime you can imagine took place in this area but burglary was top of the list. It was my first week and I'd just completed my examination of a burgled flat in one of Battersea's enormous and, frankly, unnerving council estates. The victim lived on the tenth floor, and the rule was to stick to the stairways and not use the lifts because certain criminals had no fear of targeting police officers and, unfortunately for me, although I was plain-clothed and technically a civilian, my plain minivan had been repainted with police livery, with jam-sandwich stripes along with the Metropolitan Police logo. Crime figures were rising and Scotland Yard was desperately attempting to reduce them. The idea was the more police cars on the road, the bigger the deterrent.

The criminals formed only a tiny part of the population but they kept us extremely busy. A few had started to become loosely organized into gangs, using the estates as bases from which they could operate. The architects, unfortunately, did not think about criminal potential when designing these blocks. Whenever a search warrant was executed you could see tens of people escaping via numerous rat runs from one high rise to hiding places in the other. The criminals that came from the estates were predominantly black, and they were targeted using stop-and-search tactics, particularly in the Clapham Junction area close to the huge Winstanley Estate and where commuters were targeted by violent street robbers. Although stop-and-search was targeted, often based on undercover intelligence, at those suspected of street robberies and drug dealing, it caused unrest, and the local population would come out on the streets, surrounding the police cars and proclaiming racial harassment.

As I left the building, head down, deep in thought about the day's work ahead, I suddenly noticed lots of broken glass on the road in front of me. A smashed TV was lying next to my van, which had a huge dent in its roof. The TV had been hurled from a balcony above. The culprits were no doubt watching but, as I couldn't see any obvious suspects, I calmly unlocked the van door and drove off, with pieces of TV falling onto the road as I gathered speed.

Although I hadn't a clue who I'd be meeting or even whether Dougy had bothered to warn them I was coming (he hadn't) I'd been given a warm welcome by the DCI, Tom Glendenning, who, in his late thirties, was quite young for a Chief Inspector. He gave me the grand tour and introduced me to the CID team who also seemed pleased to see me. A good team, I thought as I listened to their morning briefing which, I would soon learn, always finished with the famous phrase from US TV drama *Hill Street Blues*: "Be careful out there!"

My supervisor, the SOCO Grade 1 was Ian Walter, a quiet, mild-mannered guy who gave me good reason to hope we'd get along just fine: "Just do the work Larry, and I'm not interested in anything else," he told me in a friendly tone.

"Fair enough," I answered as we shook hands. Finally, some relief from Malcolm.

When I rolled back into the station with my dented mini-van, the CID guys gathered around laughing. Dougy was not amused however, and issued me with an old, battered olive green minivan from the original fleet. Much better, I thought; no one would ever suspect that this vehicle belonged to the police.

# JUMPER

This job was full of unexpected surprises and new challenges, for many of which I was totally unprepared. On one particular sunny spring morning, I found myself on the roof of a tower block, forensic bag in hand and a burglary victim in front of me sitting on the roof's ledge, his feet dangling over the crowds below. Some in the crowd were urging him to jump; one was even enthusiastically banging on a small drum.

It had started just like any other burglary. A call to a block of flats. Someone's TV had been stolen. But when I turned into the street, I found it cordoned off with police tape. A CID officer was already there and he came up to explain.

"Hi Larry, the guy whose flat was burgled this morning is threatening to jump. He's on the roof, sat on the ledge with his feet dangling over the side."

"Wonderful," I replied, adding with some sarcasm, "Should I explain I've come to examine his flat and I need his elimination prints? And I need him to point out anything that's been moved."

The detective thought for a moment before saying, "You know what? That's not a bad idea."

"What?"

"It might just work. He says he can't live without TV. If you give him hope of getting it back, maybe he'll change his mind."

He lifted the inci-tape and let me by. I walked up to the flats, passing a crowd of about sixty people, feeling more than a little apprehensive. After all, it wasn't as if I was used to dealing with the suicidal, let alone had training in these sorts of negotiations.

I found the Duty Officer and he agreed with the idea.

"To be honest, I'd try anything right now," he said. "The guy has been shouting he can't live without his TV and is going to jump, so be careful. Don't shake his hand or get too close in case he pulls you off with him, or you spook him and he suddenly decides to take the plunge."

So here I was, suddenly promoted to negotiator-in-chief. I cleared my throat and did my best to forget about the surreal nature of this situation, and to try sound like a normal, friendly human being.

"Hullo mate."

The man, who had his back to me, was white and had dark curly hair. He was wearing a denim shirt and was indeed sitting on the ledge, feet over the side. I expected to see him disappear at any moment as he turned his head and looked over his shoulder at me.

"What's your name?"

"Mike."

"I understand someone's taken your TV."

"I can't go on without it!" He wailed, shifting his position slightly. I could hear shouts of excitement from the people below.

"Wait!" I shouted, panicked, hardly the best of starts. "I'm a forensic officer. We're taking this crime seriously, I can assure you and we know how important TV is, so I've come to examine your flat."

He turned back at me. "You're a crime scene examiner? Like on the TV? You look like the guy from the *Rockford Files*."

This was a popular American TV detective show from the 1970s and while I appreciated the comparison to its star James Garner, this young man was clearly suffering from mental delusion. Even though I had Mike's interest, he was still just an inch from slipping off that roof.

"Yes," I said. "I'm a Scenes of Crime Officer. And hopefully I'll find some fingerprints that will help get your TV back for you. But Mike, I need your help to point out the articles that have been moved, and to show me how the burglar got in."

The man looked at me for a moment. His eyes were red from crying. Then he stood up. This led to more shouts from below. He turned to look down and slipped.

"Careful!" I yelled, as the shouts became screams.

He swayed, then caught his balance.

"Come in with me, Mike," I said, "I can't do it without you."

Mike gave me a long look, shouted some abuse at the people below and then took a step towards me. "OK," he said. "Let's see what we can find."

As we left the roof I caught the eye of the Duty Officer. "I think we should let Mike do the examination with me," I said quietly as we passed. He nodded in reply. We searched Mike's flat and found some possible fingerprints. Our would-be jumper now seemed like a perfectly normal and polite young man and we shook hands when it was time for me to go.

Two weeks later, I arrived at work and walked into the charge room at 9am to check what had taken place overnight. The reserve officer on duty excitedly told me that my 'jumper' was in the cells.

Mike had been found on the High Street, bleeding from slashes made to his wrists. He told the officers who picked him up that he couldn't live another day without a TV. Mike was sectioned and informed, much to his evident relief, that there was a TV in the mental hospital to which he would be taken (I sincerely hope this was true).

Not long after this, I received an official commendation for talking Mike off the roof, but I felt as though there was little for me to be proud about, as we hadn't been able to deal with the source of his misery and recover his TV.

# RATTED ON

I t was 1980 and the new decade continued as the old one had ended; crimes came to Battersea Nick in a non-stop stream; weekend GBH's in pubs, street robberies, burglaries, stolen cars (often recovered post-joyride in one of the communal car parks around the estates), drugs recovered using the 'sus' stop (suspicion of committing a crime) and multiple drugs raids for everything from cannabis to heroin.

We were always busiest over Christmas, which meant we got to spend precious little time with our families. In one Christmas week I dealt with eight rape allegations and sixteen armed robberies. A Lavender Hill post office was raided on two successive days. The post office hadn't even had time to re-stock its cash supply, leaving the second robber sorely disappointed.

Another robber, holding up a corner shop supermarket, was caught out by a passing police officer who walked in to buy a packet of sweets. The robber panicked, turned and started firing his gun at the officer, who dropped to the ground. The robber, having fired every bullet in his gun, legged it. The police officer, convinced he'd been shot, pressed his hands to his body to look for wounds but they came away stained green – the only casualties were the cans of peas on the shelf above.

Christmas was the worst time for really nasty domestics and family-related crimes. I was summoned to a small terraced house which had been gutted by a fire in the early hours of Christmas Day. Creeping out of the house, trying not to wake our two boys, the eldest of whom was more than ready to catch Santa in the act, I drove through deserted streets to the scene. It was truly grisly, made even worse thanks both to the date and the fresh memories of my sleeping family, presents under the lit tree as I left.

A mother and her ten-year-old daughter had perished in the smoke; their bodies were burned to a crisp in the beds they'd slept in.

It was clear to me that petrol had been poured through a letterbox and set alight. It's easy to recognize the liquid-shaped burn patterns. I took samples of burnt carpet for analysis, to confirm the presence of petrol.

The chief suspect, the squaddie boyfriend of the deceased mother was saying nothing. Forensically there was no supporting evidence. His fingerprints were all over the scene but as he had legitimate access, these were meaningless forensically. He was nonetheless arrested and left in a cell over Christmas Day.

On Boxing Day he was still saying nothing and his solicitor was agitating for his release when we heard thumping coming from his cell door. We ran to see what the noise was about and found him shouting at the top of his voice: "Let me out! Let me out! I will confess, let me out!"

Wondering what on earth had led him to change his mind and in such a hurry, we opened the cell to find the soldier cornered by a rat that had crept up through the toilet bowl and bit him on the bottom while he was 'making use of the facilities.'

Terrified of rodents, he quickly confessed to committing the crime after arguing with his girlfriend on Christmas Eve and she'd shoved him out of the door, yelling at him to never come back.

As tempting as it was to give the rat a commendation and offer it the role of station mascot, the creature managed to find its way back to wherever it came from.

# BABY LOUISE

We spent our holidays on a campsite in the south of France where we'd bought a mobile home. The children had a sixteen-acre park in which to ride their bicycles and the beach was just a mile away. It was paradise. Our time spent there was truly life-changing; work was forgotten as soon as we were 'camped' and I could let the boys run wild, safe in the knowledge that the area was free of all urban hazards.

During one such holiday, on a typically sunny morning, I opened my newspaper to see Battersea CID featured on the front pages of all the UK newspapers. They were embroiled in the nationwide search for Baby Louise Brown. Baby Louise was two weeks old and, according to her 30-year-old dad, was lying on the back seat of the family car when it was stolen from outside a post office.

I telephoned the CID and was told, confidentially, that they were treating the case as murder. The car had been found two hours later in Chelsea, without any sign of the baby and prime suspects were the baby's mother, Susan, and father, Paul, who were currently missing, along with Louise's sister and Paul's older brother, Ian.

The Murder Squad asked me to be their dedicated SOCO and I agreed.

Thirty hours later I arrived at Putney Nick and met the Detective Chief Superintendent leading the investigation, who immediately gave me my first task. I was to examine a four-foot wide circular vat of tar the father used in his job as roofing contractor.

The Chief Super asked me: "Is there any way you can tell if the baby was boiled up in the tar to conceal the body?"

"I'm on it guv," I said and headed down to the station's yard to examine the vat. As I descended the stairs I wondered whether there was such a thing as a portable X-Ray device (there is now but not then). I also wondered whether the bones would float to the surface, or if we could heat the tar so it could be sieved.

The vat, a dirty and tar-encrusted round vessel about four-feet high, was underneath a heavy tarpaulin. Peering inside, I saw that there didn't seem to be much tar left so, after measuring the outside and inside, I deduced the depth was three inches; this was not somewhere a baby's body could be easily concealed. I called a bone specialist at the forensic science lab and he confirmed my hypothesis.

That done, I was sent with a young DC called Pete to perform a brief search of the parents' address before the specialist Police Search Advisers (PolSA) were sent in to tear the place apart. Apart from Baby Louise, we were also looking for any indications as to where the parents might have gone.

The pungent smell of decay hit us the moment we stepped through the front door. We looked at each other and simultaneously said: "She's here."

The smell was coming from the kitchen. We looked in the rubbish bin, which contained nothing but food and wrappings. Then we turned to the fridge; as we drew close, it became clear that this was where the terrible smell was emanating from.

"Who's going to open the door?" Pete said in a dry whisper. He was in his early twenties and this was his first murder enquiry.

"Before we do that, I'd better go and get a brown paper sack out of the van," I replied, remembering the concealed birth from Victoria Coach Station.

After I returned with the sack, Pete bravely went to open the door but I stopped him.

"Pete, you'd better stand by with a tea towel," I said, handing him one that was lying on a worktop. "I'll open the door on three and if she falls out you'll have to catch her."

Peter, white as a sheet, nodded, and I reached out my hand to take the handle, trying not to let it shake.

"One, two, three!" I opened the door to reveal - a large wedge of rotting blue cheese. The smell made us both baulk, and I quickly slammed the door closed again.

We both went outside to get some air then continued searching the house. We found a machete hidden under the mattress of the double bed in the master bedroom - not the murder weapon but nonetheless an interesting find, which told us something about the father - but nothing else.

Dirt recovered from the wheel arches of the family car had been sent off to the Forensic Laboratory and they reported that it had recently been driven somewhere in the South Downs. Enquiries in that area revealed that Louise's parents, along with other family members had stayed at a Brighton hotel. Eventually, following public appeals and a lot of newspaper and TV coverage, the Murder Squad found them on a campsite not far from the hotel.

I'd thought of our campsite as the one place in the world where work and crime wouldn't come calling and now I was mixed up in a case were the prime suspects in a baby murder had gone to ground in a campsite packed with young families. I pushed these thoughts to one side and focussed on the job, as I now had to supervise the taking of the family's fingerprints, blood samples and clothing. They were subdued, as one might expect, and I remained professional, even when the father suddenly snapped at me and spat in my face. It was difficult to keep my thoughts in check, however. After all, he had murdered his own two-week-old daughter in cold blood.

Baby Louise had Downs Syndrome and cried a lot. This, apparently, was too much for Paul to cope with - he didn't visit her for all the time she was in hospital after the birth - and he murdered Louise after a heavy drinking session. Louise's body was never found. The Murder Squad came to the conclusion that Paul's older brother, Ian, buried Louise in a coal tip, which was then used in a power station - a witness had seen Ian and Paul covered in a black substance.

Susan, who'd loved and cared for her baby, had tried to stop Paul from murdering Louise, screaming "Don't!" over and over again.

The family members were found guilty of perverting the course of justice. Ian got nine months for helping dispose of the body. Paul was convicted of manslaughter and received a five-year sentence but was released after serving just two years.

That, unfortunately, wasn't the end of the story. In 1997, Paul who was by this time a father of four (Susan stood by her man) stabbed Ian (also a father of four) sixty-three times with a kitchen knife in a drunken brawl. Paul denied murder, claiming it was a moment of madness, that he couldn't even remember what they were arguing about, but the judge told him: "Your brother's death is the second death for which you have been responsible... Eight children in all have been left fatherless."

This time, Paul got life.

Many cops felt he should have been given this sentence the first time around.

# THE CRIME MUSEUM CASE

**M**urder enquiries are tough. One has to remain professional and keep a clear and open mind. But we're human and feelings can't help but intrude.

I was standing in the mortuary looking at the body of a beautiful 21-year-old woman who'd been found in Wandsworth cemetery lying on her back with a tree branch sticking through her stomach, impaling her to the ground.

The body had already been through a post mortem and I looked at her, fury building in me, that someone thought they had the right to take this girl's life away, causing unimaginable heartbreak to her family. Like anyone else I wanted to see justice done, but it didn't look good and this only made the feelings worse.

Her boyfriend was the prime suspect but he could claim legitimate contact in every sense of the meaning, so basic forensic evidence relating to the boyfriend was of limited use. The Murder Squad had nothing else and the boy wasn't talking, so it was down to us to come up with the goods. 'Us' in this instance was myself and Wandsworth nick's own SOCO, Howard Giles and

Detective Chief Superintendent Don Bremner, who I knew from Detective Training School. I was by this time acting up as a SOCO1 (I was getting there, despite Dougy's best efforts) and Howard asked me along because it was such a difficult case. Howard was a good SOCO who later resigned to join the Metropolitan police as a fully-fledged police officer; one of only a handful of SOCO's to make such a move. Howard pointed out an unusual wound on the girl's left cheek.

The mark was circular, about half-an-inch in diameter and had been made by an object with rows of raised bumps, which had caused contusions on the inside of the cheek. The victim had been hit so hard that the inside of her mouth had bled. We spent over half an hour scratching our collective heads as to what had caused the mark, with suggestions ranging from hairbrush to sovereign ring.

"Can you take a Silcoset cast of it?" Don asked.

Silcoset, you will recall, is a liquid rubber compound that solidifies when mixed with a liquid hardener. This was going to be tricky to say the least. It hadn't been tried on human skin before (as far as I was aware). Normally you would create a dam around the impression that was being cast, such as an instrument mark from a jemmy on a doorframe before pouring the liquid into it. The contours of the face made this difficult, however, and I didn't want to do anything that would stretch the skin and therefore the indented mark. It had to be perfect, as scientific measurements of the cast would be made to compare the cast with whatever it was that had made the impression

I created a dam around the mark using a plastic tube cut down to about an inch in depth and poured in the solution. Ten minutes later I removed the cast to find there were "blown" marks all over the cast, meaning air was in the indentations, thus compromising the cast. I had another go and the same result. Four tries later, I fashioned a semi-circular dam from the same plastic tube, and tried rolling the rubber solution across the girl's face and into the wound, forcing the air out at the same time, relying on gravity to hold the Silcoset at the dam. It worked! The cast was perfect.

Don guessed the mark had been caused by the boyfriend's signet ring and managed to get hold of it before the lad cottoned on and chucked it. Wound and ring were matched by the Forensic Science Laboratory. The boyfriend had punched his girlfriend so hard that the ring's impression had gone almost completely through her cheek. He was sentenced to life and the Silcoset cast and ring are today exhibited in New Scotland Yard's Crime Museum - perhaps better known by its more infamous title, the Black Museum.

\*\*\*

Friday afternoon and, as usual, there was to be in a drink in the office. Don Bremner was there with Bill Foreman, the DCI. Don came over to thank me for my help with the Wandsworth cemetery case and told me: "You'll be promoted as soon as Dougy Cresswell has retired."

No further explanation was given but before I could ask the obvious question, "Why?" we were joined by Bill, who then asked: "Larry, what's the biggest problem you have doing your job?"

I nearly said Dougy Cresswell, but instead replied: "Crime scene preservation, Guv."

"OK, from next week I want you to give an hour-long lecture on Wednesday afternoons for the woodentops."

"Thanks Guv, but I've never lectured before."

"You'll be fine, I'm giving you a week to write your notes."

Sure enough, a week later I was standing, with Bill, in front of twenty uniform constables and sergeants. Bill's introduction was flattering and I could only hope I would be able to live up to it.

"Gentlemen, listen to this guy, we are lucky to have him working with us."

It had been a frantic week, filled with anxious preparation. I'd been to a lecture some months previously, given by one of the Detective Chief Inspectors from the Anti-Terrorist Squad. He opened up by grabbing our attention immediately by telling an intriguing story with a brilliant conclusion and I wondered if the same thing could work for me here. So I told them an 'amazing-but-true' story I'd picked up on my travels.

"Hi Guys. Frequently pilots, particularly British Airways pilots, are asked to deliver diplomatic bags to UK embassies. One such BA pilot was asked to take a bag to Moscow during the Cold War. He was scheduled to stay at the famous Leningradskaya Hotel, and had been told to expect a diplomat to meet him in his hotel room. The diplomat duly arrived and immediately warned the pilot the hotel was notorious for being bugged by making the relevant gesture of zipping his lip.

They started to look around the room for signs of a bugging device and eventually found what looked like a metal stud underneath a rug in the middle of the floor. The pilot took the knife and fork from a tray from room service and started to remove the stud. After half an hour, the pilot managed to unscrew the stud and, after successfully prizing it out, he triumphantly showed it to the diplomat, at which point there was the sound of a huge crash. He had unscrewed the main chandelier in the restaurant below."

Amid the laughter, I said: "Gentleman, just like a scene of crime, caution should be exercised at all times, because frequently you don't know the importance of what you see until all the facts are known."

From that moment I had their attention. At the end of the hour I was satisfied that I'd got my message across regarding scene preservation and the importance of packaging or preserving evidence correctly. One particular example I've often observed on TV crime series is the poor treatment of blackmail letters, demand notes in armed robberies or any handwritten evidence placed in a plastic bag. Such exhibits, after photographs have been taken, are treated for indented impressions. It is possible to retrieve indented impressions on the bottom piece of paper from a tall stack. But placing such a paper inside a plastic bag erases the indented impressions due to the electrostatic electricity on the surface of the plastic bag.

Apart from the lectures, I also attended police station open days where I demonstrated crime scene examination to the public. The standard scenario was for a room made up as a bedsit, with a female manikin laid in a single bed with just the top of its head showing. I'd set up various clues around the scene, such as footprints in white powder and signs of a disturbance, with various items strewn around the floor. I then talked the audience through scene examination, explaining how one cleared a pathway to the body, so we didn't lose or contaminate forensic evidence such as blood, hairs, fibres and so on.

I was doing this at Wandsworth Police Station and had just reached the 'body' in the bed, revealing that the victim had been strangled with her own tights when I noticed that a young woman in the front row was crying. She was with a young man who was comforting her. I thought to myself, should I stop, or keep going? Should I ask her if she is OK? I decided in that fleeting moment that I'd better continue and not draw attention to her distress.

I realized that afternoon that many people would find my daily experiences traumatic, even more so if they had personal experience. I wondered about that young girl at the Open Day, and what upset her, but never found out.

# MY FIRST DRUGS RAID

Target: The Doddington Estate's local boozer. The plan: hit it with everything we've got on a Friday night around 10pm, when it was at its busiest.

Usually, because of the dangerous nature of these operations, SOCOs didn't accompany officers during a raid, but I suggested it might be useful to have me there for a variety of reasons, from crime scene preservation to matching discarded items to the people who'd chucked them. I also thought it would be exciting to see what went down when the boys in blue came crashing through the door; perhaps there would be some new and interesting problems for me to solve.

The Chief Superintendent, hearing of my presence, allocated the biggest uniform constable in the nick - Wally, who weighed 16 stones - to be my protector.

"Never had a civilian along with us on a raid before," Wally said cheerfully, "But don't worry, I got your back."

I parked my minivan some distance away from the pub. The plan was to call me over the radio as soon as the 'hit' went in. My protector was carrying his radio so we sat waiting for the call. 10.20pm and still no shout, so we decided to slowly make our way towards the pub. When we turned the corner we were confronted by total mayhem. A crowd was outside the pub, chanting "Pigs! Pigs! Pigs!" Constables were dragging out the arrested and shoving them into police vans.

We rushed into the pub hearing shouts of: "Where have you been Larry? It's all kicked off and there are loads of exhibits!"

Poor Wally, already mortified before he was given a good roasting by his sergeant, had forgotten to turn on his radio after the briefing. I spent the next two hours catching up; packaging, sealing and labelling drugs and despite the hiccup, my help was much appreciated and I was able to join the lads for a celebratory post-raid drink at 1am, while the drug dealer cooled his heels along with fourteen of his customers.

My next raid took place in Chelsea. The dealer lived in Chelsea but sold his wares in Battersea. It was a straightforward knock-the-door-down and rush in screaming "Police!" before grabbing anything that moved. What could go wrong? The door was knocked down and amid shouts of: "POLICE! POLICE! Put your hands above your head!" we all rushed in and surrounded the single occupant in their bed, which turned out to be a little old lady shaking with terror.

The drug dealer was next door. The building, once a detached house, had been split into two semis, 15a and 15b. The intel had said 15 and nobody had noticed that the 'b' had fallen off this lady's door. Whoops. Luckily the lady was ok once we got her calmed down and a carpenter in to fix the door (and a few other things around the house, to make up for the trauma). The-house-you-want-is-next-door-type situation happened more than once, and so we took a carpenter with us on raids, just in case. We kept him busy.

A less salubrious place for a raid was a Battersea squat. We were sure there was no mistaking this particular terraced house. It looked like a squat, with unkempt garden, sheets for curtains and lots of crusty-looking people coming and going at all hours. There was some confusion over the order of entry, however (perhaps because it was 5am and I wasn't fully awake), and I found myself third in line as we crashed through the door. I should have been last, and that was at least eleventh or twelfth.

And we were in for a surprise. Once we reached the end of the hallway, we could see the whole row of five houses had been knocked into one communal squat. The two officers in front of me legged it to the bedrooms on the first floor, leaving me all alone in this wide-open space. Sensing movement to my left, I turned to see the biggest black Alsatian I'd ever seen flying through the knocked-through walls and I instantly turned tail, climbing over Wally, who was just behind me blocking the whole hallway, eventually reaching the safety of the outside world. Luckily, one of the squatters grabbed the dog. No drugs were found; the squatters seemed pleasant enough but there were suspicions that they'd somehow been tipped off; possibly thanks to an overheard conversation among police officers in a pub.

# STEALING THE SUN

I was seconded to Brixton nick, part of a task force of SOCO's brought in to deal with the thousands of crimes committed during the Brixton Riots of 1981. We dealt with everything from looting and arson to assault of police officers and attempted murders and Battersea nick seemed very quiet after an exhausting week of scene examinations during which I faced a great deal of intimidation.

I walked back into a complex CID investigation. The LEB (London Electricity Board, as it was known then) had noticed a sudden drop in electricity consumption at certain addresses in the Wandsworth and Battersea areas. There were no apparent signs of tampering of the relevant electricity meters; the board's lead seal, which covered the wire that locked the meters closed, was still intact.

Electricity theft was common; one way was to use a powerful magnet to slow down a meter's revolving disc, and some well-known south London villains once tapped into their neighbours' electricity supply to heat their swimming pool. LEB officials brought in three domestic electricity meters for me to examine. A team of meter installers were interviewed and they all denied knowledge of any tampering.

So what to do? I seized all the seal-crimping and wire-cutting tools of the installers. LEB records showed which installer connected and sealed which meters, and I had a record of which wire cutters and seal crimpers belonged to each of the individual installers. The Forensic Science Laboratory compared striation marks on pieces of cut wire still attached to some meters and the seals with the various crimping tools. We were then able to show that a particular meter had been installed by installer "A" but sometime later the seal had been reset by installer "B" or "C," etc. Various installers were arrested as part of the conspiracy to steal electricity and the fingerprints found inside the meter boxes identified the principals involved. The guys arrested had been breaking open their mates' meter seal and reversing the dial and then resealing the meter. They never considered the power of forensic evidence to differentiate between the crimping tools. It was a large conspiracy amounting to tens of thousands of pounds of stolen electricity and I received an official commendation for my efforts.

Successes like this were celebrated down the local boozer, the Union Arms, which was usually filled with detectives of an evening and on those occasions I joined them – though I liked to head home to see Jennifer and the children socializing with your police co-workers was essential to decompress. The ethos at Battersea was work hard and play hard, and the Hill-Street-Blues-style camaraderie reinforced the feeling that we were one big family. Although Christmas was our busiest time, we usually managed to squeeze in a day of festivities, a Christmas CID Lunch that ran until the small hours. In 1983 we took over a local restaurant known as The Three Fives (the street number was 555). I was a little apprehensive as police humour sometimes got a little out of control at these dos and I took my seat expecting to have to deal with many ribald jokes but, in preparation, I'd secreted a small weapon which I planned to use on anyone who dared to take the Michael: a small but powerful water pistol.

The wine flowed like Niagara as speeches were made, congratulating the team on the year's highlights and wishing everyone a Happy Xmas, concluding with the Detective Chief Superintendent - a new guy who'd replaced Don Bremmer. Once the speeches were done and we started to relax, I started to 'shoot' the other guys on my table. A few squirts here and there and soon the whole table were laughing their heads off. Then the challenge was made: "I bet you haven't got the bottle to squirt the Chief Super in the face!"

Oh yeah? No problem! SMACK! Right between the eyes.

He looked so startled it was incredible to watch, a huge, six-foot-four guvnor in total shock. When he realized I was the culprit he stood up and pointed at me: "Larry, if you do that again, you're sac-!"

Too late! I hit him a second time with a double squirt straight in the mouth. The restaurant erupted and everybody leapt to their feet and applauded. Thank God they did! It took the heat out of the situation. Later, I apologized. The DCS stared down at me. "Larry," he said, putting his arm around my shoulder, "It showed me that we have a good, harmonious team, but don't ever fucking do that to me again!"

# DON'T MENTION THE WAR

I n 1983, Sara Keays, the personal secretary and mistress of British Conservative politician and Secretary of State for Trade and Industry Cecil Parkinson, fell pregnant to his child. The story was all over the newspapers and once it emerged the affair had gone on for twelve years Parkinson was compelled to hand in his resignation to Prime Minister Margaret Thatcher.

Sara Keays' house in the Battersea area had been broken into. The place was tidy, with no ransacking of rooms, suggesting a cool and tidy search for interesting documents and photographs. I suspected that the burglar was a member of the press, or had at least been commissioned by them. Keays was very pleasant but understandably tight-lipped when the detectives made reference to the Parkinson affair. In this case the burglars had been far too careful and the perpetrator was never found.

One Sunday I attended the home of one of my screen crushes from the sixties, Susannah York (star of *Tunes of Glory*, *Tom Jones*, *Battle of Britain* among many others). Her house had been burgled and I needed to take her fingerprints for elimination purposes. She had a badly bruised thumbnail, which she explained was the result of hitting her thumb with a hammer whilst hanging a picture.

"I'll be careful Ms York," I said as I proceeded to hold her thumb to roll it onto the fingerprint pad. I was trying not to come over all starstruck but I'd never thought that I'd be holding Susannah York's hand and I got a bit lost in the moment, which ended when Ms York let out an almighty scream. In my excitement I'd put too much pressure on her bruised thumb and now she was clutching it in agony. I was most apologetic but she was not amused and I'd blown my one and only chance for a cup of tea with my idol.

Another celebrity burglary victim was 'Ethel' from the BBC soap opera *Eastenders* (real name Gretchen Franklin). Known to the nation as Dot Cotton's lifelong friend, Gretchen was very cheerful and welcoming as she opened her apartment door, despite the fact that she'd just been burgled. She'd explained over the phone that she lived alone and that no one was with her so I got the shock of my life when I walked into the dark lounge to see a man sitting on the settee.

"Oh! Er, hello, I wasn't expecting anyone to be here, Ethel, um, I mean Gretchen said she was on her own."

It was only then that I realized that it was in fact a mannequin, dressed in an evening suit, black tie and all.

"Who are you talking to?" Gretchen asked, coming in behind me. I didn't mention my surprise at encountering the mannequin and Ethel didn't bring him up either as I took a seat next to the old chap and listened to Gretchen explaining how the burglar had got into her place via an open window. There was nothing missing and I have a strong suspicion that the sight of the mannequin in the dark would have been enough to dissuade any burglar from taking any more steps into Gretchen's apartment.

# LOST AND FOUND

I was the not-proud owner of a metallic bronze Ford Cortina estate which, since I'd bought it a couple of years earlier, had developed an unusual condition in that one side of the car started to lose its metallic sheen and twelve months later, well, it was a car of two halves. I'd been ripped off; this was some bodged cut-and-shut number. I needed to get it replaced but with a mortgage and two hungry sons to support, I wasn't quite ready to fork out on a new motor.

One day I returned from work to collect my car, oh joy of joys, some muppet had stolen it! Of all the cars in the world a car thief would have chosen to steal, I would have bet money that mine was bottom of the list. I walked back to the nick and reported the car stolen to the Reserve Officer, so it could be circulated and a crime report compiled.

"Yeah, ok Larry," he said with a smile, "Nod-nod, wink-wink!"

"It's genuine!" I exclaimed, "Somebody really has nicked my motor. I don't particularly want it back, so can you tell the guys not to look too hard for it."

I walked into the canteen where some of the CID guys were playing cards.

"Some bastard has nicked my car."

They all started laughing,

"You will be nicked for making a bogus insurance claim Larry."

"Guys, it's genuine, I promise you. Someone has done me a favour and nicked my motor so please don't find it, ok?"

Most stolen cars are found within forty-eight hours so as it hadn't been recovered by the third day I was hopeful it had been nicked for parts and dismantled. The insurance company advised me that they would pay out after six weeks. It was now four weeks and no sign of the car. Travelling to work by train each day was a pain but I was about to go on holiday to France and when I returned on the Monday in two weeks' time the insurance company would have sent me a cheque.

Two weeks later I returned suitably tanned from the south of France although having been on the beach everyday with my two sons I was now in need of a holiday. I walked through the station yard gates and my jaw fell open. There it was! My Cortina of two halves parked in the corner still intact and not another scratch on it. I ran into the Reserve's office,

"Bob my car's in the yard! Get it out! The insurance company is paying out today."

"Sorry Larry it's already booked into the system as recovered."

"What! Which idiot found it!"

"A couple of new guys straight from Hendon College were posted to the nick last Friday. On their first patrol they found the car parked in the Winstanley estate car park, and brought it in. All the regular guys had been walking past it for the last five-and-a-half weeks to see if anybody was driving it in the hope they could nick them."

Gutted, I telephoned the insurance company to advise them of the recovery.

"That's incredible Mr Henderson," the insurance agent said, "I have just this minute put the cheque in an envelope to post it to you."

Bollocks.

Not long after this, a very different kind of delayed crime solving came my way, thanks to a combination of good fortune and scientific progress. Late in 1983, the powers that be decided that two SOCOs with more than three years' experience would take it in turns to be on-call to cover the whole of the Metropolitan Police District, in other words all of London. London was divided into Group1 North and Group 2 South. The scheme started in January 1984 and I was one of the first officers on call for all jobs south of the Thames. To speed things up a bit, on-call SOCOs were allowed to park their minivans at the police station closest to their home.

My first call out was to a suspected GBH on Fulham High Street – a man had been seen dripping blood in the street. It turned out he had cut himself while chopping a cabbage. Three hours of overtime for a cabbage-related non-incident. Not the best of starts.

The next evening I was called to the scene of a rape of a young woman on Barnes Common. I arrived at 1am to find a blue-nosed, shivering police constable standing guard over the victim's clothing and belongings, which were scattered over a large grassy area. Rain was forecast, so we needed to get these items covered until they could be photographed.

"Where's the photographer?" I demanded of the constable, who shrugged amid his shivers. "And can you arrange with your Duty Officer for some flood lights please?"

It was pitch black on this part of the Common and so I made do with my heavy and cumbersome "seek and search lamp" to find and cover the articles with large plastic bags until a traffic officer arrived with arc lights. I started to find more potential exhibits, including a gent's watch; the fastener had snapped (we found out that the woman had fought back and broken it off). We then covered everything with tarpaulins.

No one was caught and I chalked this one up as one of the many unsolved rape crimes we'd had to deal with. Most unsatisfactory.

And there the story should have ended.

But…

Twenty years later I received a phone call from the Cold Case Unit at the Yard.

"That watch you found. We managed to recover DNA from it and it's given us a suspect; someone who has already done time for a number of rapes."

They needed me to make a statement so I arranged for an officer to come to my home and, sure enough, the suspect was convicted on DNA analysis.

How things have changed. I've often said that the best crime fighting force we have is science - and it's getting better all the time.

# PART FIVE

The Metropolitan Police Forensic
Science Laboratory, (C7 Branch)
Lambeth, London SE11
November 1984 – April 1985

And

Royal A District,
Cannon Row Police Station
Derby Gate, Westminster, London SW1AH
April 1985 - March 1989

# BE CAREFUL IN HERE

I t was Tony's leaving do. Tony, a permed, craggy-faced, Keith Lemon lookalike with bulldog eyes, was a CID legend. Once, during a police raid, a drug dealer aimed a loaded pistol at his head. Tony's response was to smack the guy in the face and relieve him of the handgun all in one smooth action. The gun was no imitation, it was a loaded semi-automatic Luger which I had to make safe and send to the forensic laboratory for ballistic examination and comparison with outstanding crimes. It was actions like this that had attracted the attention of Scotland Yard's Central Drugs Squad and so Tony was being transferred.

His leaving speech, given in the CID office, with bottles of booze crammed onto everyone's desks, was also legendary. He cleared a space, stood on his desk and raised his glass to make a toast.

"Four years ago, when I arrived here, I was young, recently married. I had savings, didn't smoke and rarely drank. Today, I'm an alcoholic and smoke thirty a day. I'm divorced, bankrupt, and by God I have loved every last fucking minute. Good night and I hope I never see any of you again!"

Dougy Cresswell retired a few weeks after Tony left and shortly after that I was promoted to manage a District, with a team of SOCOs and fingerprint officers below me, and more responsibilities (mostly relating to paperwork) but, before I could take up my new appointment, I had to spend six months on attachment as Liaison Officer at the Metropolitan Police Forensic Science Laboratory in Lambeth.

The attachment to the Laboratory is a two-fold experience. Firstly, one assists in the receiving of exhibits, ensuring they're correctly packaged for submission, and that there is sufficient detail in the accompanying report for the scientists to proceed with their examination. Secondly, one is expected to gain an education, to learn how individual departments operate and the services they offer. In 1984 the departments were: Chemistry, incorporating the Fire Investigation Unit (FIU), Documents, Ballistics, Biology, Drugs, Metallurgy & Physics and Specialist Photography.

The hours were 9am till 5pm, with a late turn to 6pm once a week, and every fourth Saturday morning until 1pm, which for me was a doddle compared to my 'irregular' hours out in the field. Finally, I was going to be able to spend a 'normal' amount of time with my family.

Roy Davis was the highest-ranking liaison Police Officer at the Laboratory. He was a cheerful soul; I'd worked with him at Sutton police station when he was a Detective Inspector, where we'd regularly played snooker together. He was pleased to see me, as I understood the ways of the police.

My time there mainly consisted of learning the do's and dont's of receiving exhibits. The lab teams told me their horror stories, such as fully primed firearms being submitted for ballistic examination and blood bottles with loose caps. It was no longer a case of "be careful out there" but "be careful in here."

Within a week I was up to speed on reception procedures and I started my rotation visits to the departments. It all seemed straightforward enough and the scientists were friendly and enthusiastic in the explanation of the many problems they encountered when dealing with exhibits submitted by the police.

I was even able to work on my squash game - I'd been playing international squash for the Met for some years- and made many friends in the department that way.

Although the work was plain sailing, one new and interesting liaison duty I got involved with was preparing blackmail pay-offs. Real Bank of England notes were used, with a few hidden tricks - which I'm not able to elaborate on for obvious reasons.

In one particular case, a multi-national company was being blackmailed with product contamination. The operation to catch the extortionists was delegated to the Yard's Serious Crime Squad (SCS).

The villains wanted the bounty thrown from a Kings Cross to Leeds train at a specific spot along the track, so the SCS tested this with a dummy run carried out two days before the drop at the specific stretch of railway track. They used a football which burst on impact, so we made sure the suitcase was suitably reinforced, with straps were tied around it for good measure.

The night before the ransom was due to be paid, undercover officers wearing camouflage secreted themselves in foxholes along the track and in surrounding fields. The drop was made and, after a thirty-minute wait two guys broke cover from a field and ran towards the suitcase. They were captured in an adjacent field before they were able to reach the helicopter they'd readied for their getaway.

During interview the guys admitted that they'd watched the train over the previous two days before the drop. One of them mentioned he'd seen some stupid kid throw his football out of the train. "Why on earth would someone do something like that?" he asked rhetorically.

The detectives just looked at him for a while in response, but the penny never dropped.

At the end of the six months I was posted to Eight Area, (this was Central London - I'd dropped plenty of hints over squash games and other sporting occasions to the relevant Commander that this was where I wanted to be). Even better, I'd been sent to Royal "A" District, my old haunt from the seventies, which included district headquarters, Cannon Row (AD), Gerald Road (AL), Rochester Row (AR), Hyde Park (AH), and the one-man office Wellington Arch (AW). The only fly in the ointment was that a change in the administration meant that the SOCOs now answered to the Fingerprint Department (C3 Department as it was known then, before it became SO3) but I was delighted to be back where I belonged.

# TAKING CHARGE

Cannon Row police station was at the hub of the country in policing terms. It was responsible for an area that covered Buckingham Palace, Kensington Palace, Westminster Palace (the Houses of Parliament), St James' Palace, Clarence House, Marlborough House and Downing Street. It also had the unusual and exclusive responsibility for the policing of Windsor Castle. Then there was The Ministry of Defence (MoD, our neighbours), the Treasury and the Foreign Office, various national monuments, art galleries, headquarter buildings of national and multi-international businesses, including many banks, all policed by Cannon Row, as were demonstrations and other, many and varied events.

I was leader of my own small team of two people. Gerald, the wily old fox with whom I'd shared an office with at New Malden and who was involved in my promotion board saga, in that Gerald was part of the conspiracy not to let on to me that the board was happening. Gerald was based at Rochester Row, and for the last three years had been his own master, signing his own overtime returns, deciding when he worked at weekends and generally pleasing himself.

Jacqui was a new SOCO recruit based at Gerald Road, my old station in the seventies. In the job for six months, I was told that she was a feisty strawberry blonde in her mid-twenties and that her and Gerald could not stand one another. I liked Jacqui already.

Detective Chief Superintendent Carney, head of the District, appeared to be a reasonable Guvnor, and I could see no problems there. On my first day, before checking out my office, I said a quick 'hello' to the Detective Inspector in the CID, whom I'd worked with (and got on well with) at Sutton, so no problems there either. Then I stepped into my office: a large first floor room overlooking the MOD building, Victoria Embankment and Westminster Bridge. I was in heaven.

First item on the agenda was Gerald and Jacqui. My plan was to sit both of them down, thrash out any issues and clear the air. It didn't go according to plan. Jacqui spoke to me before the meeting and let me have both barrels right between the eyes. Apparently, Gerald had implied to the CID officers that Jacqui was unsuitable for her role and Jacqui said she would not tolerate this undermining and wanted a transfer. I'd gone with Jacqui to observe her scene examinations the previous day and they were perfect and all the CID detectives at Gerald Road spoke of her enthusiastically. I wanted her on my team and I told her as much, restraining my urge to tell her that I knew Gerald was a devious git who would gladly stick the knife in when you weren't looking.

Gerald didn't turn up to the meeting and signed off duty. He then took a couple of days off as annual leave, saying he needed to visit his daughter and never returned to duty, retiring on grounds of ill health.

Weekend duties were normally shared between the SOCO1s for the Area, namely Dave Grover stationed at Paddington Green, and Nic De Silva stationed at West End Central, and myself, so we each worked one weekend in three. Unfortunately, thanks to Gerald's sudden departure, I now only had one SOCO II while C District and D District had three, (C and D Districts also had their own Divisional fingerprint officers), so I arranged for the C District duty weekend SOCO II to assist us at A district. Sundays had the potential to be busy for one person, but there was also a Grade I on duty so my message to Nic and Dave was "roll your sleeves up."

# SHALLOW GRAVE

My first weekend call came at 9am. A dead body had been found in the ornamental fountains in Kensington Gardens. According to the police officer at the scene, it looked like the British politician and trade unionist Arthur Scargill, who was also president of the National Union of Mineworkers (NUM). He was a controversial figure to say the least and it wasn't beyond the bounds of possibility that somebody would want to see him dead, but it seemed doubtful, I thought, as my minivan bounced across Hyde Park on my way to the scene.

A constable was guarding the body, which had been discovered by a member of the public ninety minutes earlier. The corpse was completely submerged, lying on the bottom of the shallow pond, which was about 200 yards long and 30 yards wide. He was face up, arms by his side in about eighteen inches of water and only about two feet from the pond's edge. He was fully clothed and wearing a beige mackintosh. I took a close look, leaning over the pond and could see he had red hair that must have been styled in a comb-over but was now covering most of his forehead.

"I don't think it's him," I said but, to be honest, it was hard to tell through pond water.

The constable then said: "He must have come by car."

It took me a moment to realize he was joking. A small Dinky toy model of a jaguar MKII was lying beside the body at the bottom of the pond.

"Anybody tried to pull him out of the water?"

"No, and he's been in it for some time. I've been told to leave him where he is and wait for the Divisional Surgeon to attend to pronounce him dead."

"How long have you been waiting?"

"About ninety minutes."

"Hm, well, I think he's dead, don't you? If you like, I'm happy to help you pull him out of the water and get him into a body sheet ready for the mortuary and PM."

"Sorry sir, my instructions are to wait for the Divisional Surgeon."

"Fair enough."

I checked the area, just in case there was anything lying around that could belong to the person in the water but drew a blank. While I was doing this, I noticed that dozens of the Canadian Geese were standing around the edge of the pond, not one of them was in the water.

The Divisional Surgeon arrived a few minutes later and immediately requested we pull out the body. We dragged it out onto the grass bank and then onto a white plastic body sheet. As soon as we'd done this, all the Canadian Geese hopped into the water and started swimming around.

The Divisional Surgeon was another Gestapo officer lookalike. In fact, he also looked just like Herr Flick from the *Allo Allo!* TV series. Thin, round steel-framed glasses, slicked back blonde hair and an attitude as cold as ice. He took out his stethoscope, popped the earpieces in his ears, opened the victim's shirt and placed the scope to the deceased's chest. He listened for a moment, then removed the rubber end that he'd placed on the chest, sucked it, and said: "Yup, he's dead!"

My open-mouthed look of astonishment at 'Herr Flick's' bizarre behaviour was broken as Jacqui rolled up in a police Sherpa van. A quick examination of the corpse showed no evidence of a struggle or any injuries, so we packaged the body in the plastic body bag and lifted it into the back of the Sherpa van for transportation to Westminster Mortuary in Horseferry Road.

I watched the Sherpa leave which, unfortunately, took longer than it should have. It was squeezed into a tight area between two ponds and the driver had to perform what turned out to be a nine-point turn. Every time he stopped a thud came from the back of the van as the corpse, in a near frictionless envelope of wet plastic, slid up and down the van's smooth metal floor. At this rate he was going to arrive at the mortuary with a flat head and broken ankles, so I handed the driver a note for the pathologist, explaining the transportation issues.

Arthur Scargill is still alive and well at the time of writing. This man turned out to be one of the many homeless people that live on the streets of central London, and had drowned whilst intoxicated. It came to surprise me just how many times I ended up in Westminster mortuary with yet another homeless man - they were nearly all men- taking their fingerprints in an effort to identify them. Sadly the nature of their lives meant this was often impossible, with no ID, dental records or police records, they were buried in a pauper's grave at the council's expense. I would sometimes reflect on the circumstances that might have led them to become homeless with the mortuary attendant, who never failed to combine my visits with his lunch break. He would eat his sandwiches while sitting at the bottom of the PM table with the homeless person's corpse laid out in all their gory glory.

# THE AYATOLLAH KICKS OFF

When Nic De Silva, my counterpart on C district phoned to ask if I could assist him with a siege at the Iranian Airways office in Piccadilly, I jumped at the chance. My first month had been interesting but, I felt, had lacked the excitement of a live operation, so I arranged for Jacqui to meet me at West End Central for a 2pm briefing.

Nic, a real gentleman, was born in Goa and had had an adventurous life. He'd worked in Kenya as a bodyguard to President Joma Kenyatta (modern Kenya's founding father) in the 1960s. After an assassination attempt left Kenyatta injured, violent unrest ensued and Nic decided the time was right to leave and moved to the UK, where he applied to become a Scenes of Crime Officer. Nic never forgot a name - he told me the trick was to associate a picture with the name upon introduction - but he struggled with decision-making, wasn't a natural leader and his forensic knowledge was questionable. He sometimes excused himself by saying: "Remember Larry I am working in a foreign language," which was hardly the most reassuring of reasons.

At West End Central, the uniform Chief Superintendent addressed the assembled room of uniformed officers, detectives and us SOCOs.

"Students of varying nationalities have occupied the offices of Iranian Airlines. They've secured the glass entrance doors with a large chain and padlock and are holding airline staff against their will in an anti-Ayatollah-Khomeini demonstration. In other words, this is a hostage situation. But they seem peaceful and we have negotiated a truce so that we can enter via the front doors and remove the hostages, before we *peacefully* arrest the demonstrators."

As far as we were concerned, we would follow behind the police officers and, in the words of the Chief Super: "Grab any exhibit close to you and then retreat, just in case it kicks off."

The students had daubed anti-Khomeini slogans in red paint on the office walls, and had lynched an effigy of the Ayatollah so that it was hanging in the airline office's front window and placed placards and leaflets all over the office. The Chief Super emphasized that we must "NOT attempt to take down the hanging effigy of the Ayatollah in the front window." Apparently, this was a condition of the truce.

"All understood?" the Chief Super asked. We replied in the affirmative.

I then turned to Jacqui. "We will need brown paper sacks, and large plastic bags, just in case as we will be looking to match paint on suspects, fingerprints on leaflets or any other propaganda. We stick together and work as a team of two and we follow the uniform guys in. No running into the premises gung-ho; let the police do their job first."

I'd never forgotten my confrontation with the squatter's Alsatian and was determined that nothing like that would ever be repeated as far as I, or any of my crew were concerned. The briefing had identified the hostage takers as "students" but in reality we didn't know who they were, or who might be in their midst. Fanatics are good at camouflage.

Despite the fact that this was his operation, Nic didn't say anything to his staff at all. Personally, I would have directed one SOCO to the Charge Room to advise officers on the taking of clothes from suspects as they arrived, and to identify other exhibits that would be required e.g., paint swabs from people's hands. As they had not attended the scene, cross contamination of exhibits could not then be alleged. As a SOCO you have to cover all bases. Best to look at the scenario and think ahead. When under cross-examination in crown court by an experienced and silky-smooth barrister - there's a reason they're called Silks - eighteen months or two years after the event, you need to know that everything was done by the book. Defence barristers will have no hesitation in attacking your integrity and the integrity of the exhibits. If they can find any possibility of contamination or incorrect procedure, then the evidence is useless and their clients are practically home and dry.

As we formed up on the pavement outside the Iranian airline building, I noticed that Nic was right at the front.

What the hell was he up to? Too late for me to do anything as the glass doors suddenly swung open and the police piled in, not exactly the orderly entrance they'd promised. Nic was right at the front and he immediately climbed onto a table and pulled down the effigy of the Ayatollah. He'd done the one thing the Chief Super had asked us not to do. Pandemonium broke out as the students kicked off and a free-for-all, cowboys-in-a-saloon-style brawl erupted; twenty students armed with placards battled twenty cops armed with truncheons. Jacqui and I threaded our way through the melee, working together, snatching leaflets, tins of red paint and brushes, and a placard that said *Death to the Ayatollah*, dodging fists, boots, batons and sticks as we went, and we quickly escaped with the evidence intact, job done.

An hour later we were back at the station busy packaging and sealing our exhibits so the detectives could use them in interviews, when Jacqui tapped me on the shoulder.

"Check out Nic," she said. I looked and couldn't help but smile. Nic looked rather dishevelled. Caught up in the brawl, he'd ended up being battered by both police (who failed to recognize him) and students. On top of this, one of Nic's SOCOs had pinned an A4 paper stating: "I CAUSED A RIOT!" to his back. Quite a few officers with black eyes and other bruises were pretty pissed off with Nic but even they couldn't help but grin at the sight of that A4 paper.

# DON'T MENTION THE WAR

Protestors of all kinds were a fact of life at Cannon Row. I was regularly called to so-called 'peaceful' protests outside the Houses of Parliament or in Trafalgar Square where I was asked to examine weapons - such as three-foot long iron railing, its end sharpened to a point - regularly confiscated from the tiny minority of protestors who were anything but peaceful.

Another common crime, often associated with protesting, was the vandalism of memorials. I was once called to examine the RAF Memorial on Victoria Embankment, something people drive and walk past everyday but barely notice, just one of the hundreds of monuments to be found in Westminster. It's Grade II listed and was originally dedicated to the memory of those RAF pilots who perished in World War I but has been extended to include all subsequent conflicts. It features a zodiacal globe bearing the gilded eagle that comes from the RAF's badge and the motto 'Through adversity to the stars.' I was called to examine the monument because someone had vandalized it with silver and aluminium paint, spraying the legend: 'Remember The JE'. From this I can only deduce that the author had been disturbed in mid-spray. I took samples of the paints and also a scraping of the memorial stone. If the culprit was caught then residue from the statue and paint could be matched to skin and clothing. Alas, the vandal was never found.

I was also called to the Cenotaph, our primary national war memorial and arguably the nation's most famous monument, after someone pinched one of its flags. It puzzled me as to the type of person who would do such a thing. Was it for the thrill or some simple villainy? I found partial finger marks on the flagpole but it wasn't enough to identify the thief.

Shortly after I returned to base after the Cenotaph job, Rochester Row CID called me to ask if I could drop what I was doing and accompany a young detective to the London home of Conservative Minister Cecil Parkinson as he had been burgled. This was only a few months after the story of Parkinson's relationship with Sarah Keays had broken, so I was interested to see who might have been responsible. Mr Parkinson lived just around the corner from Rochester Row and, after picking up the detective, I warned him not to use the word "keys" when talking to Cecil, or his wife Anne.

"OK Larry, no problem," he replied confidently.

It was a horrible wet evening and we ran quickly from the car up the path to the front door, which was answered by Anne Parkinson. She told us that the intruder had gained entry by forcing one of the sash windows, which were secured with a lock. Although the window had been forced, it was still possible to lock it and I asked for the 'implement' that would open the window. Examination completed, and convinced that this time it actually was a burglar (as opposed to journalists desperate for a story) as several valuables had been stolen, I returned the key to its place on the hallway desk.

The detective explained how he would circulate the list of stolen property and would be in touch within the next day with an update.

We were walking out of the front door when the detective turned and said: "Oh by the way, my colleague did return the keys, didn't- Oh, sorry Mrs Parkinson, I didn't mean to say that!" He paused for a moment, turned bright red and added, "I think you are very brave!" as I pulled him down the pathway under the inflamed gaze of Mrs Parkinson only to bump into Mr Parkinson who'd just alighted from a black cab.

"Oh- er- excuse us!" the detective said as we legged it through the rain to the minivan.

"Oh very nicely done," I said to the mortified young detective who remained hopelessly flustered during the short journey back to the station. "No problem, you said."

"I'm so sorry Larry."

I've always wondered how that evening went for the Minister after our foot-in-mouth encounter with his wife.

# SMELL THE MONEY

I n 1972, the annual total of armed robberies in the Metropolitan district was 380. By 1978, it had risen to 734 and by 1982 it more than doubled to 1,772 (that's five a day) – a 466 per cent increase in a decade. Changing attitudes to authority, the growth of motorways and the arrival of cheap, fast cars, helped robbers stay ahead of the law. Two of the most notorious were Ronnie and John Knight.

The Knight family grew up in Hoxton. Ronnie ran clubs and successfully kept a life of crime secret from Barbara Windsor, his movie-star wife – even though he was spending nearly every night out with East London gangsters Ronnie and Reggie Kray.

Ronnie Knight's younger brother John owned a garage and ran the Fox Pub in Shoreditch. In 1983, John mastermind-ed what was then Britain's biggest cash robbery.

The Security Express depot in Curtain Road was known locally as Fort Knox. Knight found an empty build-ing in the alley that overlooked the depot. He broke in and watched the place for more than a year before striking and escaping with five tons of cash, £6 million in total. "When them doors opened it was beautiful," John said later. "It was like Aladdin's cave." John's share was £400,000. He buried most of it in his garden and took £100,000 to Ronnie asking him for help to get it out of the UK to Spain. Then the Flying Squad, the Met Police's robbery specialists, got a tip-off and John was arrested. Ronnie fled for Spain – which, at that time, had no extradition treaty with the UK.

I received a call from the Flying Squad asking if I could assist them by examining the basement of The Fox Pub in Shoreditch, owned by John Knight. They had received a tip off that the money had been taken there immediately after the robbery. I was looking for any evidence that could connect the pub to the stolen bank notes, such as the plastic the money might have been wrapped in, or anything that appeared unusual in the basement area, the only place in the pub where there was enough room to hide six tons of cash. There was a lot of brick dust and I found a partial shoeprint. I took samples of the dust from various locations, swept the whole floor and retained the sweepings as an exhibit. An enthusiastic young photographer who was new to the job asked - once he'd finished taking photos of the scene - if there was anything he could do to help.

"Take this," I said, handing him a large glass jar. "And stand in various locations around the basement taking air samples. Make sure you close the lid tightly when you're finished."

He looked at me like I was taking the Michael.

"I'm serious," I said and he set about his task.

I know this sounds like a joke but I promise you it was not. That basement had a distinctive smell of damp and beer. During John's trial, the jurors were taken to the Fox to see where the money had been hidden and – in a legal first – to smell it: the smell in the basement matched the smell of the money. Scientists from the forensic laboratory matched the brick dust to traces of dust found on the £2million that was eventually recovered, proving the money had been stored in the Fox Pub (and thereby linking it to John Knight), where it had been divvied up between the robbers.

In 1985, five men were found guilty of robbery and handling money from the Security Express robbery and sentenced to a total of 66 years. The judge singled out John Knight for the harshest sentence: 22 years. Ronnie returned to Britain in 1994 after losing most of his money, and after a newspaper agreed to pay him £20,000 for his story. The police were waiting at the airport. He pleaded guilty to handling £384,000 and was sentenced to seven years. None of the other stolen cash was ever found and the police failed to convict other members of the gang, including drug smuggler Clifford Saxe, the former manager of the Fox. Police arrested Saxe in Spain on Boxing Day 2001 but the 73-year-old died before he could be extradited.

# ZUT ALORS!

I'd come too far to turn back now. I was on a one-foot wide ledge sixty feet above the ground with a one-metre jump to get to the evidence: a single footprint left by a burglar who'd struck the previous night at the Prince of Wales Theatre. They were currently in the midst of the stage adaptation of the popular BBC TV show *Allo Allo!*, with the original cast.

A thief had gained entry from the roof of the theatre and had ransacked the dressing rooms. The stage manager had discovered the burglary early in the morning and I'd arrived at 10am to find a constable already there, telling me that he'd seen a footprint on the roof, which *may* have been caused by the burglar. To get to the roof I had to climb a sixty-foot ladder at the back of the stage, tip-toe past dozens of counter weights that helped move the scenery, then onto this foot-wide ledge.

"What am I doing?" I muttered to myself as I made the mistake of looking down. "It's too early in the morning for this sort of stuff."

I jumped the small gap to the other side and quickly found the shoe mark. It was almost certainly left by the burglar, but there was no way I could ask a photographer to climb that ladder and jump across from that ledge carrying his equipment. So I sketched the shoe in detail then carefully jumped back to the narrow ledge, clinging to a piece of scaffolding upon landing for support before descending the ladder in great relief.

I found various finger marks in the dressing rooms and so had to take the cast's fingerprints for elimination purposes. I returned to the theatre early that evening and met the actors who were already in, or half-in-half-out of costume. A surreal moment was taking Gestapo Officer Herr Flick's (Richard Gibson) fingerprints (I had met two Herr Flick lookalikes in my career but didn't think to mention this at the time); he was very jolly, in stark contrast to his character, and knocked back the white wine at quite a rate. They peppered me with questions about crime scene examination as they swigged back the wine and I left the theatre with a sore throat, having spent the entire time answering questions and having forgotten to ask them anything about their fascinating careers.

Disappointingly, despite my death-defying leap and subsequent footprint recovery, the thief was never caught and, even more disappointingly, I returned to the station only to find that one of my Herr Flick lookalikes was about to make a sudden and most unpleasant reappearance.

# MRS THATCHER'S TIGHTS

In-between a never ending stream of burglaries, I was often asked to examine anonymous malicious letters sent to HRH The Queen and Prime Minister Margaret Thatcher as well as MPs, Peers of the Realm and various showbiz personalities. I was busy one afternoon, examining one of several such letters sent to Prime Minister Maggie Thatcher (a confusing missive about something called 'Pratt's drinking beer' but the words 'threat' and 'kill' had been highlighted in the text, so the author had our full attention) when in waltzed Malcolm. This was Malcolm from my Wimbledon/New Malden days, the Herr Flick lookalike who had it in for anyone who failed to share his opinion (particularly where overtime budgets were concerned). Some idiot had made Malcolm a temporary Senior SOCO and posted him to my area, making him my boss. I wondered if this was a deliberate act by the Fingerprint Branch to sabotage my management style. I was probably being paranoid. Wasn't I?

"Larry, Mrs Thatcher is performing the official reopening of Cannon Row police station in two days' time and I want you to deliver a twenty-minute crime scene presentation."

Cannon Row had just been through a major refurbishment and I was aware that an official ceremony was coming up but this was too much.

"What? Only two days' notice! The Ceremonies Office never mentioned this. You should be doing it," I said, thinking that he must have been asked but had decided to bottle out at the last minute.

"No, as I said, I want you to do it".

No point in arguing. Sod it. I was fuming but there was no time to throw a wobbly as Malcolm would not sanction any overtime for this. That would be like admitting he hadn't given me enough notice to prepare.

I called the Ceremonies Office who were really helpful and gave me a full briefing on addressing the Head Girl, before I ran my idea for a presentation past them, just to check its content. They approved and, with my plan signed off, I was good to go.

On 17 June 1985, at 11.30am, Prime Minister Margaret Thatcher officially opened Cannon Row Police Station. In her speech she said she appreciated the courtesy, and dedication of the officers of Cannon Row, concluding: "In the prime duty of safeguarding liberty, yours is the most important task of all. For unless the law-abiding citizens are protected, and the law breakers apprehended, there is no security, there is no freedom."

'How true,' I thought to myself, 'As I'm currently dealing with a bunch of threatening letters addressed to you.'

She then rambled on a bit about the pay of police in 1900, three shillings a week for a constable, and finished by saying: "I should like to express our gratitude and admiration to all who serve here and wish them well in this new building."

Then she entered the charge room and, after a minute spent chatting to the officers, she entered a room normally reserved for the interrogation of suspects with me nervously waiting to receive her and all of the members of the COBRA Cabinet, (Cabinet Office Briefing room A). Her husband Dennis was also in the group. No journalists or photographers were allowed into the room.

One hour earlier, at 10.30am I was in a panic. I'd borrowed cutlery, crockery, kettle, tea towels, box of cereal, flour, and other bits from the canteen to help create a bedsit. The Detective Chief Inspector loaned me his-half drunk bottle of whiskey and two glasses. I had borrowed the single bed from the Divisional Surgeon suite, as the examination couch did not look right mocked up as a bed. I'd brought a duvet, pillow, and a couple of ornaments from home, and a Victoria Street boutique had loaned me a female manikin, wig and all.

The scenario was to feature a young woman living in a bedsit, with signs of an argument, possibly with her boyfriend, as there was a man's jacket on a chair, two glasses on the table with a small amount of whiskey in one glass and the other glass knocked over with spilt whiskey on the table. There was a partial shoe mark in white powder on the floor, and fibres on the duvet cover. The female was in bed under the duvet with just her nose and head showing.

The room was oblong in shape and my plan was for the entourage to file in from the right and they would stand behind a ceremonial blue rope running the length of the room, looking directly onto the 'crime scene.'

My reason for panic was that I was missing one piece of equipment: a pointer. I didn't want to have to push past the PM or turn my back to her to explain the scene and demonstrate examination techniques. Then I had the bright idea of using a snooker cue. I bolted up to the snooker room (a key part of any London nick in those days) and chose the newest cue available and dashed back to the scene to practice. At the last moment, I decided that the snooker cue was a bad idea, so I leant it up in a corner beyond the rope.

Maggie entered the room followed by her Cabinet and a smattering of Generals, with Dennis bringing up the rear. I then explained the scenario and how we create a path to the body so the Divisional Surgeon, pathologist and photographer can work without contaminating the scene. I pointed out the various clues and explained the techniques involved with regard to fingerprints and other forensic evidence, and the possibility of the presence of drugs (the white powder). The climax of the presentation was the reveal that the woman in the bed had been strangled with her own tights (I had completely forgotten about the tights as I was leaving home that morning, so I nicked Jennifer's, which had been drying on a radiator).

Presentation complete, I invited questions. The Prime Minister, as a former chemist, raised a number of technical queries and, as a former chemist myself I was able to answer them. An Army General asked if I had any involvement with the military. The first thing I thought of was the suicide in Knightsbridge Barracks but obviously not a good case to bring up here.

Thinking quickly, I said: "Yes sir, I have been involved with the RMP, (Royal Military Police), dog section, and a brilliant Springer spaniel and dog handler who assisted me in finding a firearm discarded in undergrowth following an armed robbery. I was also involved with an investigation where we used military equipment."

The equipment was the man-seeking radar I'd used in Surrey to catch the cat burglar. The General seemed pleased and smiled smugly at his Rear Admiral colleague who was standing next to him.

Dennis chirped up next. "Mr Henderson, what is the significance of the snooker cue here next to me?"

Oops. "Sir, I have to be honest. I was lacking a pointer so borrowed the snooker cue but two minutes before you arrived I decided not to use it as it looked unprofessional. So it has nothing to do with the scene. You've caught me out there, sir."

Dennis and Margaret were both delighted and roared with laughter. I could glimpse the press through the door who were clearly desperate to find out what was so funny about a murder scene.

We all filed back into the charge room and mingled for a few minutes where I found myself cornered by the Head Girl. Whilst I was talking, her gaze and attention never left mine, even when an aid started whispering in her ear. I later learned that he'd been updating her on the TWA flight hijacked by Hezbollah and Islamic Jihad earlier that day, which was at that moment on the tarmac in Beirut with 26 British nationals on board although one person was murdered and thrown from the plane onto the tarmac, the rest of the 146 crew and passengers were rescued unharmed.

After a short discussion about my work, she leaned in and said: "Mr Henderson, the criminal must never know what you know."

"Yes Ma'am, but unfortunately television educates the criminal every evening and that's a worrying issue for me."

These days, the danger created by the Internet is far more pernicious than TV ever was - TV shows like CSI, while giving away the odd snippet, are wildly inaccurate.

She nodded, and said that the media sometimes played into the hands of our enemies before thanking me for a "most interesting presentation" as her entourage readied to leave. I breathed a sigh of relief, which lasted for about twenty minutes as I dismantled the scene and returned all the articles to their owners.

When I got home Jennifer said: "A peculiar thing happened today; the tights that I washed last night and left on the radiator have disappeared."

"Oh that was me, I took them for Maggie"

"Maggie?"

"You know, the presentation."

"Yes, I remember that, but what did she want with my tights? Was she wearing them?"

I turned to look at Jennifer in exasperation and saw she was grinning.

A few weeks later, it became clear to me that when Mrs Thatcher was talking to me about how media can sometimes play into the hands of criminals, the hostage situation must have been at the forefront of her mind. In a speech she gave to the American Bar Association on July 15, 1985, she said:

"For newspapers and television, acts of terrorism inevitably make good copy and compelling viewing. The hijacker and the terrorist thrive on publicity: without it, their activities and their influence are sharply curtailed [...] they see how acts of violence and horror dominate the newspaper columns and television screens of the free world. They see how that coverage creates a natural wave of sympathy for the victims and pressure to end their plight no matter what the consequence. And the terrorists exploit it.

"We must try to find ways to starve the terrorist and the hijacker of the oxygen of publicity on which they depend. In our societies we do not believe in constraining the media, still less in censorship. But ought we not to ask the media to agree among themselves a voluntary code of conduct, a code under which they would not say or show anything which could assist the terrorists' morale or their cause while the hijack lasted?"

Whatever one might think of Maggie, I had to agree with her on this point - for those who are wondering, I've been careful not to let any trade secrets that would assist criminals come out in the writing of this book. I once saw an episode of a popular TV crime series, in which a character accurately demonstrated a simple way to destroy

DNA. It may have satisfied the script writer in terms of providing a decent plot point on which to hang a story but this also brought the technique into the public domain, possibly educated terrorists, murders, rapists, robbers, kidnappers and burglars. But now we have the Internet, so we can forget all about Maggie's suggestion of a voluntary code of conduct.

# ELEPHANT IN THE ROOM

**D**rug dealers are, sometimes, extremely inventive people, and will go to great lengths to protect their empires. I experienced an example of this when a DI based at Rochester Row approached me about a possible raid against a notorious drug dealer.

"This is not an easy job Larry," he said. "This guy is dangerous, and the flat is fortified with a steel door with four mortise locks and reinforcing bolts."

He asked if I would handle the exhibits, as he knew his squad would have their hands full on the day. This was right up my street. I loved proactive policing, i.e., taking the fight to the criminal, so I readily agreed and said I'd also bring Jacqui along, as she'd already shown me she worked well under pressure. Then it was time to tell Malcolm the boss.

"No! No! No!"

I was not at all surprised at his predictable reaction. He did not like getting involved in pro-active policing and hated it when I offered to support the Area Crime Squad on their operations because, more often than not, it involved overtime.

"I am not authorizing overtime for one SOCO, never mind two."

"Malcolm this is a serious target, we should be there!"

"I will not authorize the overtime and that's it!"

I left him and headed straight to the DI's office,

"Guv' can you fit me and Jacqui into your budget for this op? That bastard at the end of the corridor won't sanction the overtime."

"Yeah no problem Larry, I want you there".

Result! I returned to Malcolm's office.

"The DI is paying our overtime so Jacqui and I are supporting the Crime Squad tomorrow night. The briefing is at 8pm, and the hit at midnight. We should be finished around 3am so we won't be in till later in the morning, I will brief Nic De Silva to cover any early burglaries or incidents."

"I expect you in at the normal time Larry."

The flat was on the second floor of a two-storey block. The drains from the block of flats had been covertly surveyed and filters were in place to catch any drugs flushed down the toilet.

Our role was simple. React to the situation as it unfolds and take responsibility for the anticipated drug exhibits and paraphernalia such as the weighing machine and plastic bags.

"Always remember," I told Jacqui, "The better the evidence, the longer the sentence."

The target was a heavily-tattooed white guy in his thirties. I have to admit, he looked terrifying and I would not like to have been his neighbour. Local people were understandably scared of this guy. Although he had a long history of violence, all the intelligence indicated that no firearms would be in the flat.

We were driven to within fifty-yards of the premises in a transit van, and quietly filed onto the road. More officers were ferried in another transit van to the rear of the apartment block. Back up uniformed officers in marked police cars parked two roads away.

The plan was for two uniform officers from the assault team, wearing protective vests, together with a dog handler and Ben, a very large Alsatian, to lead the charge, once the Entry Team had jacked the door off its frame using hydraulic jacks.

The stench of urine in the stairwell was almost intolerable - and I've smelt more than my fair share of dead bodies - and once we were lined up on the walkway to the flat, the two guys from the entry team quietly made their way up to the steel front door, at which point one of them dropped his hydraulic jack. We might as well have rung the doorbell. The element of surprise was lost but the looks of horror on everyone's faces turned into determination as the two lads hurriedly positioned the large jacks against the vertical frame of the door and blew it apart. The steel door was forced open; Barks, shouts and screams: "POLICE! POLICE! Remain where you are and put your hands above your head!" We charged in but I could already hear the fading sound of the flushing toilet.

Although we recovered ten small packets of cocaine from the blocked drains, it wasn't a lot, just a few grams. We'd been expecting a kilo or two at least. There was also a trail of white powder leading to the toilet, which was useful, but we needed more if this guy was going to spend any time in prison. After an hour of searching, even lifting floorboards, and no sign of any drugs, I decided it was time to mention the elephant in the room.

Well, it wasn't an elephant per se, but a huge bloody great big snake: a fully-grown python in a huge aquarium.

Someone was going to have to search the aquarium for the stash.

"Um, so are these poisonous or what?" one burly officer asked.

"Dunno," said another "But I saw one eat a donkey by dislocating their jaws on David Attenborough. Should I take the lid off then boys?"

Everyone took a step back.

I called the nick. No snake specialist was on our emergency list. So we called London Zoo's emergency number and eventually someone was seconded from the reptile house to the Crime Squad for the examination of said snake and its lair.

"She's asleep," the Zookeeper said. He was a tough looking outdoors-type in his 30s and looked like he very much wanted to be back in bed and asleep himself. "They're not always happy when you wake them," he added before turning to look at the big tough police officers that filled the room. "She's over eight feet, so I'll need some help, otherwise she might have me for breakfast." He smiled evilly. "Any volunteers?"

Uncomfortable looks were exchanged amidst muttering. "How about you?"

'Why is it that I always end up at the front?' I wondered to myself. I couldn't refuse this challenge in front of the cops, so I shrugged.

"Sure, she's not poisonous is she?"

"No, but you need to watch out for her head. She's an Indian Python, quite rare, and if she bites she can't let go, thanks to her backwards-angled teeth. Then she'll try and eat you."

Two minutes later I had four feet of the rear end of a snake wrapped tightly around my left arm and I was starting to panic.

"She likes you, doesn't she?" the zookeeper said with a fixed smile as he struggled to unravel her and place her in what he called his faunarium, a huge plastic box lined with newspaper.

Eventually, the python was finally in its faunarium from where, so it seemed to me, it gave me the evil eye.

In the tank, underneath eight inches of sawdust, we found heroin and cocaine worth £80,000, clearly tie-able to our chief suspect, as he was the only one who handled the python. Pats on the back all round.

Once the criminals had been booked, the evidence been logged and the python entrusted to the care of London Zoo, we went for a celebratory drink in New Covent Garden, where the pubs open at 3am for the shift workers. I can't say a pint of lager before breakfast is exactly refreshing, but it did help to reduce my adrenalin from the stratospheric levels to which the raid and subsequent snake handling had boosted them.

I arrived home at 5am and was back on duty by midday. I re-checked the exhibits from the raid, which included poly bags, plastic bank bags, spoons, aluminium foil stained brown, a cigarette lighter, straws and two weighing machines. I then checked with Nic De Silva who'd had a quiet morning, returned to my desk and fell asleep. My phone woke me.

"You've turned up then." No mistaking who this was.

"I was in by twelve, even though the operation finished later than anticipated."

He did not ask if we'd had a successful evening. Instead, that snake in the grass 'reminded' me that the monthly stats for scenes visited were due on his desk before close of business.

# THE FIT-UP

One of the more unusual places I've been called to deal with a break-in was Wellington Arch Police Office, which is in the middle of the Hyde Park corner roundabout, and has room for one (or two thin) constables. I was pretty certain that the culprit was a homeless person trying to escape the winter.

Police stations seem like an unusual place for criminals to want to strike but one day I was called to New Scotland Yard to investigate the theft of two bottles of wine from the fifth floor catering stores, which was just down the corridor from the Commissioner's office. The Commissioner at that time was Sir Kenneth Newman (GBE, QPM) who had been a Detective Superintendent at Gerald Road a few years before I rolled up and had, as Commissioner, instigated some major reforms of the police.

The store room door had been forced, so I searched and found some finger marks and took some impressions of the marks left by the tool used, probably a 9mm screwdriver, as well as samples of paint and wood. With me was a Detective Chief Inspector from the Serious Crime Squad based at the Yard. Job done, we walked back along the corridor, past the Commissioner's office where I saw two bottles of red wine tucked in a corner next to his office door.

I turned to the DCI and pointing to the bottles said: "Looks like somebody's fitted up the Commissioner, will you be interviewing him later?"

I examined both bottles for fingerprints but they had been wiped clean. We never identified the thief. Whomever he/she was they had a lot of bottle, not only thieving just yards from the Commissioner of the Metropolis, had tried to fit him up to boot. That really was taking the proverbial.

# BAPTISM OF FIRE

After Gerald departed, I shared jobs from Rochester Row with Jacqui for nine months, until we at last received a new recruit; Rhianna, who was in her twenties and originally from Aberdeen. Her training course reports were good but a note had been made that she had a tendency to speak her mind at the wrong moment, in front of the wrong people. I met her at Rochester Row and introduced her to everyone, including Malcolm. After inviting her for lunch, I left her to organize her equipment and made sure she understood she could call me if she was ever in doubt.

She called me two days later and asked if I would accompany her to the scene of a fatal fire. I agreed, as this was hardly the best scene to have to deal with in your first couple of days.

The fire had taken place in the ground floor flat of a tenement block. The victim, a woman thought to be in her eighties, was sitting in a lounge chair, and badly burnt. Rhianna took one look, panicked and asked to leave.

I followed her out to find her in tears, and I walked her slowly back to the police station. As we walked along, she grew more and more upset and so I instinctively took hold of her hand, explaining how her reaction was perfectly natural.

"Yes, I understand," she said, "It's just that I visualized my grandma sat in the chair."

We had just turned the corner into Rochester Row when she started to regain her composure. I stopped.

"Do you feel like returning to the scene with me?" I asked. "I will do the necessary and then call the Fire Investigation Unit at the Laboratory. I think it would be good for you if you could manage."

She agreed, so I let go of her hand and we walked back to the scene. We did the necessary examination together and I then called the FIU at the Lab explaining the circumstances (they would conduct their own examination to establish the fire's cause and the point at which it had started). I admired Rhianna's resolve. It wasn't easy to walk back into that terrible scene, to confront the twisted shell of the dear old soul who'd lived there. Once our examination was complete I suspected I knew the way her death had come.

"It was quick," I told Rhianna. "She fell asleep and died before the flames even touched her, from the smoke inhalation. It's a peaceful way to go. As carbon dioxide builds up in the blood, the brain starts to shut down the vital organs. It was probably over in less than five minutes."

Rhianna nodded. "Doesn't make it any easier though, does it?"

I had to admit, she had a point.

# SABOTAGE AT THE CASTLE

C annon Row had many sensitive enquiries, which in the main concerned Members of Parliament and the post they received via Royal Mail. Occasionally, we would have to investigate a crime that had occurred at Windsor Castle.

A senior member of the Household Management had become suspicions about the number of sudden breakdowns of electrical equipment that occurred at the weekend or on bank holidays. It was always something related to the residential section of the Castle, such as the central heating or lighting circuits. This man, as one would expect, was extremely well-spoken and reserved but couldn't help get a little excited when he revealed he'd done a spot of detective work and had retained a particular electric motor that had caused a problem over the previous weekend. He had it under lock and key in a workshop.

"That's incredibly useful, thank you," I said, "Can I take a look?"

This was easier said than done. Windsor Castle sits on a maze of underground tunnels, through some of which runs an electric train, providing quick delivery of certain bulkier and heavier items, from crates of wine to bedding. When we finally arrived at the workshop, I examined the device along with the service manager, who'd called us in and who had once been an electrician. Upon removing the motor's outer case, we could see a severed red wire with a small piece of red insulation tape underneath it. Remembering my LEB enquiry and the success of matching tools such as pliers and wire cutting tools, I immediately consulted the DI and suggested that all the tools of all of the maintenance staff needed to be taken immediately. The purpose of examination and comparison with the cut edge of the terminal wire in the motor needed to be compared with all maintenance staff, not just the electricians. Not an easy task, as different teams were on duty at different times.

The DI's enquiries highlighted one particular electrician whose records showed he was regularly called out. If our reckoning was on target, this electrician had a lot to lose by his actions. He lived in a grace-and-favour cottage on the estate, and had a reasonable wage and shift hours. I searched his locker, tool bag and car. I also took possession of all the tools that could possibly have made the cut on the red wire, along with a roll of red insulation tape I found in his tool bag. The Forensic Laboratory matched a pair of pliers to the cut edge of the motor wire and mechanically fitted a cut edge of the tape back to the cut edge on the roll, proving it came from that specific roll.

Our suspect was number two on the list of staff to be interviewed, but it was engineered so that he was interviewed first and we managed to do this without raising his suspicions. He eventually admitted to deliberately causing problems to boost his earnings. If called out on a bank holiday, for example, his pay tripled. The disgraced electrician was fired and evicted from his cottage but was spared criminal charges.

In a minor royal coincidence, I was called to Kensington Palace first thing the following morning after I returned from Windsor, as a stamp album had been stolen from a glass display cabinet. Although glass is an excellent surface from which to retrieve a finger mark, it had been wiped with a cloth and the dastardly philatelist was never caught.

# OUT OF CONTROL

On the evening of Sunday October 6, 1985, I was resting at home after an enormous roast beef dinner, and the only thing on my mind was contemplating whether I had the energy to get up and get ready for bed. My lethargy got the better of me and I decided to wait until the news came on the TV, as I'd heard there was a bit of a riot kicking off on an estate in Tottenham.

A young black man, Floyd Jarrett, had been arrested by Haringey police, having been stopped in a car which they thought might have been stolen, as the tax disc didn't match the vehicle. Four officers went to his home on the Broadwater Estate in Tottenham to search for further evidence. Floyd's mother Cynthia opened the door and while she might not have been best pleased to have four police officers in her home, she nevertheless allowed them to conduct their search.

The situation deteriorated as soon as Floyd and his brother Keith arrived along with their sister Patricia. They shouted at the police to get out and some pushing and shoving started. Cynthia, who was twenty stone, collided with a detective, fell to the ground and stopped breathing. She was pronounced dead on arrival at hospital

No stolen property was found in the house, and the vehicle Jarrett was in when he was arrested wasn't stolen. Cynthia's death, seemingly at the hands of the police, sparked outrage. The next day Haringey's black mayor, Bernie Grant, said, "A black woman has been killed by officers of the state. Police behaviour is totally unacceptable. The force is out of control." The area suffered from high unemployment - up 82 per cent within ethnic minorities in one year -, high crime and poor housing.

Violence began after a coach-load of black and white youths arrived on the estate to be greeted by locals. At 6 p.m., at a packed meeting held on the estate, Grant appealed for calm. Someone shouted, "It's too late for words!" and the estate erupted into violence.

When the news came on I sat up in amazement. It was mayhem. Hundreds of police and rioters going at it hammer and tong, fires everywhere you looked. Then my phone rang.

"Larry, we need you in Tottenham. I know it's not your weekend on call but we've got officers down and injured and need help with evidence collection."

"Of course," I said, "I can leave in ten minutes."

"Ok, get ready and I'll call you back."

I put the phone down, staggered through the house cursing my over ambitious appetite, got changed, packed my bag and awaited instructions.

I was ordered to the A&E department at North Middlesex Hospital, Tottenham to vet casualties and preserve and package forensic evidence, such as burnt uniforms for petrol (fuels are chemically marked by the retailers and are traceable). I drove to Cannon Row, picked up my van and burned rubber to the hospital. It was only when I reached Tottenham that I realized driving on my own in a small van marked with the livery of the Met police into an anti-police riot was akin to Colonel Custer riding his horse through a Cheyenne village. I then realized, thanks to the bangs and thuds on the side of my van, from fists, boots and the occasional half-brick, that if I were to stop, my van would be overturned. I drove as fast as I dared, hoping I didn't knock someone over and thereby create another crisis.

The hospital looked like it was in the middle of a war zone. Young police constables were arriving by the dozen. All had burns from petrol bombs and although most were not badly injured, all of them were angry with their commanders. They felt abandoned, with no clear orders to attack or retreat while petrol bombs rained down upon them. It was terrifying to hear and rumours had already spread that at least one police constable had been killed. Someone had at least made sure that no injured civilians were sent to the same hospital, as I'm sure the riot would have carried on right there.

As more injured officers arrived, the stories grew worse and worse. They'd been attacked with bottles, stones and petrol bombs. As one officer fell trying to escape a hail of bricks a concrete slab was dropped from the second floor of a tower block; it landed on his back and ruptured his spleen. A few minutes after this, shotgun blasts sent the police scrambling for cover; two journalists were hit with pellets. Every time the police tried to advance they were sent packing by a hail of petrol bombs and bricks thrown by more than four hundred rioters

At 9.40 p.m. Scotland Yard's firearms squad were issued plastic bullets and CS gas - the first time the police had been authorized to use CS gas on the UK mainland. Nine minutes later a policeman was shot and seriously injured. By 10.10 p.m. the first floor of a block of flats was on fire but the fire brigade couldn't get close enough to tackle the blaze because they were pelted with missiles.

The injured officers continued to arrive at hospital, one with gunshot wounds, until about 4am, and things finally seemed to have calmed down. I left the hospital at around 6am and drove through the smoke left by many fires to Tottenham Police station for the SOCO debrief. It was then we heard that a police officer had been murdered.

A team of policemen led by thirty-four-year-old PC Keith Blakelock, a father of two, had been sent to attempt to clear a path for the fire brigade so they could reach a flat that had caught fire, but they'd been overwhelmed by dozens of men who appeared on the smoke-filled landing. Blakelock suddenly found himself cut off from his colleagues and surrounded by several masked men and some boys armed with machetes and baseball bats. His head was practically severed in the attack. The dying PC's helmet was taken as a trophy. As PC Blakelock lay dying, the fire he'd tried to help extinguish caused a huge gas explosion, destroying someone's home. Moments later another officer was shot.

I volunteered, along with my Area colleague Dave, the D district SOCO1, for night duty for the rest of the week, working on evidence that was still being collected. I was also asked to remain on standby, just in case the riots kicked off again. Fortunately, it remained reasonably quiet, with the odd skirmish producing few new exhibits, including a number of live rounds of ammunition.

Following the Broadwater Farm, the police's riot tactics were improved, and police were issued with fireproof riot gear. As for the murder of PC Blakelock, detectives are still working on finding the perpetrator. In October 2004 his bloodstained uniform was removed from Scotland Yard's Crime Museum for DNA testing but, despite three trials, justice has yet to be done.

The riots of Broadwater Farm did irreparable damage to the community. This was the moment a young minority turned their backs on civilized society and embraced crime, using the rapid influx of drugs such as crack as a financial base, keeping people like myself busy for the rest of our careers.

# HOWSABOUT A BULLET?

The new SOCO, Rhianna, had settled in splendidly at Rochester Row and as a team, the three of us regularly lunched together and sometimes had a drink after work with some of the adjacent District's scene examiners. Christmas was approaching, so I volunteered to organize a festive lunch for all the SOCOs in 8 Area, including our divisional fingerprint friend Matthew, who was an integral part of the team.

I had paid many professional visits to the Charing Cross Hotel, next to the station of the same name, as professional thieves have a habit of targeting hotel rooms and arranged for a private room with a traditional lunch and drinks to order. We got on like a house on fire, inevitably entertaining one another by sharing stories relating to the job and talking shop in general. Even Malcolm was smiling, until he overheard one of the guys ask me: "Who invited that fucking idiot? We can't relax with him here, everything we say will be on our files tomorrow."

"Buy him a drink, then and talk him round," I said. "It is Christmas after all."

Malcolm left twenty minutes later making the excuse he had a prior appointment. Then the party really started. For thirteen people, in 1985, the food bill was a reasonable £150, and you could not complain at the three-course menu and coffee. The drinks bill was £500. I said it was a good party. In fact it was an excellent party because in that one afternoon and evening we all got to know each other. That was important to me.

The next morning, walking over Hungerford bridge that linked the South Bank to Victoria Embankment, I was thinking about the positives from the party, and promising myself a couple of paracetamol with my morning coffee. I was also thinking about an idea I'd had for A and C districts to be run by one SOCO1, not two. It would make us more flexible and provide more experience for the junior SOCOs. Nic De Silva had been transferred a couple of months ago, and the new SOCO1, Alan, had hinted, for family reasons, that he preferred being at the Forensic Laboratory on liaison duties with regular hours and most weekends off. The "A" team's Christmas lunch was the following day, and we were going to discuss it then. It was at this point that I realized it was past 9am and my pager had been unusually quiet. I reached into my suit pocket to check I had turned it on to find I had picked up my TV's remote control instead of my pager.

The "A" team's Lunch was postponed thanks to a hoax bomb that had been delivered to 10 Downing Street, the mail-room of which has extremely sophisticated detection equipment. After being cleared by the bomb squad guys, all suspicious packages ended up on my desk for forensic and fingerprint examination. Regardless of the sender, whether crank, fanatic, protestor, or genuine assassin, they are all unpredictable and even the cranks have to be taken seriously, if for no other reason than to give the subject of their attentions some relief from the constant bombardment of this extreme version of hate mail.

It's tricky and delicate work. We can identify individual specs that would fit on a pinhead and can therefore recover a huge amount of scientific info from a single device. This latest package contained fifteen items, including a three-inch detonator-like cylindrical object, a small paper clock face, electrical wiring, a flash bulb, and pieces of plastic all made to look as if they were wired up together. Not the most sophisticated arrangement but it was accompanied by a letter stating:

"....and the thing you must realize about the Gods is that they are all interconnected spiritually and genetically."

It rambled on to say that Margaret Thatcher was falling into the pit of horror, and the Gods hold the planets together before concluding "...so Super Nova to you Thatcher, From the Guys of Iran."

The handwriting was that of woman and she continued to send packages for some time in re-used jiffy bags. The messages escalated in their violence, e.g., "Perhaps I should kill you," and "Oh my goodness yes." Another message contained, "I've got my fingers in my ears and my eyes closed," and over twenty components had been used to make it look like a bomb. One of the packages even had a surplus to pay for an incorrect stamp. That really is taking the Michael. Eventually, the packages stopped arriving and the sender was never found.

Politicians were seen as fair game by the crank brigade. Labour Leader Neil Kinnock once received a postcard from Holland which stated 'they' could not 'necklace' him but 'howsabout a bullet?' The sender had even written: 'Don't look for fingerprints, you won't find mine, sorry chum.' They may have been harmless cranks but we simply couldn't take the chance. The task was almost overwhelming, so many of these letters and packages were delivered to 10 and 11 Downing Street, as well as the Palace of Westminster, that examining them was part of my daily routine. Anyone caught was prosecuted under the Malicious Communications Act (1988), which makes it an offence to send a letter or other article which conveys an indecent or grossly offensive message, or a threat where the purpose of sending it is to cause distress or anxiety, even if the information conveyed is false. The maximum sentence is six months in prison and fine.

The worst series of threats came shortly after Section 28 of the Local Government Act (1986) was introduced, which stated that local authorities: 'shall not intentionally promote homosexuality or publish material with the intention of promoting homosexuality,' or 'promote the teaching in any maintained school of the acceptability of homosexuality as a pretended family relationship.'

Over 180 Peers of the Realm, including Earls, Baronesses, Marquesses and various Lords and Ladies received letters with the words: 'Destroy Section 28 or

we will destroy you,' made up from a newspaper cuttings. Some lobbying! The work involved was phenom-
enal, as each one of the 400 letters and packages had to
be examined individually (each one was an individual
offence of 'sending threats to kill' through the post). No
one was ever prosecuted and Section 28 wasn't repealed
until 2000.

I dealt with letters sent to Minister for Sport Colin
Moynihan, Prime Minister John Major, Chief Secretary
to the Treasury David Mellor and the author Salman
Rushdie among many others, with several letters arriving
at the homes of MPs.

John Wakeham, now Baron Wakeham, was the government's Chief Whip when he received a threatening
letter from which finger marks had been developed. As
he had opened the letter personally I needed to take his
fingerprints for purposes of elimination.

Mr Wakeham, as he was then, was, like many politicians, used to receiving threats but he had been on the
receiving end of threats that had been carried out. He had
been in the Grand Hotel in Brighton in October 1984
when the IRA had tried to assassinate Mrs Thatcher and
as many of her cabinet members as possible. The bomb
had killed Mr Wakeham's wife, Roberta, and Mr Wakeham
had been left with serious leg injuries.

When I arrived to take his prints, he was at his desk, in
the middle of a lively telephone conversation. He paused
for the moment whilst I explained what I was there for.

"OK, but can you do it now, whilst I am on the telephone? I'm very busy and this telephone call is important."

I prepared a brass plate with black ink. I did have a non-ink chemical pad and sensitized paper for such occasions but at this time the results weren't that great as the fingerprints started to fade quickly as soon as they were exposed to light. So I started to ink Mr Wakeham's right hand with a roller whilst he held the telephone in his left hand. He laughed as I did so and interrupted his conversation to tell the person on the other end of the line: "You should see this! A police officer's taking my prints and my fingers are black with ink."

I rolled each finger individually on the elimination fingerprint form in the appropriate box, and then pressed down all four fingers together in another box followed by the right thumb in another box. The process became quite fiddly as I had to work around the telephone and Mr Wakeham was quite animated as he continued his conversation. When I cleaned his right hand with kitchen towels and white spirit I was conscious that his immaculate white shirt-cuff was precariously close to becoming indelibly inked. I repeated the process with Mr Wakeham's left hand as he continued to chat away without inhibition. Once he was cleaned up, I thanked him for his cooperation and he replied: "Thank you for yours!" and carried on chatting.

We identified many of the senders. Throughout the 1980s, one particularly malicious person sent strange objects through the post in pizza boxes (such as egg shells and unused condoms) to famous people. They seemed to have a particular desire to target actresses in stage plays and a handful of news readers who made tiny guest roles in pantomimes at Christmas (victims included the BBC's top TV newsreaders Jan Leeming and Sue Lawley). The boxes came with notes, which described how the sender had been watching them from the fourth row of the theatre and had videoed them. The recipients were understandably spooked and maintaining the traditional theatre motto "the show must go on" has probably never been so difficult. It took twelve years to catch the man who was sending the boxes, but he was finally successfully prosecuted under the Malicious Communications Act, thanks to forensic evidence.

# BARNEY AND ME

My idea for A and C districts to be run by one SOCO1 was accepted and Alan, the SOCO1, at West End Central returned to his favoured posting at the Forensic Science Lab while I took on A & C districts.

One of my first requests from C district was to assist the Vice Squad operating out of West End Central, just a minute's walk from the heart of Soho, that well-known den of the sex trade.

The Vice Squad, suspecting that a porn shop was renting illegal videos , including suspected snuff videos, where someone is murdered, or commits suicide while being filmed, or contains footage of executions, had sent some undercover officers to infiltrate the shop, win the owner's confidence and then join their 'exclusive' membership scheme. They had successfully managed to rent illegal porn videos but no snuff movies were seen. As soon as the detectives returned the videos, the shop was raided. This had so far been done twice but on both occasions they'd failed to find the cassettes.

Apparently, after a video was returned, the shopkeeper disappeared into a back room, returning to the counter in seconds. So how could it be that despite a comprehensive search, no videos were ever found? I had fluorescent grease markers that would transfer to anything the video came into contact with and would perhaps provide a trail to the hiding place but this wasn't foolproof. My preferred method was to coat the object of interest in a specific scent, which would allow a police dog, trained to follow this specific odour, to track the package.

The Vice Squad were up for it, so I dabbed scent on a porn video rented by an undercover officer. The only problem was that it did leave a rather strange, pungent smell. The undercover officer said he'd just explain that he'd kept in his shed so it wouldn't be found.

The video was duly returned; the shop was hit a minute later and in went Barney the Springer Spaniel.

He could not find the video.

When I heard this I went back in with Barney and the dog handler to have a look for myself. The shop was small and nondescript, a few shelves lined with sex toys and soft porn for the tourists. Barney led us through to the back office and to a wall covered by a piece of ply. Behind it was a letterbox-sized hole in what appeared to be a closed-up chimneybreast.

"Surely it's in here," I said.

They had looked through with torches but said there was nothing behind the hole, just an empty chimneybreast. The Chief Inspector running the operation came up to me, saying that it looked like we'd blown it. We timed the route from counter to back room: four seconds. According to the undercover officers the shopkeeper always returned to the counter with the video within fifteen seconds. It had to be in the back room somewhere. Barney knew what he was doing too and he was resolutely focused on the hole in the chimneybreast.

"Well," I said with a shrug, "As Sherlock Holmes put it: 'When you have eliminated the impossible, whatever remains, however improbable, must be the truth.'"

"What are you suggesting Larry? Knock the chimney breast down?"

"Yes, or at least put a big hole in it."

After someone had ran back to the station to find some sledge hammers, we set about opening up the 'letter box' until I could get my head inside. I glanced to the left and saw two switches. I pushed one and something started to whizz at me with a whirr from above. A dumb waiter with a pile of videos on it.

"Gotcha!" I said in triumph. "This isn't a chimney breast, it's a lift shaft."

A dumb waiter operated from the loft and passed through two separate companies on floors above the shop, without them ever being aware of it.

I gave Barney a pat of congratulation and he licked my face in return. Our reputations had been saved.

As the storekeeper was led out to the waiting police van, I said "Somebody give that dog a biscuit," adding, "And me a pint of Kronenbourg."

Another dog-related criminal investigation took place shortly afterwards when I was called to a sumptuous terraced house in Chester Square, home to many British icons. Leading up to the large, immaculately-polished black front door were three broad concrete steps. Sitting on the top step, by the door, was an enormous black Alsatian. I was wary as, although an ardent dog lover, I have seen police Alsatians at work and they have yet to be bettered by a human in a fight.

I placed my aluminium equipment case, between the dog and myself and rang the doorbell. The householder, a guy in his sixties, opened the door and the dog ran inside. I went in and we chatted as I carried out my examination. I had just packed my equipment away and was about to leave when the house owner came up to me, clearly quite flustered.

"Mr Henderson, I am not impressed with your police dog. He has left a rather large message on a very expensive Persian carpet in the drawing room."

I was by now in the hallway with the door open. The smell wafting in from the drawing room told me all I needed to know as the Alsatian ran out of the house, leaving me to explain. "Sir, I've never seen that dog before in my life. It was sitting by your door when I entered, and I assumed it belonged to the house as it ran inside so quickly."

The man was left somewhat speechless and so I quickly said goodbye, legged it downstairs to find the dog sitting on the pavement, tongue out, tail wagging, as if waiting for me, as if I were his owner. I didn't dare look back and I have no doubt the master of the house didn't believe me as he watched us walking down the road before going back in to clean up the "message" left on his "very expensive" Persian carpet.

# DUMB AND DUMBERER

**W**estminster Cathedral - not to be confused with Westminster Abbey, opposite the Houses of Parliament - sits back from Victoria Street, a short distance from Victoria Station and Buckingham Palace. A striking building dominated by its brick facade, it opened in 1903 on the site of the old Tothill Fields Bridewell prison and is the mother church of the Catholic Church in England and Wales.

Rhianna called me to ask if I could help set a trap to catch a thief or thieves who were targeting the Cathedral every two or three weeks. They'd break in and empty the large oil drums that were used to collect cash donations from the public. This was a serious amount of money, running into thousands of pounds.

I took a look at the Cathedral and decided it could be done but there was one issue: the many lit candles would have to be extinguished an hour before the alarm was set, as the system I had in mind - which I'd used many years ago to catch a persistent burglar - would be set off by candle flames and it needed an hour for the thermal movement of air to stabilize after the candles had been extinguished. The alarm, which was silent, simply alerted the duty officer at the local nick, who would then order officers to move in to make the arrest/s.

Getting the go-ahead for this operation took some time to achieve - the votive candles, lit by Catholics in memory of loved ones or as part of a prayer, were normally allowed to burn out - but I was eventually given the nod by Cardinal Hume, the Archbishop of Westminster and set the alarm one Friday evening . The candles were extinguished at 8pm, as the last of the public left. Max, a police Alsatian then searched the building to make sure no one was hiding or had possibly fallen asleep in a confessional box. I noticed that Max, although an excellent search dog, left a little to be desired in the marking-his-territory department as he seemed to be 'christening' many of the pews, along with a confessional box.

By midnight the building was judged to be empty and the alarm was set, tested and armed. The alarm did go off, but this was due to a lit candle we'd failed to spot, and the thieves failed to appear.

On our second attempt, however, the alarm went off at 2am on a Saturday morning and two guys, both in their twenties were nicked inside the Cathedral. The men, who were from Liverpool, claimed innocence and denied breaking in but when detectives checked their building society accounts, they found that these two prize idiots had actually banked the money. Each entry in their building society passbooks was made on a Monday morning, which tallied with the date of the burglaries the Saturday before.

Both the Chief Super and the Cardinal's staff were buoyant. The Archbishop invited everyone involved in the case to a Friday lunch as a thank-you. It was a tremendously jolly affair and I have to say I was surprised that the Cardinal's staff not only outdrank the cops, they also outdid them on the dodgy story and bad language front as well, and I suspect there was a queue for the confession box the following morning.

# THE LORD DEVONSHIRE

**O**ne Sunday, I found myself with time to spare when Rhianna at Rochester Row telephoned with her morning round-up for A & C district.

"The Lord Devonshire was burgled last night," she said, "Do you want to join me at about eleven? If the place is any good we could have lunch there."

"Great idea."

So at eleven we set off to the address, which was close to Shepherd's Market, a posh residential district in the West End. We drove up and down the short road looking for the pub, and quickly gave up,

"Let me check the address," I said. It was definitely number 26. "Well that's where we are, but it's clearly someone's home. Why don't you knock on the door and see if you can clear this up?"

So Rhianna went and knocked on the door and a smartly-dressed gentleman opened it a moment later.

"Good morning sir, sorry to trouble you but we're looking for the Lord Devonshire and this is the address we've been given."

"That is me, young lady," he said smoothly. "I presume you're here about the burglary."

Ah, it was Lord Devonshire not *the* Lord Devonshire who had been burgled. Lord Devonshire was one of the richest people in the UK, who'd served in the government of Prime Minister Harold Macmillan who was married to Lord Devonshire's aunt, and had opened his fabulous country home, Chatsworth House, to the public. He was quite charming, as was his wife Deborah Mitford, one of the Mitford sisters.

The Duke's extramarital affairs became public shortly after our visit when he appeared as a witness at the Old Bailey in 1985, at the trial of a son of a former butler who had been accused of stealing cheques from him. The Duke had to admit, under oath, that he was on holiday with one of a series of younger women when the crime occurred at his London home. The Duke also claimed, during the trial, that his marriage's success was due to the Duchess's tolerance and broadmindedness.

When the Duchess of Devonshire gracefully offered coffee, we gladly accepted in the knowledge we weren't about to have a pub lunch anytime soon.

Shortly after having coffee with the Devonshires, I was called to deal with someone whom it was suspected, would have gladly blown them both up, an alleged IRA terrorist, who was being held at Paddington Green's high-security police station.

IRA suspects, no matter what part of the country they were arrested in, would always end up here. As part of my examination, I had to check the prisoner for traces of explosives. The technique in those days involved dabbing the hands and face with pieces of pre-cut sticky tape and placing them in glass bottles for chemical analysis and examination under an electron microscope - with 500,000X magnification it could spot and analyse the slightest trace of explosive chemicals. After this, fingernail scrapings were taken using cocktail sticks (they did the job just fine, trust me) and were placed inside separate glass phials.

I was chatting to the IRA suspect as I was placing one such stick into a phial and as I closed the top it exploded. Unable to contain my shock, I lost by non-biased attitude and exclaimed: "Bloody hell mate, you're using good stuff!"

# BRACE YOURSELF

Occasionally I would receive a call from one of the Specialist Squads at New Scotland Yard and, because I was local, I could drop into the Yard at a moment's notice. I rolled in one day in 1987 after a detective whom I'd worked with on the Soho porn shop bust asked if I could help with an enquiry that related to a case being worked on by TO15 (Obscene Publications). He explained he was involved with something called Operation Spanner and was about to receive a great many exhibits from Manchester Police regarding a sadomasochistic ring made up of at least sixteen men (that they knew about so far) who were committing horrendous and illegal acts. TO15 had been directed by the Home Office to eliminate the ring "at all costs". The operation started when Manchester Police had accidentally come across a video as part of another investigation. They thought the video was a snuff movie; that the 'victims' in the footage had been killed. They launched a murder enquiry only to find that the 'victims' were alive and also claimed to be consenting adults, in that they wanted to be tortured to the point of unconsciousness.

The acts were wince-inducingly awful and those of a mild disposition might want to skip to the next story. Those with sensitive dispositions should most definitely Stop Reading Now. The name Operation Spanner came about because, according to the detective, "Every time you talk about it, it makes you want to tighten your nuts!"

He explained how some of the gang sliced out a testicle from the scrotum of one of their fellow members, and then the 'victim' jumped on his own ball.

It got even worse. I repeat my warning. There were photographs of penises cut along the urethra so the penis was in two longitudinal halves. I also examined some horrible pieces of equipment, such as leather rings with large sharpened metal studs on the inside of the ring, through which you were supposed to push your John Thomas. Most of the exhibits were bloodstained. I packaged them for further forensic examination and presentation to the courts.

At the trial, the accused argued that they were consenting adults in a private place but they were found guilty of assault occasioning actual bodily harm and sentenced to four-and-a-half years' imprisonment. They took their appeals all the way to the European Court of Human Rights (ECHR) via the House of Lords. At the Lords, they were told: "Society is entitled and bound to protect itself against a cult of violence. Pleasure derived from the infliction of pain is an evil thing. Cruelty is uncivilized." The ECHR agreed. After all, according to UK law, "a person does not have the legal ability to consent to receive an act which will cause serious bodily harm, such as extreme activities of a sadomasochistic nature."

This investigation, which provoked much debate in legal circles, is now referred to as the "Spanner Case."

# THE THAMES TRAGEDY

Around 3am on the twentieth of August 1989 I received a call from the Reserve Officer at Cannon Row. "Larry, there's been a shipping disaster on the Thames, a collision between a pleasure boat and a dredger; the pleasure boat has sunk and many people have drowned. The Detective Chief Super wants you to attend."

The party on board the Marchioness had only just begun when the tragedy happened. Most of the passengers were in their twenties and all of them were celebrating the 26th birthday of banker Antonio de Vasconcellos. People were just starting to dance when the pleasure boat lurched and was pushed down into the water, before she started to turn on her side. People screamed as the lights went out and the boat started to sink.

The fact that the dredger Bowbelle's anchor had torn through the upper decks of the Marchioness made it possible for some people on these decks to quickly escape the sinking boat and swim to shore, by which time the Marchioness had vanished from view. Those left in the water found themselves being dragged upstream by the powerful currents which, as the river was an hour from high tide, were at their strongest, and people who had managed to cling onto lifebuoys found themselves being swept west as the tide continued to rise. Eyewitnesses, including the landlord of a riverside pub who'd run out to help, and many survivors who were already ashore, spotted dozens of people in the water.

I rallied my troops and we headed to Leman Street Police station where we met Board of Trade officials who briefed us on maritime law, which dictated the method and type of evidence we would need to collect. This done, I asked Ashley, a SOCO temporarily posted to Bow Street to fill a vacancy, to go to the Bowbelle and seize all navigation charts and logs, and remove all writing implements so no original logs could be altered. While he was there he would also check to see if and how many bunks might have been slept in and to record the amount of alcohol on board, such as whether there were any open or half-drunk cans of beer, and so on.

Once Ashley had left, a trade officer took me to one side. "Larry, the Captain of the Bowbelle, was a Douglas *Henderson*. We just need to make sure he's no relation."

He wasn't, and so I joined a police patrol boat to search the Thames for the deceased, starting from the collision site close to Cannon Street railway-bridge. The river, black and silent, refused to give up the dead. It was a truly eerie experience, no doubt fuelled by our mood of shock and sadness. Somewhere below us were the bodies of dozens of young people who, just a few hours earlier, had their whole

lives ahead of them. I expected to see a head break the surface at any moment, but there was nothing. We were stood
down at first light after failing to find a single body.

Later that day, I joined the crew of another police patrol
boat at Wapping Police Station, the centre of operations
for the river police, and set off to examine the Bowbelle.
Eyewitnesses reported that the starboard side of the
Bowbelle had struck the Marchioness amidships and its
anchor had literally sliced through the pleasure boat.

Collecting the evidence wasn't easy, a bit like walking a tightrope in a high wind. I had to balance atop the
police boat's cabin and carefully remove specs of paint
and small pieces of wood from the starboard anchor
while the swell lifted and dropped me several feet. One
moment I was above the anchor and the next I was far
below it. I managed to recover broken glass, specs of paint,
wood splinters and rope fibre, all of which was eventually linked to the Marchioness. I also decided to seize the
navigation lights; it would be worth checking to see if any
weren't working at the time of collision. Forensically, it's a
straightforward job to establish if a light was working and
subsequently broken in an impact. When the glass breaks
it hits the filament wire, which operates at a temperature
of 2,000-2,500°C, so if it was lit at the time of impact then
melted glass would be found on the filament as proved to
be the case.

Bodies started to be recovered the following day, miles
downriver and even though extra cops from Battersea

were drafted in to join the search teams, it still took several days before every body had been recovered with one of the last to be found was recovered close to HMS Belfast. Fifty one people of the one hundred and thirty one people on board the Marchioness lost their lives with the average age of the victims just twenty-two. Twenty-four were recovered from inside the hull. Twenty-seven were recovered from the river.

Among the dead were Antonio de Vasconcellos, his older brother Domingos and Francesca Dallaglio, the older sister of future England rugby captain, Lawrence.

It was impossible to imagine how the family and friends, not to mention the survivors must have felt. Seeing the unavoidable newspaper and TV coverage only compounded our feelings of helplessness. One survivor later said he spent a month going to the funerals of his friends. A mother of another victim said she kept thinking her child was out there somewhere but she was unable to reach him. She hadn't been able to sleep or eat since the tragedy and I couldn't blame her. Their deaths were totally avoidable. They had been robbed of the long, successful and happy lives that were ahead of them.

Also, things didn't go much better for the families in the immediate aftermath. It was only revealed some years after the Marchioness Disaster that - as part of identification procedures - it was standard practice for coroners to order the removal of the hands of the deceased after a mass disaster so they could be sent to the Fingerprint Department Laboratory for printing (due to the lengthy immersion in water, they could only be fingerprinted at the FDL), a grisly task for the fingerprint officers. Of the twenty-five individuals who had their hands removed only three were identified through the use of fingerprints, the rest of the identifications being made through dental records. Some of the hands were removed even after this positive identification had been made. In a number of cases the hands were not returned to the body before the body was released to the family. Policy and procedure have long since changed, thank goodness, but this was small comfort to the families who had to come to terms with this controversial decision. One of the parents, speaking of her son, said: "He was a brilliant musician. It's unbearable to think they cut his hand off, but nothing was said about it."

Westminster Coroner Dr Paul Knapman was strongly criticized by Lord Justice Clarke in his 2001 report into the circumstances surrounding the collision. That this report came about at all was thanks to the Marchioness Action Group, formed by relatives of victims and survivors, who had to fight for a full inquest and public enquiry, which came over a decade after the disaster. The recommendations in Lord Justice Clark's report into the *Identification of Victims Following a Major Transportation Accident* have had a highly significant impact on the way in which individuals are treated following disasters. Without the commitment of the Marchioness survivors and bereaved, the public enquiry would not have taken place and Lord Justice Clark's recommendations - which have influenced policing for the better - would not have been made. Those of us whose lives have been unaffected by disaster owe them a debt of gratitude. They have helped to make the river a safer place. The inquiry also found that the Metropolitan Police were 'ill-prepared' and had no contingency plan for such an event and, thanks to the Marchioness Action Group, four lifeboat stations were installed on the River Thames by the Royal National Lifeboat Institution in 2002. New laws on being in charge of vessels under the influence of alcohol were also introduced.

No one was ever prosecuted for what was regarded as an unlawful killing of these fifty-one young people. After two trials in which the juries could not agree on a verdict, the captain of the Bowbelle was acquitted of failing to keep a proper look out. Evidence had shown that he had drunk five pints of lager the afternoon prior to the collision.

# JOINING THE SWEENEY

There were no police counselling services available then as there are today, and no one ever mentioned that there might be a need. Two pints of lager, a chat about the day's events with colleagues and a few jokes was the only remedy. I was lucky; I didn't have hang ups or nightmares despite the many mutilated bodies I dealt with, the drownings; the man shot point blank in his anus with a shotgun by his partner after an argument; an overdosed heroin addict undiscovered for a week; a child killed by his mum's heroin addiction. But the psychological effect of these experiences did come out in my already-mentioned overprotectiveness and I displayed over-the-top nervousness whenever we went caravanning. If our boys were playing close to a riverbank or started climbing a tree, I starting seeing 'scenes,' the aftermaths of tragedies, and was beside them in a flash, full of warnings and ready to tell them off for behaviour that was quite natural to children. I can see how I was a bit of a spoilsport to live with in that respect but I did my best to always make sure I left work outside my front door, even after particularly tough days. I would normally be welcomed home by our two

Labs, Honey and Tanya and I'd make a fuss of them until the boys, Richard and Robin, found me and, with Jennifer, we'd play a variety of games and they'd tell me what they'd been up to that day.

My work life was going from strength to strength. I felt a bit like I was in charge of Charlie's Angels as, thanks to the addition of Rose at Vine Street and Daniela at Bow Street, I now had a team of four women. My one male co-worker was Pete the fingerprint guy, based at West End Central, and we got on just fine. We met regularly at a lunchtimes and enjoyed after work drinks together in the Victoria Embankment's floating pub, The Tattershall Castle, or in Strutton Ground's wine bar, where the manager would keep a bottle of pink bubbly on ice for us, or in Gordons Wine Bar in Villiers Street, next to Charing Cross station. Reputed to be the oldest wine bar in London, with its Dickensian, candle-lit atmosphere, I still visit today for a glass of Shiraz. Another favourite was the Red Lion in Whitehall, at the Parliament Square end and, when Prince Andrew married Sarah Ferguson, the landlord allowed Jacqui, Rhianna, Rose, Daniela and Jennifer to view the procession from an open bedroom window above the pub. We had a perfect view with drinks to hand, although I remained sober as I was technically on standby with the 'Fast Response Team' at Cannon Row, just in case anything kicked off. The Red Lion was also famous among locals for its 'Division Bell,' which warned the MPs that vote was about to take place in Parliament. Drinking on the job is no problem for some.

I wasn't wearing rose-tinted spectacles when it came to assessing my team. Their fingerprint and forensic identifications were excellent and the number of visits per month was well above average. Taking into account the fact that central London attracted professional villains, not just the neighbour-next-door-type who would screw your gas meter for five pounds, the team was 'flying'.

They weren't perfect of course (and neither was I), and I'd learned a great deal about team management from Buster Geering at Gerald Road in the seventies and from Bill Foreman at Battersea in the eighties. They trusted me from the start, displaying as yet un-earned confidence in my abilities, and cared for and encouraged me as much as anyone else on their team.

I don't care what anyone says, in my experience managing four women is different from managing four men. They spoke their minds much more than the men did and yet I found that the best way to maintain the harmony when one of them had caused an issue, was not to meet them head on, like you would with a bloke - hit a guy between the eyes with a problem they're causing and nine times out of ten they'd understand.

My preferred method with my team was to call a meeting, about once a month on a Friday at 4pm. I would get through the official stuff, open a bottle of wine and then bring up whatever problems I felt had to be addressed - without naming anyone - and explain the consequences of certain actions. Discussions would develop, and these would sometimes become heated but by the end of the meeting the issues were resolved. I never pulled rank but acted as 'chairperson', and did my best to steer discussions to common sense decisions. That done, it was off for a drink at Gordons or the Tattershall.

The team worked and played well together and, as a result, our successes with both fingerprint identifications and forensic 'hits' were impressive.

It couldn't last, of course.

I was cutting back some trees in my garden and burning the debris. The fire was smoky and I ended up breathing too much of it in. Suddenly unable to breath, Jennifer rushed me to hospital where we learned that I was having a serious asthma attack. It became was so severe that I ended up in intensive care. It took a week or so for me to recover, during which time I received a call from Jacqui. "Larry, I've been transferred to Tottenham."

I was livid as there'd been no discussion with me about the transfer, or discussions on a preferred replacement. I knew that Malcolm wasn't happy with my team's good working relationship, particularly Jacqui and Rhianna. They were geographically the closest to my office, so it was natural that I saw more of them and we had become friends as well as colleagues.

It was a *fait accompli*. There wasn't even going to be a replacement; instead my brilliant team was going to be broken up.

So Jacqui had gone and Daniela soon followed and now I had Ashley, based at Bow Street. I was moved to a new unit based at West End Central. The unit was the Forensic

Scientific Support Unit, (FSSU) and comprised a Senior and Grade 1 Fingerprint Officer, Senior and Grade 1 SOCO all sat looking at each other across four desks. Worst of all, the person I was sitting opposite to was Malcolm. It was a recipe for disaster. We pussy-footed about, trying not to tread on each other's toes and when we did (which was often), we argued. In no time at all I wanted to leave, even though this was the best posting in the UK. The idea behind the unit was that as a self-contained 'team' we could attend all the serious crimes in the area. The reality was quite different. Malcolm stayed in the office organizing planning meetings and I did all the work. We were also the admin centre for the area and as part of this we were expected to train uniformed police officers in crime scene examination. I was allocated this job too and, despite protests about my workload, I lectured twenty or so uniformed officers on a regular basis.

Our unit was also supposed to compile intelligence from evidence gathered at crime scenes. An index card system was used to record coded shoe mark patterns and instrument marks (such as 6mm screwdriver blade with blue paint or 9mm screwdriver with red paint, etc.) so they could be compared with shoes and instruments taken from suspects or villains. Who was allocated the task of maintaining the card system? I'll give you one guess.

I was saved when Malcolm suddenly decided to return to the Liaison counter at the Forensic Laboratory. With Malcolm out of the way, I made a bid to transfer to the Flying Squad (a team of specialist detectives who investigated serious robberies and hunted some of the UK's toughest villains, it was seen as the Yard's most prestigious specialist unit, along with Special Branch) as senior SOCO. Nic's replacement was Bernie Lilly, and we'd always got on well. I also endorsed Jacqui's application to fill one of the vacant SOCO II posts on the Squad. Senior management rejected her initial verbal enquiry on the grounds that she did not have sufficient experience, and was a woman. Make that a reason today and you'd be in court before you could say 'discrimination'.

I endorsed Jacqui's written application and tried to persuade Bernie that she would be an asset to the Squad. She had the temperament and, despite her 'lack' of experience (she had been in the job four years), thanks to the areas in which she'd worked she was probably superior to another SOCO out in the sticks with twice the number of years under their belt. Bernie agreed and, to my delight, Jacqui was transferred to the Tower Bridge office of SO8 Flying Squad.

Then it was my turn. I had to fight off a challenge from the Fingerprint Department, now called SO3, who wanted one of their officers on the Yard's most prestigious squad. I pushed and pushed. I wrote up a report detailing how, during a window of twenty months out of the four years I spent at Cannon Row, I had assisted in twelve murder enquiries, over three hundred threats to kill, sixteen rapes, twelve armed robberies, ten confidential enquiries other than threats to kill, six arsons and two fatal fires, ten drugs raids, nine aggravated burglaries, too many burglaries to count, various hoax explosive devices, fifteen sudden deaths, and umpteen examinations of persons in custody, including terrorists. In addition there were the training lectures, countless checks against shoe marks and instrument marks on records from crime scenes and shoes and tools found in the possession of suspected criminals. I had no idea what the final figures amounted to but I now had no time for squash. Although I felt that central London was the best area in the country to work, I had blinding ambition to work on the "cutting edge" of pro-active policing – and that meant joining the Flying Squad.

A few weeks later, I got the news: "Larry you are being transferred. Report to Commander SO8 Flying Squad, eighth floor at the Yard on Monday morning."

"YES!!"

# PART SIX

Specialist Operations Department 8 (SO8)
Flying Squad
New Scotland Yard, London SW1
1989 -1992

# WORKS ALONE

Commander John O'Connor was in charge of the Flying Squad. I knew John from my time at Sutton; as I mentioned previously, today you can often see him on Sky or BBC News, called in to explain the police response after a major crime has taken place. John introduced me to the rest of the staff, a Chief Superintendent, two Superintendents, and a DI Staff Officer. In the general office were crime analysts Les and Tony, along with Mick, a Crime Prevention Officer.

A number of civilian support staff covered communications on a shift basis. They manned the office radio, sent out pager messages and responded to direct requests from detectives carrying out enquiries. The support staff also had access to a support services directory, which included contacts for everything from a safe opener to a Consultant Medical Physicist (a person who compares surveillance and video photographs to establish identity), as well as specialist dogs from the Royal Military Police.

The Squad operated four regional offices: North East at Finchley; North West at Lea Valley; South West at Barnes; and South East at Tower Bridge. Each office had a dedicated SOCO II. These were Steve, Paul, Simon and Jacqui.

My job description was five A4 pages long but in one section regarding supervision, a single sentence stood out: "Works alone but receives advice from Senior Identification Officer (SIDO)." This SIDO resided in the Fingerprint Department, SO3, so even though I was now part of the Flying Squad, SO8, I was still subject to the whims of the Fingerprint mafia, even though they didn't have a clue about my job. Part of my new role involved submitting a great deal of paperwork to SO3, including monthly statistics, such as scenes visited, arrested suspects examined, successes in fingerprint identifications and forensic successes, as well as overtime returns, making sure I didn't exceed my budget.

Although I was now officially part of SO8, I was also still an SO3 Officer but, as far as I was concerned, I was only answerable to the SO8 Investigating Officer on each case, and the Commander of SO8. The rest were colleagues who I would advise and help as necessary.

My first action upon joining the Flying Squad was to have a covert, 100-channel radio, capable of communicating with all the UK's Police Forces, fitted to my car at a specialist police garage. The registration number of my car was also blocked on the DVLA system.

The next was to talk to my staff. They were all experienced Flying Squad SOCOs and were considered *la crème de la crème* of our profession. And the Squad kept them busy. I found out that my predecessor rarely visited scenes, was not into pro-active work, and let the SOCOs be. As a result, there was no co-ordination between the SOCO's, no socializing and no team spirit (although distance was an obvious problem). Each operated virtually as a separate entity and looked inwards to their respective office.

I was also responsible for the SOCO2, Judy, on the Central Drugs Squad, (SO1, Department 4). Judy had received zero supervision from my predecessor, and she simply supported the Drugs Squad by packaging their exhibits and transporting them to the laboratory.

I was going to be a very different boss: sleeves-up and hands-on, close communication with my staff and senior officers, and do whatever we can to improve the effectiveness of the support we provided the police.

From the Kray twins to Kenneth Noye, the Flying Squad has been at the centre of British criminal investigations for over eighty years. The squad was formed by Detective Inspector David Goodwillie in 1919, as the 'Mobile Patrol Experiment', in response to growing concern about an influx of organized crime from overseas into the capital. The group's original twelve detectives were allowed to pursue criminals into any police division area. In 1920 the Daily Mail referred to this group as 'flying squads of hand-picked detectives' and the name stuck. Criminals dubbed it 'the heavy mob' because it handled some of the Met's most high-profile cases, concentrating on armed robberies and organized crime, and later the Sweeney Todd (Cockney rhyming slang: Sweeney Todd = Flying Squad). The Flying Squad officers themselves never referred to themselves as *The Sweeney*, just 'The Squad'.

The unit's officers have always been chosen because of their knowledge of the underworld. Extensive contacts with paid informants have been the jewel in the crown of the squad's intelligence operations for years. The Flying Squad is unique in that it solves forty per cent of its cases through informers. Other non-dedicated units solve only about five per cent of crimes this way. Sometimes, however, this close relationship with the criminal fraternity backfires, with truly disastrous consequences. The relationship between policeman and informer is open to abuse from both sides as detectives allow criminals to continue their careers uninterrupted in return for information. In February 1972 the head of the Flying Squad, Commander Kenneth Drury, was revealed to have spent a two-week holiday in Cyprus with James Humphreys, one of seven porn barons named by the British press. Drury claimed they were looking for Ronnie Biggs, the escaped train robber. But on 7 July 1977 Justice Mars-Jones stated that Drury was the 'chief architect' behind the porn syndicate in Central London and sentenced him to eight years' imprisonment. Another twelve Scotland Yard detectives were jailed for accepting bribes.

By the early eighties it was virtually disbanded and renamed The Central Robbery Squad. However, without its pro-active approach to organized gangs of robbers, crime started to soar. The Squad was reformed and I was fortunate to arrive when its strength was at its greatest, the golden years of the early nineties.

The Flying Squad's brief was simple: investigate and prevent armed robbery. Cash robbery was at all-time high with robbers regularly hitting cash transit vans, jewellery shops, post offices, banks, betting shops and building societies. Tiger kidnappings were also on the rise - so-called because the robbers stalk their prey like a tiger. Tiger kidnappings involved targeting people who had access to large amounts of cash, such as bank managers, and then kidnapping their wives and children, holding them hostage until the target has provided access to cash, jewels or safety deposits.

Detectives were recruited to the Squad by invitation. This was a rugged outfit, in every sense of the word and, apart from the Tactical Firearms Unit and Special Branch, the only permanently armed squad in the land. The word in the underworld was the Flying Squad meant business. So if you had a gun and fired, then they would fire back; if you didn't put the gun down when ordered to, they would shoot. Criminals had good reason to be afraid of the Squad.

Squad detectives faced considerable dangers. They specialized in the 'pavement ambush', catching robbers in the act of committing a crime as it was much easier to convict them this way. Although their sheer speed usually won the day, it was a high-risk form of policing and certainly not for the faint-hearted.

Being aware of the Squad's history, I could only 'judge as I found'. I was uniquely placed as I was a civilian but I was also part of the Squad's senior management, so attended all high level meetings and was privy to a lot of confidential information.

My first management meeting took place in the Commander's office just three days after being posted to the Squad. I met the respective Detective Chief Inspectors of the four offices and we talked about my role and I stressed that I was keen to get involved in proactive policing.

I never discussed The Flying Squad policies, operations, and activities outside of SO8, not even to my own department, SO3. As far as I was concerned I was an SO8 officer doing an SO8 job. I never forgot that job description: 'works alone'.

My first hurdle was getting used to the police jargon that poured out of my radio in a torrent of codes, abbreviations and TLAs (Three Letter Acronyms). Many jobs were called in by the office's patrolling 'gunship'. This was an unmarked car, driven by the most talented uniform advanced drivers who were able to keep cool while being shot at. They were an elite, all to their own, usually at the rank of constable, and it was considered a plum job in terms of sheer excitement. Apart from the driver, an unarmed detective observer sat in the front passenger seat, handling communications. Two armed detectives, normally a detective sergeant and constable sat in the rear.

I stopped when I saw the gunship's abbreviation on the police code sheet. Fast Armed Response Team. FART? Really? And it was.

On pro-active operations the Squad used encrypted handsets and maps with coded grid references. This was because both journalists and villains listened in, tuning scanners to police frequencies. On one occasion I recovered four A4 sheets of paper explaining the call signs - including my own - and the police codes from a robber's house. Professional gangs also used 'spotters' to record details of Squad cars.

Jacqui was just about to go on leave, so I covered for her at Tower Bridge, a good way for me to get some on-the-ground experience with the Squad. I was used to handling armed robbery crime scenes as, when at Battersea, I'd attended sixteen armed robberies in one week. So here we go!

# SITTING TIGHT

The robberies came thick and fast. The examination of vehicles involved in these crimes was time-consuming as we literally took the vehicle apart. Most cars had been stolen and 'ringed,' i.e., the number plates had been changed. The false plates frequently matched the make and model of the car and careful examination of the plates revealed a great deal of evidence, such as fingerprints and clothing fibres. Guns and ammunition were found underneath seats, behind sun visors, inside glove compartments, underneath the rear seat, even inside engine bays. All examinations had to be exhaustive - there could be no exceptions.

Squad jobs had a reputation in the world of forensic examination. The level of commitment needed, along with the extensive forensic and fingerprint knowledge, frightened off a lot of fingerprint officers and most SOCOs. Trials were often bloody (metaphorically) as the finest defence barristers in the land always attempted to get their clients 'off' by questioning the integrity of exhibits, and they made allegations of contamination as well as the use of incorrect procedures. The accused had nothing to lose because they faced up to a twenty-five-year prison sentence, so would say anything they could think of that might help overturn a case or would establish 'reasonable doubt' in the minds of a jury. For SOCOs, this was policing at the sharpest of ends. If I contacted a local Identification officer (IDO - a Fingerprint Officer trained in forensics) for assistance I would hear the fear in their voice. They usually said they were "too busy," "couldn't do any more overtime," and on one occasion, an officer struggling to come up with an excuse blurted out that "I have to meet my wife at the shops!"

Funnily enough, this problem didn't arise with women officers; it was always the men. Even with the potential for courtroom nightmares, the offence of armed robbery itself - apart from the obvious firearms aspect of understanding wadding, shot and cartridge cases from a shot gun, or striation marks on bullets or casings - was no different to any other scene examination. So why was there such a lack of confidence by our male colleagues? It was thanks in part to the Squad's expectation that nothing would be missed and the subsequent issue that one would end up with a mind-boggling number of exhibits, which needed to be coordinated for the courts. You also needed a detective's instinct to see the potential for evidence in everything, from a plain plastic bag found at the scene - these can be traced to manufacturers and outlets - to video footage where a consultant medical physicist can match photos and video footage to a suspect.

And then there was the examination of arrested suspects. These were some of the most terrifying men in the UK. They had been known to attack people even while being held in a police station. On top of this, the Squad's bad reputation went before them and officers didn't want to get caught up in allegations of corruption, such as fitting-up a criminal to secure a conviction as had happened in the not too distant past, so it was down to the SOCOs to make sure the evidence was watertight.

My first serious test came not from the Flying Squad however, but from the Regional Crime Squad (RCS), who closely associated with the Squad in that they did the same thing, but outside of London.

At about 11.30pm that night I met Jim, an undercover officer in Waltham Abbey. Jim explained that I was to mark some lifting equipment that was going to be used in the theft of a large safe. The theft was due to take place in a couple of days' time. I was not told where.

Shortly after midnight we arrived at a large detached house which belonged to the chief villain with some garages in a separate compound around the back.

We parked in an out-of-the-way area and I followed Jim who had some 'special keys,' which opened the garage of interest. He let me in, and then locked the garage door behind me and retreated to the car, telling me I had ten minutes. We had no radio communications, so it was a case of: "Any problems, sit tight Larry. I'm right here and a full team is less than a mile away."

Trying not to think of the many worst-case scenarios lurking around the edges of my consciousness, I searched the large garage and soon identified the lifting equipment. I'd come armed with a specialized fluorescent liquid - the marks would show up under UV light - and had just finished marking the lifting gear when I heard a large dog, probably an Alsatian, barking in the yard outside. It must have picked up my scent. I squatted down at the rear of the garage, taking cover behind a large tarpaulin stretched over a large wooden box. I hoped that this tarpaulin, which was filthy, would help dampen my odour. Ten minutes became fifteen, then twenty and soon forty minutes had gone by and the dog was still right outside. Jim clearly wanted the dog to bugger off before coming to get me; otherwise all hell would break loose.

'That dog might be there all bloody night,' I thought to myself.

Finally, after an hour, it went quiet. I carefully picked my way to the front of the garage using the UV light, thinking 'Where the hell is that detective?'

Suddenly a key went into the lock. Jim? Or was it the villain?

I quietly retreated to the back of the garage, picking up a steel bar as I went, telling myself I would have to put it back exactly where I found it, otherwise the villain might be alerted.

If it was the villain, all I could do was sit tight, hoping the guy would see nothing had been disturbed and leave. If I was discovered, well, that didn't bear thinking about. I'd try to pretend I was dossing there for the night and if it turned nasty it was best to have the iron bar close by, just in case.

The door opened. It was Jim.

We had just got back into the car when the villain appeared, walking down the road, obviously on his way home. He was a six-foot, fifty-something, fat-bellied guy with a crew-cut. Would he rumble? Before I could think of anything, Jim put his hand around my neck and snogged my left ear! Luckily, instead of telling him to get the hell off, I cottoned on and instantly responded by shouting at him, "No more tonight, you've had enough!" and I started the engine, seeing a look of utter disgust cross the villain's face. Jim's gambit - that we were gay lovers looking for an out-of-the-way-spot for some privacy - had worked.

We drove back to the nick and Jim thanked me for my night's work. I advised him that I had the control sample of the marker I'd used. If they recovered the equipment after the job was done then I would handle the submissions to the laboratory.

As it turned out, I was never asked to submit any exhibits, so I assume the job didn't come off. Perhaps our ruse didn't work after all?

# OFFICER DOWN

O ne of the first observations I made was that the Flying Squad SOCOs frequently handled firearms that had been abandoned by criminals at scenes or had been seized after the arrest of a suspect. After twenty years' experience, I was used to making firearms safe but my SOCOs had no formal training. While some had experience and were fine with this role, others weren't and left it to experienced Squad officers. It was important that the SOCO did this, as they knew how to preserve weapons for fingerprint and ballistic examinations. So I thought some proper training was in order, just in case a SOCO accidentally left a bullet in the chamber or encountered an unfamiliar weapon and accidentally fired it when trying to disarm it, so I arranged for my team to attend Lippits Hill, the training centre for SO19, the Tactical Firearms Unit.

SO19 frequently supported the Flying Squad. Their standard equipment was a Heckler and Koch MP5 9mm sub-machine gun. The MP5 has both single-shot and semi-automatic modes, so is a versatile and popular weapon – it's used by the armed officers who patrol our airports. Another popular sidearm was the Glock 9mm automatic handgun, favoured by Special Branch. The Squad's principal firearm was the classic Smith & Wesson revolver which had limited rounds, and each officer was limited in the number of rounds he or she could carry, hence the need for SO19 back up, especially with villains managing to get hold of more and more deadly firearms.

At Lippits Hill we fired and dismantled an array of weapons: the MP5, Lugers and Mausers, Austrian Glocks, Smith & Wessons, British Webley revolvers, the Israeli Uzi, Purdy shotguns and an array of sawn-off shotguns. We learned how certain guns developed certain problems if they were not cared for properly, or were modified. By the end of the session we felt like we could handle any-thing gun-related.

All Squad detectives knew the dangers involved in going after serious criminals and did all they could to minimize the risks but sometimes, an operation would fall apart with catastrophic consequences.

The call came midweek at 10pm. It was Judy.

"Larry, I need your help urgently. A large operation has gone tits-up and we have an officer down."

Judy, normally pretty much unflappable, sounded truly shaken

An undercover officer had been about to complete the purchase of a substantial amount of drugs from a high level dealer who operated on a large north London estate, when an argument had quickly escalated into a one-sided shooting match. Dealing large amounts of Class-A drugs such as coke and heroin carries the risk of decades-long sentences, so major players didn't surrender without a fight.

The protocol dictated that I call the night duty SO3 officer at the Yard for extra support.

"Larry the guys on this week are not experienced enough to handle a shooting of this nature, it sounds very involved," the officer told me.

"It's ok, I'll supervise," I said, "Just send me a SOCO2 and tell them to bring as many Firearms Residue Kits as they can carry. And I'd appreciate it if you could call the duty photographer for me."

The estate was in Wembley and I arrived at 11.15pm. I found Judy in the midst of chaotic scenes, with dozens of police officers in attendance.

"What's the news on the officer who was shot?" I asked.

"It's serious; touch and go."

"Anyone in the bin?"

"Eight suspects arrested so far."

"OK, let's start at the top" I said. "Hospital first. We need the officer's clothing, the pre-transfusion blood sample taken for cross matching, if he's been transfused. If the bullet is still in him we obviously need it when it's removed, along with the instrument used to extract it in case it's left any extra striation marks."

We also needed to find out if the wounded officer was armed. If so, then we needed to take firearms residue samples from his hands and face, and also get hold of his gun and ammunition. At that time we still didn't know what had actually occurred, as we were still waiting for the detectives to turn the scene over to us. I had to think of all possibilities, even the case that he'd been shot with his own weapon, if he had one.

Luckily, a Laboratory Liaison Officer turned up and he agreed to go to the hospital and collect the exhibits from the wounded officer. Judy stayed at the scene and later joined the drugs squad who were raiding other villains' homes as a result of this op having gone belly-up. It was hardly the ideal end to such a complex operation and the shooting would mean an even more complex trial than normal, with hundreds of exhibits that would be used to tell the night's story.

As Jacqui lived close by, I called her out to assist with examination of the prisoners. Standard procedure dictates that arrested persons be taken to separate police stations. This avoids suggestions of contamination from one person to the other by being in common places, such as the charge room. They all had to be examined for firearms residue straight away. Other non-intimate samples would be taken, i.e., hair, as a couple of woollen hats had been recovered at the scene of the shooting. Problem was we had eight suspects, all at different stations; it would take all night to examine them all. With no time to lose, I was able to arrange, thanks to a helpful Duty Officer based at Wembley police station, the services of seven constables. At 3am, I gave them a lesson on how to take firearms residue samples from live suspects, how to use a comb kit to take hair samples that could be compared with hairs and fibres recovered from the woollen hats.

By 6am I had the kits back with all the samples correctly packaged, and entered officially into the property system. I released Judy and Jacqui, plus the night duty SOCO - who'd coped well with his first major scene. At 8am I debriefed the Chief Super about our actions and the exhibits we'd taken. He thanked me for the night's work and I set off home some twelve hours after receiving that first call from Judy.

I walked through my front door at 11:30am with just enough time to shower, change, have a bite to eat and be off again. I had been 'warned' to appear as a witness at the Old Bailey at 2pm - 'warned' is the official way of saying you have been ordered by law to attend.

It was another drugs-buy-gone-wrong case, involving the RCS, this time in Camberwell, southeast London. The seller realized the buyer was a police officer and, as he legged it, had fired a gun to warn off his police pursuer. The drug seller didn't get far before he was arrested, as armed officers had the area surrounded. I was in the vicinity so attended the scene but the local SOCO seemed to have it all in hand, so I left him to it. Now the cops needed a SOCO at short notice to give evidence about how difficult it is to find a bullet at a scene, as the SOCO and the RCS officers hadn't been able to find any sign of it, despite several thorough searches.

The trial was taking place in Court One, known by the charming name 'The Hanging Court', for obvious historical reasons. Within minutes I was sworn in, and then Prosecution Counsel asked the Court Usher to give me a bundle of papers about twelve inches thick. He then asked me to turn to page 121. Before me was a photograph of the scene, a concrete jungle of nondescript blocks of two-storey flats. The first question was to do with the geography of the estate. I looked down at the photograph but couldn't quite figure it out. The Judge, who was just to my left, looked over my shoulder and said: "Mr Henderson if you turn the photograph up the other way it may make sense to you."

"Oh! Thank you my Lord."

'Bollocks!' I thought, reddening, 'I'm really paying for that late night!'

After that hiccup, I answered questions about clues and indications, such as ricochet marks or bullet casings; explaining the difference between an automatic handgun expelling a metal shell case as it is fired, and a revolver that didn't and that finding bullet fragments at a large, open scene like the one in the photograph was extremely difficult.

Job done, I escaped the Hanging Court and returned to the office where the latest update was that the shot officer would survive but had suffered life-changing injuries. He wouldn't return to active duty.

A couple of days later Peter Jones, Head of SO3, wrote a personal note to me thanking me for "turning out" as he phrased it, and upholding the good name of SO3. I was surprised he even knew about the incident, but there is a night duty log, so presumably the info was passed to him. Too often in the police, detectives, police officers and their various support teams are expected to perform extraordinary duties without so much as a thank you, so Peter's comments were much appreciated. But, having said that, thinking about these two shooting incidents, my job was nothing - in terms of sacrifice - compared to those officers who put their lives on the line over and over again, all in the name of justice and to keep us civilians safe.

# DEATH ON THE PAVEMENT

A number of well-known armed robbers, driving a stolen car, were under surveillance by the Squad, accompanied by tactical firearms officers. I was in a back-up car with unarmed Squad officers.

The robbers parked up outside a bank and entered, leaving the getaway driver with his engine running.

The Squad guys moved in and quickly surprised the driver, dragging him from the vehicle, handcuffing and hauling him away to another car, parked out of sight. He was not armed and the arrest went very smoothly, despite the tense situation.

Seconds later, the robbers, wearing balaclavas, ran out of the building with bags of cash, only to be confronted by plain-clothed police shouting: "Armed Police! Put down your weapons!"

They were wearing 'plot caps,' which are the baseball-style black caps with a black-and-white chequered band, which IDs them as police.

One of the robbers turned his weapon on the police officer nearest to him.

There is no choice. No time to wonder whether lives are in danger. No time to think. By that time your enemy will have pulled the trigger. The officer opened fire, hitting the robber a number of times, and he fell to the floor. His accomplices surrendered immediately. One was unarmed and the other dropped his shotgun, putting his arms in the air.

Recovering from the shock of what I'd just witnessed, my professional self got into gear. As soon as the robbers were handcuffed, I ran over and moved the weapons out of the way before checking the injured robber. His blood was choking him. I was sure he was dying but I needed to try something. To stop bleeding you have to push anything that comes to hand into the wound and apply pressure. A sock from the injured person, as in this case, was a typical choice. It would later become an exhibit and retained for forensic examination, as it would contain both firearms residue and the pre-transfusion blood of the robber - DNA would also be recovered these days.

The robber died in hospital. A Laboratory Liaison Sergeant was sent to attend the Post Mortem while SOCOs examined the prisoners and took firearms residue swabs as well as possession of their clothing. Their homes were searched with SOCOs on hand to assist. All vehicles associated with the robbers were removed to various police stations for examination and once the scene had been photographed and examined, I turned my attention to the armed police officers. All their weapons and ammunition, whether or not they'd been discharged, had to be taken as exhibits and were submitted to the Forensic Science Laboratory for screening, so that the identification of the weapons that had been fired could be confirmed. This was done to comply with the subsequent Independent Police Complaints Commission (IPCC) investigation. The bullet(s) removed from the deceased would identify which gun or guns delivered the wounding and fatal shots. Then there was liaison with the appointed Exhibits Officer and attendance at the de-brief followed by a welcome pint with your colleagues at the end of a twenty-hour day (everyone still shaking with adrenaline), bearing in mind that you needed to be ready tomorrow when it could all happen again.

The Squad didn't take any satisfaction from days like this. A professional outfit, they'd analyze the events that had led to the shooting to see that everything had been done correctly but, as the armed robber had raised his weapon in anger, he had crossed a line and the officers were - and still are - trained to shoot without hesitation, to kill to protect others. It remains a terrible but necessary power but the consequences of inaction are far worse.

# LUCKY SHOT

To say we were busy would be some understatement. The Squad's SOCO team often dealt with up to sixteen to twenty armed robberies *every day* across every part of London. I found myself frequently called upon to assist on busy days when my team was feeling the pressure, and I was only too happy to help, especially if it was a complex scene, e.g., if shots had been fired.

Friday at 5.30pm, and the Barnes gunship was in hot pursuit of an armed gang who'd just robbed a Hammersmith building society and were fleeing via the enormous Hogarth roundabout to the westbound side of the A4, towards the start of the M4 and out of London.

As the getaway car approached the roundabout, a gunman leaned out of the passenger door window and shot at the gunship, shortly before a second gunship hit the robbers' car side-on, bringing the chase to a dramatic end. The two robbers were dragged from the car and nicked in no uncertain terms. Fortunately, the bullet hadn't hit any of the pursuers, nor had it hit the vehicle. Unfortunately this incident caused one of the worst traffic jams London has ever seen.

Apart from the scene at the building society, there was a mile-long stretch of the busiest route out of London to examine - and we had to try and find the bullet. And then there were the prisoners. Photographs of suspects wearing the clothes they were nicked in would be needed. This was so they could be compared to CCTV footage and eyewitness statements.

I decided to take the scene at the A4 and left the building society and the prisoners to Simon, the Barnes SOCO to organize. I contacted the Squad Central Reserve and requested two traffic units to close the A4 while I performed my search. In the meantime, it was left to a local constable to hold the traffic heading out of town. We had to wait for the traffic officers to hold the other side of the road, as everyone else was busy with the scene, collecting witness statements from other drivers, whose cars I would have to examine to see if I could find the bullet.

If I found that bullet then the robbers were guaranteed substantial jail time. Witness statements are good but unreliable and the criminals were bound to say they hadn't fired a shot. All they needed was reasonable doubt. The bullet was the difference between being done for robbery and robbery plus attempted murder.

I had just under a mile of road to search. It was summer, which meant the light was good for another three hours, so no pressure there.

As soon as the traffic guys were set up with their control, I started to examine the cars that had been stopped after the pursuit had come to its spectacular end, releasing them one at a time, with myself on the off side and one of the constables on the near side, checking, amongst other things, the tyres for any sign of a bullet lodged in the tread. This was completed in half an hour. No bullet, so I walked the rest of the route, checking the road. Nothing. Neither bullet nor shell case. I finally admitted defeat and, after thanking the traffic guys for their assistance, I removed the roadblocks so the traffic could at last start to move again. I then searched the small gardens in front of some of the houses along the road, looking for signs of a bullet impact or ricochet. Nothing. Bollocks. 'Oh well,' I thought, 'Have to hope those eyewitnesses will sound convincing in court.' After a final check with Simon to make sure he had the building society and prisoners under control, I headed home, arriving around 8pm. Toby, our Spaniel (our labs had long since passed away) was pleased to see me and gave me a knowing look, which, roughly translated, said: 'A nice walk followed by a packet of crisps and a pint or two?'

Then my pager went off.

An hour later I was in a first floor flat on the Great West Road section of the A4, a bemused American watching me as I walked around his bedroom. His bedroom window had a hole in it. The wall opposite had a large space where a piece of plaster had fallen off. Then there was a half-open wardrobe door with a long dent in it, then a hole on the opposite wall and finally, there it was, in the middle of his bed: a bullet.

"You expect this sort of thing in Chicago," he said as I took measurements of the bullet hole in the window, "Not in London town."

"It's not something one sees every day, I have to admit," I replied, noting the point of first impact on the bedroom wall, just in case the ballistic boys needed to pinpoint the shot's direction of travel.

"Guess I'm just lucky then," the American said with a smile.

"Those robbers most certainly aren't," I replied. "This little piece of metal is going to send them to prison for a very long time indeed."

# THE KNEE BONE IS
# CONNECTED TO THE...

There were risks to what we did too, of course and I sometimes found myself close to the action. Not long after my appearance in the Old Bailey's Hanging Court I supported Judy on a huge drugs squad operation. The plan was to raid a Brixton crack house on the second floor of a block deep within a troubled estate. Judy and I would follow immediately behind officers from the Territorial Support Group (TSG, extremely tough police officers trained in public order) so we could start gathering exhibits before evidence was destroyed.

When the door went down, it soon became clear that the house was packed with men and women in various states of inebriation, who promptly ran in all directions shouting and screaming back at the TSG who were yelling at them to submit or feel the wrong end of their batons.

What threw Judy and I was that the flat was without light. There were no bulbs in any of the fittings, no lamps, just some candles which had been extinguished when the front door came crashing down. Some officers had torches but we did not and, as we entered the hallway, I noticed a black guy hiding in a recess just next to me. He'd been missed in the rush and thanks to the darkness. I instinctively yelled "OI! Over here!" before thoughts about whether he might have a knife or gun could stop me, but before any arresting officer could reach us, the guy broke cover and legged it into a bedroom, opened a window and, in one smooth movement, without any hesitation, jumped out.

We were on the second floor and so we expected to find a body on the ground below but there was no one in sight. TSG officers ran down to have a look but there was no sign.

Meanwhile, Judy and I borrowed a torch and set about claiming exhibits in what was a truly filthy flat, littered with debris. It stank of urine and the horrible, acrid smell of crack that stayed in your nostrils for hours afterwards.

A dog handler had gone through the flat and it was decided, after ten minutes of searching outside, that he should have a look for our jumping criminal. The dog, Rex, a three-year-old Alsatian was at the peak of his game and two minutes later he was barking at a large, six-foot-high communal bin. I walked over, joining some other TSG officers, and when they looked inside, they found our jumper with his tibia bone sticking up through his knee. He must have been in agony but had not uttered a sound as he crawled down the street and then clambered into this bin. Not his best night on earth, I'm sure he would agree, especially as he had a thick file of warrants out on him for drug dealing, amongst some other, violent offences. A sergeant from the Drugs Squad came over to take a look and recognized him immediately.

"Alright Cyril?" he said, peering down before sucking through his teeth in mock sympathy. "Oooh, I suppose not. Looks like you'll need to spend a few months in a cast. You definitely won't be skipping bail this time!"

# A STOPPED WATCH AND A STOPPED HEART

**W**hen Judy was transferred from the Central Drugs Squad, which was now 9 RCS (Department 9 South East Regional Crime Squad) only four people out of four hundred eligible officers applied for her job. It was made very clear to me that, if and when SO3 found a candidate, it would not be a SOCO of my choice. It would be a Fingerprint Officer.

'Another efficient and experienced team about to be broken up by politics,' I thought.

The Fingerprint Department (SO3) had engineered the end of the SOCO system and they were now trying to 'sell' their fingerprint officers as scene examiners, equipped with fingerprint and forensic knowledge, the 'Omni-Competent Officer', as they put it. Fortunately, before a fingerprint officer could even think of making a forensic scene examination, they had to complete an advanced forensic evidence course. Thanks to a backlog in training, and with all SOCO-trained officers in jobs, very few people had the necessary experience to join the RCS elite.

I was asked to lecture on armed robbery and Specialist Operations to the students on the advanced forensic evidence course. As it was only six lectures a year, and because I'd given up squash long ago since work had become so busy, I agreed.

In my first lecture I outlined the responsibilities of the SO8 SOCO's as well as the newly-appointed Fingerprint Officer to 9 Regional Crime Squad. The look on the students' faces was a picture. I could see them all thinking: "Will I have to do *all* that?"

Many fingerprint officers freshly trained in forensic examination found it hard to think broadly when looking at a crime scene. SOCO's have to think ahead and anticipate potential problems, even obscure ones because that was exactly what barristers would ferret around for once they got their hands on the case files.

Fingerprints, although important, had finite use. They were binary in that they either matched or didn't match. Other forensic evidence varied from 'possibly' to 'definitely.'

In major cases, both the evidence and the procedure used to recover it would always be challenged in court. Many of the fingerprint guys and gals didn't realize this and it was developing into a major problem, so I took my duties at the training school very seriously.

I always based lectures on my personal experience and when talking about firearms, I recounted a recent appearance at the Old Bailey. I'd been called to give evidence about a robbery case that had gone wrong. After a robber had escaped the immediate scene, he'd ended up facing a Squad officer, threatening him with a revolver. He didn't fire the gun and surrendered when other, armed

Branch officers appeared behind him. The villain had been charged with robbery and attempted murder. His argument against the attempted murder charge was that his gun was not fully loaded. He claimed he knew there was no bullet in the next chamber and therefore it would not have fired if he had pulled the trigger.

Giving evidence, I was asked if I had made the gun safe at the scene.

"Yes my Lord." Answer the question and no more, is my advice to anyone in a similar position.

"And how would you proceed after the gun was safe?"

"Ordinarily I would make the gun safe by emptying the bullets from the chamber, and then package gun and bullets separately for ballistic examination. I'd also make a note that the gun was made safe at the scene, record the bullet-shell ratio, i.e., six bullets removed, or five bullets removed and one empty shell and so on and label each with an exhibit number, and detail the place and time they were recovered.

"And what was the position of the bullets in the chamber?"

"There was a bullet to the left of the 12 o'clock position of the barrel, and the chamber to the right was empty."

"And what would happen if the trigger had been pulled?"

"The gun would have fired."

"And how can we be certain that you are remembering accurately?"

I had to stop myself from smiling, partially from relief, partially from smugness.

"I sketched the chamber and the sequence of bullets. I made the sketch because the chamber was not full and was aware this could be significant."

By making the sketch at the scene in my pocket book, I stopped any suggestions that the gun was subsequently tampered with to fit the later charge. Most revolvers rotate clockwise, as did this particular model, so the next pull of the trigger would have fired a bullet.

The defence accused me of tampering with the gun at the scene but I stood firm and the jury accepted my evidence.

I made it clear to the students that they did not, as a rule, have to make guns safe as long as a firearms officer was present - to their evident relief - but that they should be as thorough as possible with their contemporaneous notes.

"It can only help you months down the line when you're brought before a packed courtroom at the Old Bailey. You do not want to be the reason a major case fails."

Even I half-dreaded the phone calls that started: "Hi Larry, do you remember that armed robbery case from six months ago?"

My heart would always perform a little jump. This question more than likely meant that the trial was under way and the defence was going to town, questioning the forensic evidence any way they could think of, and I'd be dragged in to testify about something I'd worked on months ago. This was good enough reason to make sure one's notes and exhibits were a hundred per cent water-tight, above question.

One "Larry, do you remember that armed robbery?" phone call demanded my urgent presence at Croydon Crown Court, where four armed robbers were being tried after being nicked in a pavement ambush that had taken place outside a post office.

"I thought it was a straightforward job," I told the caller, "They were nicked on the pavement."

"Apparently your notes show that your examination took place an hour before the robbery. You will need to explain the timings."

I dug out my original notes and, sure enough, the time was fifty-five minutes before the actual robbery. I could remember the robbery happened at about 12.40pm, but for the vehicle examination I'd written down 11.45am, which wasn't right. It must have been 1.45pm. It was a genuine mistake and I was going to have to put my hands up to it, but I knew that even if the defence accepted it, they would want to know how I'd managed to get to the scene so quickly.

Courts are intimidating places. I've seen plenty of cool, calm and collected people fall apart on the witness stand after being put under pressure by a wily barrister. I was experienced enough to remain calm when the barrister implied first corruption and then poor workmanship. I explained that it was a genuine mistake on my part, explaining that, in twenty years of scene examination, I always made sure to record the time clearly and always did this by checking my watch.

"On that particular day my watch must have been running slow and I simply hadn't noticed," I said. "And the reason I was there so quickly, was that I was in the area at the time."

It all seemed to be going well. I could see the jury accepted my version of events. The four robbers stared daggers, but there was no way I was going to let them intimidate me. The defence barrister sat down and I was about to leave the witness box when he jumped back up.

"Just one more question Mr Henderson," he said pausing, a knowing look on his face.

My heart started thumping. Bollocks. What the hell had I missed? I could just tell the bastard was going to hit me right between the eyes with some overlooked fact, Columbo-style.

He smiled. "No, actually, it doesn't matter, Mr Henderson," he said. "I won't ask the question officially, but for the Courts' benefit I was going to ask you the make of your watch, so the people present know which make they should avoid!"

# NIGHT OF THE SHERBET LEMON

A long-running operation to arrest a gang of armed robbers from South London demanded a briefing every Monday morning at 2am at a police station on the edge of the City, where the Tactical Firearms Unit (SO19) had a base.

The robbers were planning to take out a cash-in-transit van around 7.30am one Monday, somewhere in Kent. Their plan was to box the van in on a slower part of the road, which was also a hill, using two vehicles front and back and a juggernaut-sized lorry that would drive alongside, leaving it no room to manoeuvre and then force it into a slip road where other gang members were lying in wait with a JCB, ready to gouge open the van's armour to get to the cash (close to £20million) inside.

Armed officers would control the robbers, but I'd asked them not to touch the gang. The robbers should then be transported in vehicles that the armed police officers had not used. A case had recently occurred where a robber had been able to hide his firearm before he was arrested - it was never found - and then his barrister had managed to convince the jury that the firearms residue found on his clothes could have come from an armed arresting officer.

We made an impressive convoy; our unmarked cars included two three-litre Vauxhall Senator gunships each loaded with four Squad officers, a three-litre Volvo Estate with four Tactical Firearms officers, a dog handler and Bruno, his Alsatian, in another Volvo estate, the Control car (an Audi 80 Quattro) with three senior officers and my car, a 2.8 litre Ford Sierra estate 4x4 containing Jacqui and myself. We all had encrypted radios, so there was no chance of us being scanned.

Our first rendezvous was in the grounds of a hospital three miles from the scene of the planned robbery. We lined up with the rear of the cars to a wall, turned off the engines and sat waiting for the go signal. It was 3.30am in February and about minus six outside, so occasionally we would start the car engines to get the car heaters going. Jacqui was already cat napping on the passenger seat by the time I pushed my seat back to give me a bit more room in which to doze but, before closing my eyes, I ran through my own operational checklist. Jim, the Detective Super, had closed the briefing with a warning: "We have to take control of the armed robbers extremely quickly. They are all facing twenty-five year sentences and they will not hesitate to shoot their way out." If a shoot-out did erupt, then both colleagues and robbers were likely to be casualties. To avoid cross contamination issues, I'd need to call all the A&E departments of the local hos- pitals to advise them about forensic preservation as we'd need separate ambulances and separate medical teams for robbers and police. We'd also need pre-transfusion blood from all of the casualties; firearms residue samples taken from robbers and armed police; firearms would have to be made safe and recovered, every last bullet would have to be collected and clothing bagged and forensically preserved as soon as possible, and the instruments used to do the recovery would have to be forensically bagged; then I would need to liaise with the Super to find a suitable location to hold the armed police officers while the Independent Police Complaints Commission (IPCC) began their investigation (as they do in all cases where the police have fired their weapons). The robbers' vehicles would be removed and I'd have to make sure I had a list from the transport guys advising me to which police stations they'd been taken. I would also need to fingerprint the outside of the Security vehicle so it could be handled for removal. Oh! Then there's the small matter of the estimated £26million on board, which would have to be removed and stored somewhere extremely safe. Best to speak to the Super about that, I thought. I had the heater on and was just dozing off, these thoughts all turning through my mind, when there was a knock on my window. I lowered the window and looked out sleepily to see an angry looking nurse staring at me.

"Who are you and what are you doing?"

I was tail-end Charlie and so I referred her to the control car, the Audi at the opposite end of the line. However, before she hot-footed it to speak to the Detective Super, she leaned down so she was just at the window's edge and said: "Could you please turn off your engines as the children in the hospital ward behind that wall are all coughing with the fumes from your car exhausts!"

Whoops. So, to avoid killing a bunch of sick kids with carbon monoxide poisoning, we froze our asses off until the go-ahead came and the control car, one gunship and the tactical firearms guys took up their position with a view (known as 'eyeball' in cop parlance) on the main road and the slip road. The rest of us parked up out of sight about a mile away.

Radio contact confirmed that the robbers' vehicles were front and rear of the security van. The convoy was travelling towards the slip road position but no juggernaut in sight. It was a dummy run but it looked as though this operation was definitely a goer.

It seemed less like a goer some weeks later, after five 2am Monday briefings. Once again, we were in position outside the hospital by 3.30am, remembering to leave our engines off so as not to poison the kids. We were absolutely freezing, even though everybody was dressed for the occasion, including thermal long johns and I heard that one or two hot water bottles also made an appearance.

The gang was being extremely careful. They were slowly leading up to the raid, rehearsing and checking everything they could think of, including the juggernaut's closing speed . On the sixth Monday Jacqui and I were joined by a detective constable, Colin, who would help us deal with the prisoners, as we were expecting to nick at least a dozen people.

For some reason, I had two bags of sherbet lemons in the car and, I don't know if it was the cold or the boredom but, by 5am, we had eaten the first bag. The second bag had gone an hour later and, by 7am about half an hour before the hit was due, I started to feel unwell. My stomach bubbled and popped and I suspect the same was true for Jacqui and Colin and soon the car was filled with the sound of muffled wind. We were freezing but I was nonetheless wondering whether I should wind down the window, to prevent total suffocation, when we were given the go ahead. The lead car with the eyeball gave us a running commentary as we moved to our secondary position, a mile from the hit. Soon the robbers' cars were in place, front and rear, with the juggernaut closing up fast.

"We are on, all units stand by, gunship one and tactical on my count," came the command.

All I could do was wince as more wind filled my stomach and then the car. The sooner this job got under way the better. I could not wait to get out of this bloody vehicle.

And then we heard that the juggernaut hadn't yet managed to close the box; it was half way across, but it was struggling to get up the hill fast enough to close the last section of the gap. We were cheering it on: "Go on! Go on! For fuck's sake just DO IT!"

And then we heard: "All units stand down, juggernaut has failed to close the gap."

We all then went to RV2 (Rendezvous Point 2), where it would be decided whether to nick the gang for 'conspiracy to rob' but rush hour traffic was building up and I got caught three cars back at a red traffic light. I couldn't just jump out of the queue as I was in an unmarked car and the road we were now on was narrow with cars coming the other way at 60mph. I got through the first traffic lights but I turned the next corner to be confronted with a queue about a mile long that lead to another set of traffic lights.

I don't know if it was the sherbet lemons, but I'd had enough. Out I came on the wrong side of the road, head-lights on, one hand on the horn and one hand on the steer-ing wheel. I flew down the road between oncoming traffic and stationary cars. I don't know if it was any help to us at this speed but Colin was leaning out of the open window holding out his warrant card for the oncoming motorists who no doubt wondered what the hell this lunatic in a Sierra was doing. A couple of days earlier, the head of the fingerprint department had warned: "If you have an acci-dent exceeding the speed limit the department won't sup-port you." I remembered these words as I blasted through a red light, but was relieved to spot the convoy a short dis-tance ahead and a few minutes later we had diverted from RV2 into a supermarket car park to discuss whether to hit the would-be robbers.

The crime of 'conspiracy to rob' is very difficult to prove, hence the 'pavement ambush' strategy. The decision was eventually taken to run the op for one more week. The DI running the show was conscious the overtime bill for over forty officers was astronomical, especially as by now it was now over five months since the beginning of the oper-ation. Jacqui and I had only been involved for the last six weeks and our overtime was coming out of SO8's budget. The DI believed, rightly I feel, that it was necessary to catch the gang red-handed. He could have 'shown-out' warning them off and they would have abandoned their plans, so no crime would have been committed but then they would have simply vanished and there would be no way of finding out where they'd vanished to. Then they'd plan an equally audacious or dangerous robbery, be it a cash-van, a bank, a post office and so on, and then there was the danger that a cashier or security guard would get killed. This raid had the advantage of taking place in a remote location, so it was possible to hit them in a secure enough way so that no one would get hurt and this would prevent them from harming anyone else in the future. There was risk to it, but to the DI, the greater risk was to let them get away.

By the time we wrapped up for the day it was 10am and I never wanted to see another sherbet lemon ever again in my whole life. At 2pm I gave up on the day, telling Control I was going off duty to sleep off the sherbet.

The gang didn't attempt the blag the following week and the order came to nick them and charge them with conspiracy to rob. Three weeks later they were all arrested in the car park of an M1 service station. They'd been sussing out a new blag, but nothing prosecutable. All the Squad could say was that they'd dissuaded them from attempting anything for a while.

One learns to cope with frustration in this Job. It's not an exact science, it's expensive, tiring and dangerous but when it comes to protecting the public and putting the bad guys in prison, no job is too difficult.

# HYPODERMIC BLACKMAIL

G eorge, the new fingerprint officer, telephoned one morning to ask if I could accompany him on a RCS9 blackmail operation outside the Metropolitan Police District. The job involved dropping off a million pounds in a suitcase, at an as yet unknown rendezvous, and then support a rolling operation to catch the blackmailer.

This was right up my street. "No problem George, when do we go?"

"Erm... In thirty minutes."

Bloody hell!

After a quick call in which I left a message for Jennifer - "I'm going out of town, could be gone couple of days, won't be able to contact you, ok? Bye then" - I told George I was ready to go. We met up and loaded his car with equipment then joined the RCS lads and, before we headed off to darkest Gloucestershire, they gave us the low-down.

Someone was blackmailing a high street bank for a £1 million. The blackmailer was threatening to walk into a branch at random and inject the first customer he saw with the HIV virus. Communications with the blackmailer had taken place through the personal columns of one of the broadsheets.

The first point of contact was at 9pm that night at a public telephone box identified using ordinance survey map references. The instructions then took the form of the Bruce Willis film *Die Hard with a Vengeance*. The negotiator had to decipher the map reference and be at the next public call box in fifteen minutes. The negotiator was supposed to be alone but there were SO11 surveillance guys following him in two teams who came at each location from separate sides in a pincer movement; even Bruce Willis wouldn't have spotted them, they were that good.

The rest of us, which included the RCS guys, a Gloucestershire Police Superintendent and a local detective team, followed at a safe distance to ensure we didn't compromise the drop. We were supposed to be supported by the eye-in-the-sky, a police helicopter but, due to low cloud, it couldn't fly and a fixed-wing light aircraft had been sent in its place. Although you couldn't see the small plane you could hear it. Not the wisest move for a covert operation.

The running around went on for about six hours, as the negotiator darted between various location markers on motorway hard shoulders. These are the markers you see every hundred metres, which give your exact position to the police or breakdown services. George and I were kept busy, picking up and fingerprinting the letter drops after the negotiator had moved on, and then fingerprinting the phone boxes.

At 3am we regrouped. The negotiator and surveillance teams had been run around the houses and were feeling the pace. George was feeling sick. I advised him to have something to eat, "But for God's sake don't go anywhere near sherbet lemons they're a killer." George looked at me like I was mad and I offered him a bar of chocolate from a stash I kept for long-running ops. "Your brain needs sugar to keep going. This'll stop you from falling asleep."

George couldn't face it. So I ate one. By 4am we were finally in place to do the 'drop.' We were racing through a forest in the car with no lights on and I bounced around in the passenger seat as our police driver carried on regardless of the moguls we were driving headlong over. George looked like he was either about to be sick or pass out. We finally reached the RV and followed the instructions to drop off the million-pound suitcase, after which time we retreated and headed to another RV point. The negotiator would collect the case and perform the final drop at the precise spot as dictated by the blackmailer.

I knew the SO11 guys were all around us but, after hours of looking, I never spotted a single giveaway. After two hours the money still hadn't been collected and as dawn started to break, we knew it wasn't going to happen.

Then, just as we were about to give up, we got a call. A team of local detectives had been performing a sweep of the forest when they came across a guy asleep in his car. They'd taken him to the local nick.

It couldn't be, could it? George and I legged it to the suspect's car and gave it the once over, finding nothing of interest, just a couple of cans of coke. On to the local nick. The man claimed he'd had a row with his wife the previous night and she'd "kicked him out." He refused to give his address until threatened with charges of obstruction and we all stormed around to the house, which was on the edge of the Forest of Dean, the guy handcuffed and in the back of a panda car.

We watched as the uniformed police knocked on the door and a woman in her twenties answered. She confirmed the story. The guy, by this time a nervous wreck, was led into the house where his handcuffs were finally removed. He burst into tears and apologized to his wife who hugged him.

Not the happy ending we were hoping for but one had to take something positive from the night. If we hadn't found the sleeping man then perhaps he wouldn't have gotten back together with his wife. By the time we stood down, George and I had completed thirty three hours of duty without sleep although I did catnap every chance I got; catnapping is an essential skill, as long as circumstances permitted. Two days later the blackmailer posted a communication in the personal column: "I heard your eye in the sky."

We never heard from him again and no attempt was made to injure a bank customer in the manner he described.

I finally arrived home at 4pm and, forgetting the fact I'd eaten nothing but a couple of chocolate bars for the last fourteen hours, had two hours of blissful sleep after which time I had to join Jennifer for a parent-teacher evening, to hear how our boys, Richard and Robin, were doing. I prayed they were doing well, but only so I could get this over with quickly and dash back to bed. While we were waiting to see the teacher, a short boy with enormous grey shorts sat next to me with a bag of sherbet lemons. I almost threw up.

# THE KRYPTON FACTOR

The message from Jacqui said I should get over to the Squad's Tower Bridge office as soon as possible. We were needed to covertly examine a room at the Penta Hotel, Gatwick airport, with armed back up in the room next door. The DI thought we had a ten-minute window to identify, from finger marks, who was in the room. No other information was available. I dashed off before remembering I was wearing a Flying Squad tie (a swooping eagle on a plain blue or red background) and dashed back to swap with someone. Less than a minute after meeting Jacqui at Tower Bridge we leapt into a fast car with its blues and twos screaming all the way on a hair-raising journey to the airport's outskirts where we were met by a detective from Tower Bridge and completed our journey in an unmarked car.

I entered the hotel disguised as a service engineer, carrying an aluminium case with all our gear, ostensibly here to check a room thermostat, while Jacqui, who followed a few steps behind, was now part of the hotel's management team. Jim, the detective was booked into the room opposite our mysterious hotel guests, where two armed

Squad officers were already ensconced, ready and waiting to intervene if we were compromised.

All they would tell us was that a man and a woman had been in the room for three days without leaving it, apart from two fifteen-minute trips to the bar. They had, in that time, received two other couples, and the current room service bill was over £2,000. The guys from the Squad suspected they were planning a hit somewhere near, or even on, the airport site. Tons of cash, jewellery and precious metals move around the UK's major airports every week so there was no shortage of targets. The dirty tricks department had managed to install two listening devices but, because they'd only had a few minutes in which to work, they weren't well placed and the officers hadn't been able to hear much.

Our role was to attempt, in ten minutes, to find and lift sufficient fingerprints to identify the occupants of the room.

"There's one other thing," Jim said, as we got ready, "We'd also like you to search the room for firearms," before adding, almost as an afterthought, "Oh, and we'd like you to check for explosives as well."

I like a challenge as much as the next fellow but this was asking a lot. The room would have to be left *exactly* as we found it. This mission reminded me of the *Krypton Factor*, the popular 1980's TV game show where brainy contestants had to come up with practical solutions to tricky problems before competing against each other on an assault course. I discussed the examination with Jacqui and we decided not to speak to each other while we worked as, if the couple were as paranoid as the Squad imagined, they might leave a recorder going while they were gone.

Then Jim, headphones on, lifted up his finger. They were leaving. We heard the door open and close. Jim checked and saw the couple walking down the corridor. Colin, sitting in the downstairs lounge, confirmed their arrival with two clicks on his concealed radio.

In we went, Jim opening the door with a key card supplied by the hotel director. We checked for any sign of a video camera or audio equipment, saw nothing, and so Jacqui went straight to the bathroom as mirror surfaces gave the best chance of finger marks. I searched the drawers, wardrobes under the mattress for firearms. Nothing.

There were a couple of *Sun* newspapers from the last two days stuck in a bin so I carefully took a couple of pages from inside the papers for chemical treatment to develop finger marks. Jacqui gave me the thumbs-up. She'd found finger marks on the mirror. I quickly examined four drinking glasses on the coffee table and lifted marks from three of them. I cleaned the glasses removing the aluminium powder and held up three fingers to Jacqui; she indicated three also. That should do nicely, I thought. We packed our equipment away and took a final look around the room. No firearms, explosives, maps, sketches, timetables, so nothing to interest us.

The couple returned five minutes after we were back in the other room with Jim.

We had lifted the finger marks with special tape and we rolled them onto 6"x 4" plastic sheet. These were then labelled with the hotel name, hotel room number, date and an individual exhibit number e.g., LH/1, LH/2 (LH being my initials), etc.

Another fast car was arranged to take us to the Yard where the finger marks would be compared against known criminals and then the Sun newspaper pages were transported on to the fingerprint laboratory near the Elephant and Castle.

That done, it was time to debrief.

"Gordons?" I suggested to Jacqui.

She nodded and the driver dropped us off at the wine bar. It's impossible to head home to a normal world after an afternoon like that. To join the commute, to arrive, head still spinning, trying to come down, with adrenalin still pumping through your veins, is simply hopeless. You just don't want to be there. You can't have a normal conversation with your wife, partner, kids and/or pets and sit down for dinner or watch TV.

It was equally bad with long-running, high-pressure ops and I would sometimes return home thinking of an operation that was due to take place the following day, completely absorbed with the requirements I needed to cover, whether it be SOCO manpower or briefing notes, or back-up plans if the local scene examiners did not cooperate. You just don't turn off and talking about 'everyday' matters with your family is nigh impossible.

That's one reason why there are so many divorces in the police. Fortunately, Jennifer was as independent as me and we knew to make the most of the time we had together because we never knew if I was going to have a heavy week, so we really made sure we enjoyed our holidays and free weekends as a family.

Once I'd had a few drinks and we'd had been able to talk through the events of the day, we were able to go home in a much calmer state and, as Jacqui didn't drink like the Squad guys, I wouldn't be in too bad a condition by the time Jennifer saw me.

Unfortunately, for reasons I can't give, I'm not permitted to tell you too much about the hotel case, except that the two guys were later identified from the finger marks as major players in the drugs world. The subsequent police operation led to convictions for the supply of controlled substances.

# GET-OUT CLAUSE

Somehow I learned to balance my operational commitments with my managerial role. Apart from statistical compilation, overtime budgets and liaising with the Fingerprint Branch's Scenes of Crimes team as well as the Met's Forensic Laboratory in Lambeth, I had to complete individual performance reports and provide suggestions as to their career development.

I was nearly overwhelmed with data as the team submitted huge quantities of exhibits to the lab for examination. A 'typical' murder case might have twenty to thirty exhibits, whereas an armed robbery conspiracy case could easily have over a hundred. And then there were always official police reports that required checking from a forensic point of view, so my desk was always loaded with a large pile of files awaiting my attention.

Our new Commander was George Ness, who'd been instrumental in putting the Kray twins behind bars and, not long after his appointment, he asked me to reply to a Royal Commission report about the integrity of exhibits presented to the Criminal Justice System.

"Let me have your report in seven days."

The report was not just about Squad work, it required an examination of the whole police exhibits system - how they were found, preserved, recorded, handled, examined and presented to a jury.

"Guv, I think this will take longer than a week!"

"OK Larry, and it would also be good to include safety procedures for firearms."

There were so many topics to include, such as the correct packaging of an exhibit in an appropriate medium. For example, a ransom demand should not be stored in a polythene bag due to the electrostatic electricity that will remove indents; wet clothes don't go into polythene bags, otherwise mould will grow; a glass sample bottle needs to be signature-sealed around the cap to preserve its integrity (and the scientist who breaks the seal has to record his or her action in the correct manner).

Most of these practices were in place, but had never been written up into a single document. The firearms safety part meant I would need to spend some time with the Tactical Firearms Unit and talk to the laboratory about how weapons should be handled before being submitted to the Ballistics Department. I also thought about establishing arrest protocols of armed suspects by armed officers to avoid contamination and prevent accusations of contamination.

After multiple meetings with scientists, superintendents, the Flying Squad, the Tactical Firearms Unit including their Chief Superintendent and, of course, my own team, I managed to finish the report in four weeks. It was well-received and was eventually turned into a booklet on official guidelines for the handling of exhibits.

When I learned the book was being printed, I spotted a problem and went to see George Ness.

"Guv, these guidelines might do us harm. At some point a bent barrister will get hold of a copy. Then an officer will face the question: 'Did you comply with official guidelines on the handling of exhibits as per this official book?'"

George told me not to worry. "I'll write a get-out clause as the opening paragraph, stating something like: 'these guidelines are to be followed on all occasions. However, there may be occasions, due to special circumstances, where it is not possible.' That should cover officers facing cross examination."

I disagreed but George was happy to go ahead, so I spent some time warning the Squad to always stick to the guidelines because if we didn't, we would be in trouble in court.

Eight years later, I was in the South of France when I received a telephone call.

"Larry, I'm at the Old Bailey and we've got a big problem! A defence barrister has a copy of the guidelines and is grilling all the Squad witnesses. It's to do with paragraph five... Is there any other interpretation?"

"No, there is no other interpretation. If the officer didn't follow the guidelines, then there's no arguable excuse."

A get-out clause will never suffice. You can't have it both ways in a court of law.

One of the problems identified from working with the SO19 firearms guys and SO8 was the arrest procedure.

The usual method was to make the suspect lie on the floor. This meant we would lose microscopic particles associated with firearms and explosive residues, fibres, and hairs, etc. I recommended the 'crucifix position' used by the Royal Ulster Constabulary (RUC) in Northern Ireland. The arrested person kneels with their hands extended out to the side and their legs crossed behind them. This would minimize the loss of forensic evidence. Unfortunately, SO19 weren't keen and so I came up with the idea of a Forensic Evidence Preservation Suit (FEPS). The RUC used a paper jacket but that only did half the job as, with rough handling, the paper jacket was easily torn and the legs remained exposed.

This was easier said than done, of course, and I had to come up with a design that would satisfy SO19, SO8 and the ballistics section of the Forensic Science Lab. It had to be easy to put on, transparent so the suspect's hands could be seen and tough enough to survive rough handling.

It would take some time for me to bring this idea to fruition and, shortly after securing the support of Dr. Geoff Warman from the Forensic Lab's Ballistics Department (also a former squash partner), I was forced to drop everything to assist with an urgent field operation involving a Tiger Kidnap.

# TIGER, TIGER

A shley, who had assisted me on the night of the Marchioness disaster, was now at the NW Squad office in Finchley. He called one day with the news that the NW office was about to embark on a 'Tiger Kidnapping' investigation. This occurs when a person is abducted to coerce someone else to commit a crime, or divulge confidential information, most commonly the spouse and/or children of a bank manager who would be able to provide robbers with the keys and/or combination to the safe. As well as a lot of planning, Tiger Kidnaps usually involve inside information, things like when the safe is at its fullest.

This particular investigation had an extremely interesting but at the same time, extremely worrying complication: the kidnapper was a Met Police officer, a uniform sergeant, so he would be wise to the sorts of methods we would use to catch him in the act. He was working with at least three non-police accomplices.

His plan was to gain entry to a house of a bank manager (so it was thought, the intelligence was a little sketchy when it came to identifying the target beyond doubt), kidnap his wife, and keep her handcuffed to a metal rail in a transit van. The manager, who lived in Devon, would then be expected to hand over the contents of his bank's safe after closing.

The police operation to catch him would be run jointly by the Squad and Devon and Cornwall police. The Technical Support Unit (SO7) had already 'lumped' the kidnapper's van (lumped = installed a tracking device, a 'lump') and as the gang were about to travel to Devon from Heathrow the next day we met at Heathrow nick at 6am for a pre-op briefing.

The SO7 guys would track the kidnappers from a distance. Surveillance officers from SO11 on unmarked motorcycles and in an unmarked BMW 5-series would keep a closer eye on the kidnappers' van and car, overlapping one another, keeping enough ground between them so as not to arouse the suspicions of the surveillance-savvy cop.

Our convoy, which maintained a three-mile distance, consisted of a control car with the DI, Squad driver and two Squad officers; two Vauxhall Senator gunships with three armed officers in each car, and myself and Ashley in my Sierra 4x4. I was to liaise with the local SOCOs on arrival and put them on standby for the following day, without revealing the actual op and suspected target. This was all very much on a need-to-know basis, as we didn't know how far this bent cop's tentacles stretched.

We cruised along the motorway, dropping back as ordered whenever the target cars slowed down to see if they were being followed. Then we would close back up again, travelling at speeds up to 120mph (all the forces on route had been alerted to our presence and were under strict instructions to ignore us) before suddenly pulling up in a lay-by once the targets had stopped for fuel.

The SO7 officers took what would seem to most people to be an extraordinary chance and decided to affix a second device to the Transit van that would allow them to stop the van by remote control. They managed without any problems and soon we were off again at 100mph, until we reached Tiverton, where I peeled off to visit the Constabulary Headquarters at Exeter and the local SOCO offices. To my relief, one of the local SOCO's was an ex-Met officer, someone I knew and so I was reassured he'd be able to handle the mess were about to dump on his doorstep. Without giving details, I made sure they'd be available from 10am the following morning to examine a number of cars and possibly three or four prisoners.

I also made sure the SOCOs had their own Firearms Residue Kits. I'd brought my own but I'd seen defence barristers questioning their use. They'd ask something like: "Why did you feel it necessary to use the Firearms Residue Kits supplied by the Flying Squad? Did you have your own kits?"

"Yes, we have our own kits."

"So why did you not use them?"

They would then try to open a line suggesting that I, as an SO8 officer, insisted on using our kits because they had been tampered with to give a positive result. All's fair in love and court.

I also suspected that the local lads had probably only given evidence two or three times in their whole career.

We attended court regularly and we were used to our evidence being attacked by the finest legal brains in the land. That's why we were there: to ensure all the evidence was collected correctly, with no loopholes. Look after the evidence and the trial will look after itself.

I also asked the SOCOs to bring shallow boxes to pack any firearms, and lots of large paper sacks for clothing. My final words, after thanking them for their co-operation, were: "Don't do anything without consulting me first!"

We were then shown our accommodation for the evening, a small twin room in the police Section House, with communal showers at the end of the corridor.

At 8pm we met with the rest of the Squad. The gang was holed up in a farmhouse that the police kidnapper had bought some time ago. There were four vehicles parked up in a large area in front of the house. The SO11 guys were in foxholes with eyeballs on the farmhouse. The kidnappers were under control so, time for us to eat.

We chose an Italian restaurant in a small town between Tiverton and Exeter. There were thirteen of us in total and we sat at tables arranged in the middle of the restaurant. It was a busy place and the atmosphere became quite boisterous. It also grew increasingly hot and so I took off my jacket and jumper, followed by Ashley and then the rest of the guys - which led to a hush falling over the restaurant as the guys' holsters and therefore their Smith and Wesson revolvers ended up in plain view.

A nervous restaurant manager, who was Italian, approached the table but before he could speak, the DI held up his hand and said: "Sorry, coats back on, chaps," before reassuring the owner that we were police officers.

We left the restaurant at 10.05pm with a view to having a quick drink in the bar at Exeter headquarters but we had to race there as last orders were 10.30pm and the licensing laws were strictly upheld - no exceptions.

As I knew the way, I led the convoy at 128mph and I walked into the bar at 10.28pm and got the orders in - but there was no sign of Gunship Two. They arrived ten minutes later. A local traffic officer had pulled them for doing 125mph! The traffic officer was hit with the full force of the Squad's outrage: "Officer, you should be aware who we are and why we are in your area. You are holding us up from a meeting at your headquarters could you piss off please, and let us on our way!"

The day of the hit started with a 6am briefing, at which point the Devon police stated that they would not sanction a pavement ambush. The Squad had worked out the probable target, but could not be one hundred per cent certain, so Devon police argued that the pavement ambush was too risky. They would only agree to the kidnappers being taken out that morning. A few chicken sounds came from the back rows but the Devon Superintendent remained adamant.

"Take them out this morning or go back to London and we will put a cordon around the suspected victim."

By the time we trundled out of the headquarters at around 8.30am our mood was black. Proving conspiracy before the act was incredibly difficult. It would almost all come down to the quality of the evidence, so the expectation rested on the shoulders of Ashley and myself. I was to take control of the scene of arrest. I had already briefed the arrest team on taking the kidnappers' shoes and clothing, along with any other article of interest, once back at the designated police stations.

The SO11 guys reported that three men had climbed into the white Transit. No weapons had been observed. After examining the kidnappers' likely route to the probable victims' house, the local Superintendent selected a country lane for the ambush. The gunships would lie in wait, out of sight, while the SO7 car would drop in behind the transit and activate the remote device, bringing the van to a gradual stop. As soon as the van was stationary, the gunships would quickly move in, front and back.

The shout went up "GO! GO! GO!" Ashley and I were behind the control car and we arrived at the 'stop' to find the three suspects spread-eagled on the ground. One of the kidnappers was apparently having a heart attack and was rushed off to hospital where it was discovered that he was faking. This was a clever move on his part, but I can't explain why - remember Mrs T's words. The Squad guys found no weapons, so a fairly straightforward arrest. The two remaining kidnappers were taken by Panda cars to separate nicks with the Squad officers following.

I took a look in the back of the Transit. An iron bar had been welded onto the side-wall, midway down the interior, and a mattress lay on the floor. I then found a pair of handcuffs and a heavy cardboard box filled with

Lakeland slate. This would probably have been their way into the house, i.e., "Delivery for you Mrs so-and-so, I'd better carry it inside as it's so heavy."

I took tapings from the driver's seat, sweepings from the driver's foot well and examined the driver's door and controls for fingerprints. The Transit van, after the remote device had been removed, was to be driven to the headquarters where it would be 'sealed' and would await my full examination.

We then travelled to the farmhouse, which was completely empty except for three sleeping bags. Not even a pot of tea or a bottle of beer.

There were three cars to examine. Ashley took the Vauxhall Cavalier, which had been driven by the bent cop and I allocated the others to the two Devon SOCOs briefing them that, in addition to a full fingerprint examination of the vehicle, we required tapings, sweepings, and a comprehensive vehicle search.

I heard over the radio that the prisoners weren't saying anything and so the Squad needed something to help them get these guys talking. The longer the silence lasted the more likely we would fail to secure a conviction. I was about to leave Ashley and the others to it and return to headquarters when I noticed both doors of one of the vehicles open simultaneously.

"Whoah! What's going on?" I shouted, running towards the car. Both the Devon SOCOs were about to examine the same vehicle between them, as they put it, "to save time."

"You can't do that," I said. "The defence will have a field day alleging contamination from one vehicle to the next, negating all of your evidence. Examine the cars separately and exhibit everything separately, got it?"

That done, I was walking back to my car, keen not to waste any more time, when Ashley shouted "Larry! Wait up!"

"Christ, what now?" I said. I turned to see Ashley with a huge smile on his face, waving me over.

"This had better be good," I muttered to myself.

It was. He'd found a hand recorder in the driver's door pocket of the Cavalier. In it was a cassette with a message that they were obviously planning to play over the phone to the bank manager. Ashley, wearing gloves, clicked the play button. The recording was eerie, heartless, deliberately distorted and menacing: "We have kidnapped your wife and you *will* comply with our demands, otherwise you will *never* see her again."

It then went on to give specific instructions how and when the kidnapper would be contacted.

Yes! This would do nicely. I telephoned the Superintendent with the good news.

By 11.45pm that evening Ashley and I had completed our contemporaneous notes, packaged and sealed all the exhibits, and logged them into headquarters' property system. I'd also checked with the Devon SOCOs to ensure their exhibits were packaged and sealed, and comprehensive notes completed, making sure they'd taken the tax disc, which matched the number plates, even though the vehicle was a ringer with false plates and had been stolen some weeks ago. We would need it for fingerprints as it would hopefully tie at least one of the gang to the vehicle and they would therefore have known it was stolen - all useful material for a conspiracy to kidnap charge. They had done everything perfectly as far as I could see and so I thanked them and reported to the Super that everything was under control. The Super told me that a celebration was in order and that a local licensee had agreed to open his pub for a private party.

"Sounds good, but I'll probably only stay an hour," I said, "I'm due to give evidence on another case at the Old Bailey at 2pm tomorrow."

About forty officers were transported to the pub along with the local Superintendent, his girlfriend, and a few local detectives that had assisted during the day. Everybody was on a high and the drinks flowed freely with a few snacks thrown in. I was ravenous, having only eaten a petrol-station-sandwich all day. The last thing I remember was watching the Squad sing a series of rugby songs and then the next thing I knew I was looking at my watch to see it was 6am! I was packed and ready to go by 8am but I felt rough as hell, as did everyone else who, although coherent, were still drunk by the time we assembled for the post-op briefing, during which I explained the case from the forensic perspective. I explained the significance of the voice recorder, the box of Lakeland slate, the handcuffs, mattress, etc., and confirmed that all the vehicles had been examined and the clothing of the detainees taken, before confirming that no firearms had been found and therefore there had been no need to take any firearms residue swabs.

The local Detective Superintendent was in a foul mood and couldn't wait to get rid of us. Shortly after the briefing I found out why. His girlfriend had been a little too friendly with one of the Squad guys the night before. Apparently, while we were all celebrating the result, they'd shared more than a pasty.

I finally left Exeter around 10.30am and barrelled back to London. I'd been called to give evidence on my covert examination of a car used by an armed robber. While under surveillance, the robber had left his car in a road close to Waterloo Station. We had no way of knowing how long he would be gone but we decided this was a good opportunity to have a look inside the vehicle. Four armed Squad guys stood guard at strategic locations while a SO11 officer discreetly opened the driver's door. I quickly and carefully searched the vehicle for weapons, maps and any other information that would indicate what the robber was planning.

There was a white plastic beaker in the passenger foot well, upon which I found finger marks. I subsequently cleaned the beaker, so there was no sign of aluminium powder. There was a large bunch of keys under the dashboard, but no indication as to what they were for.

As I was leaning into the car searching underneath the seats, there was a tug on my leg. Time to go as the robber was on his way back. The car was relocked and we legged it. It was only six minutes after I had started. The finger marks were subsequently identified as belonging to a person who was involved with our target. They robbed a Post Office the following week and were arrested – but at different times. Both men had denied knowing one other, so this piece of evidence was crucial to their conviction.

By 1pm I was still on the M4 due to a hold up following an earlier accident. Any hopes I had of a quick wash and brush up and fresh suit were abandoned and I dropped my car at the Tower Bridge Office before taking a black cab to the Old Bailey. Once I was sworn in, I apologized to the court for my appearance, explaining that I'd been on a pro-active operation in another part of the country, and that I had driven 150 miles to get here.

I then gave an account of how I found the fingerprints before it was time for my cross examination by the two defence barristers, hoping they wouldn't have uncovered any inconsistencies. One of the barristers stood up and asked me why it had been necessary to have armed protection when examining his client's car.

"My colleagues were of the opinion your client was an armed and dangerous person who could be carrying a gun."

The barrister then said: "No more questions," and sat down.

Really? I'd driven 150 miles for that? Was that the best they could do? I was grateful of course, but…

I got home at about 5pm, a red-eyed and dishevelled mess. Showered, shaved and fed I went to bed. 'What a day,' I thought, followed by, 'I wonder what will happen tomorrow as I have a - ' and everything faded to darkness.

Once the jury heard that tape play, they'd as good as stopped listening to anything else that was said. The bent cop and his friends went down for long stretches that ran into double figures.

# PART SEVEN

Specialist Operations Department 8 (SO8)
Flying Squad
New Scotland Yard SW1
1992 - 1994

# IDiOts

A shortage of qualified SOCOs meant a new system had been imposed by SO3 whereby Fingerprint Officers were posted to local police stations. These officers, IDOs (Identity Officers), had until then been used to a 9-5 office existence, sitting at a desk looking at finger marks and prints through a magnifying glass, searching for a match through hundreds of forms. They weren't trained for the 'real world', nor were they able to make tough decisions or face the challenges demanded by live crime scenes - and they did not like being called out after 5pm, as I found on numerous occasions when I asked for help examining a Flying Squad scene or suspect. I was a manager and my responsibility was to the Squad. If my team couldn't carry out a particular examination, and I wasn't available, then I expected my Branch, SO3, to supply officers in the IDO scheme who were competent to deal with my requests. Senior SO3 officers insisted this was the case but in reality it was anything but.

One particular Friday evening, I had reason to contact the IDO at Peckham police station. An armed robber had robbed a betting shop and, as he'd fled, he'd thrown away his balaclava and gun. Both items were quickly found by the attending uniform officers who'd arrested the fleeing robber after a member of the public, seeing he was being pursued, bravely tripped him up about a half-a-mile from the betting shop.

I explained the scenario to the IDO, all standard stuff: Head to the Custody Suite and liaise with the Custody Sergeant who would confirm the Superintendent had given permission under PACE (Police Criminal Evidence Act), to allow him to take non- intimate samples of the robber's head hair. Once that was done, he should take possession of the robber's clothing and exhibit and record the items in the property system, or hand the sealed exhibits to a Squad officer, not forgetting to get their signature for the exhibits in his pocket book/job sheet to ensure continuity. All straightforward stuff for any forensic officer.

Dave, the IDO, told me he'd never examined a prisoner before.

"No problem Dave, just remember your training. Once you've finished with the robber, you need to attend the scene and carry out a fingerprint examination of the betting shop. The shop manager's waiting to show you where the robber was standing, pretending to make a bet, before committing the robbery. His gun's an imitation, so no need to take any firearm residue samples, and we're not looking for fibre evidence at the scene. It's all straightforward stuff."

Dave sounded like he was in a real panic.

"Dave, what's wrong with you?"

"Sorry Larry, I can't go, I'm supposed to meet my wife at 6pm to do the shopping!"

"Does she work, and is she still at work now?

"Yes"

"Then telephone her and explain you are going to be late."

I was amazed. The job was sometimes inconvenient to our personal lives but the weekly shop was hardly the end of the world; it wasn't as if it was his son or daughter's school play or sports day. I was even more amazed when the IDO complained and I was summoned to see Len, my SO3 line manager and the Principal Identification Officer (PIDO).

This was shortly after the Devon Tiger Kidnap but there no pleasantries about how well this job had gone, just straight in with,

"The IDO has complained about your aggressive manner last Friday evening. This is not the first such complaint I have received."

'Aggressive was I? Right, I'll give you aggressive,' I thought.

"Len I have a responsibility to SO8. The job is accepted as demanding and on a Friday night at 4.45 pm, I had a problem. You as my line manager were not around because you had fucked off home at 4.30pm and turned your pager off - I didn't know for certain that this was true but this was fairly typical behaviour. I had to make a decision, which I accept is not popular with some of the new IDOs, but I am here to do a job, not be popular. You say that your IDOs are up to the job and committed. In my opinion, your IDOs lack confidence and training and if they were fucking committed, you would not be receiving complaints about me asking them to do a job they've been trained to do. I don't hear any SOCOs complaining when I ring them in similar circumstances. Is there anything else to discuss as I have a meeting with SO19 Officers regarding arrest procedures?"

I was pleased to see he was lost for words and so I left.

The following Wednesday, at 4.15pm, a Building Society robbery took place. Two robbers decamped with cash leaving their demand note behind. My team and I were busy on various operations, so I contacted Central Reserve, requested they contact the PIDO and that he arrange for a local scene examiner to the Sutton area, ZT to attend the scene. The gunship attending had been advised by the Central Reserve that a local scene examiner was being arranged, but I knew they had the experience to take forensic possession of the demand note, just in case the examiner failed to turn up.

At 7pm I checked back in with Central Reserve. The PIDO had got back to them at 5pm stating that a local scene examiner hadn't been sent, as he'd not been able to contact the IDO covering the area. He suggested Central Reserve contact the SO3 night duty at 8pm when they came on duty.

Two days later I visited Len the PIDO in his office.

"The Chief Superintendent SO8 wants to submit a formal complaint via Commander SO8, through Assistant Chief Constable Crime (ACC), to Head of Department SO3 complaining about the availability of local SO3 Scene Examiners and SO3 working hours' policy. I have been asked to request from you the full details of your efforts to task a local examiner last Wednesday, when no officer turned up to examine the scene. They were not impressed Len. The cleaners went into the premises later that evening and could have binned the demand note left at the scene. It could have been on its way to a landfill site by now. Fortunately the Squad guys retained it for fingerprint and hand writing examination."

Len had turned pale and said nothing, so I plunged ahead with my final thrust of the knife.

"My suggestion Len, would be for you to organize a late turn amongst your team up to 6pm Monday to Friday. There used to be a late turn system up to 8pm, so 6pm should be a doddle. I can then tell the Chief Superintendent you are formulating a scheme to cover this difficult time period, otherwise the shit will be hitting the fan and dropping down from the ACC's office onto your desk!"

"OK Larry," Len said weakly. "I see the 'big stick'. I'll look into it."

Throughout my career, the Fingerprint Branch had fought to scupper the work of the SOCOs. I'd had to fight to keep the SOCO role alive and, realizing the best form of defence is attack, I fought to expand the role of the Squad's SOCO into more specialist ops, principally the Anti -Terrorist Squad, and possibly MI5, who were developing new approaches to their counter-terrorist operations.

Squad SOCOs were the most experienced forensic officers in the country and had unparalleled experience in dealing with complex operations involving firearms and explosives. Unfortunately, as was to be expected, the fingerprint dinosaurs in SO3 were against any such progress and wanted any new roles for *their* chosen ones. My one advantage was my experience and related confidence in complex operations and I so I leapt at every opportunity to take on the most challenging missions that came my way, knowing that only this way could I win the war, so I had no hesitation when 9RCS contacted me to ask for my support regarding a long-term covert operation with some of the most mind-boggling exhibits I'd ever seen.

# SUPERMARKET FOR SCOUNDRELS

**M**y dedication meant that I did not see enough of my family but whenever I had a free weekend we made the most of it. We owned a touring caravan and the boys, along with Toby the dog, thoroughly enjoyed a weekend of freedom - as did Jennifer and I. We were heading off to the New Forest at 8am one Saturday, just approaching the M3 when I received a pager message to contact Central Office Reserve urgently. I pulled into a service station. If there was a public telephone then the Yard had a free number I could call. If not, I would show my ID and ask to use their telephone.

It was Geoff, the Squad's Superintendent. "We need you in ASAP. Can't say why over the phone. Will explain when you arrive."

I walked back to the car, looking at the kids, Jennifer and Toby; they were all excited and fooling around, laughing. I hated myself as I explained and watched their faces fall in disappointment.

"Can't someone else do whatever it is?" Jennifer asked, not unreasonably.

"Maybe, but it must be important if they're asking me to come in on a Saturday. I'm so, so sorry. We have to turn around and go home."

We drove back in glum silence and I then raced to the Yard and spent the day in wait for an operation, which did not come to fruition. Because of this I can't tell you the details - if it had then it would have been front page news - which I understand is frustrating but that is nothing compared to the frustration I felt travelling home to my family that evening.

I had little time to reflect, however, as the following week another major operation reared its head and I was off again, supporting over a hundred officers in an extremely complex series of raids, which led me to handle some unique exhibits.

Operation Mensa involved the infiltration of an organized crime syndicate that controlled "supermarkets" for villains. As Commander Roy Penrose, head of the South East Regional Crime Squad, who led the twenty-month undercover operation of the London-based network put it: "Their motto was 'If you want it, we can get it.'" The villains running the scheme, a bunch of loosely interconnected criminal entrepreneurs, were making hundreds of thousands of pounds.

Armed officers were due to take part in the raids, so I was on high alert and waited anxiously in the operations room as, close to midnight, the various assault teams synchronized, confirming they were in position to launch their respective raids in London, the Home Counties,

Dorset, Devon and the Thames Valley. Then: "Go! Go! Go!"

The first hour was pandemonium as suspects were arrested and venues searched. Then requests started to flood in. Drugs found at one location, cash at another, weapons, machinery, unidentified substances and so on. Twenty-seven people had been arrested and were being questioned at several different police stations.

I sent in my SOCOs and they were beavering away when I got a call from the team at Dorset farm. "We've got a walk-in safe and no way of accessing it, any ideas?"

A safe cracker at 1.30am?

"No problem Guv I'll deal with it."

I called the aptly titled Back Hall Inspector at the Yard. The Back Hall Inspector, part of a round-the-clock team, has access to an incredible and unique index of emergency personnel. Thirty minutes later a locksmith was on his way to the venue. An hour after that we were looking at £2million in forged UK and US currency (the counterfeiting and forgery operation would turn out to be one of the biggest ever discovered and produced notes of exceptional quality), over forty guns, including a machine gun and AK47 assault rifles, military explosives, and forging equipment so diverse they could offer everything from driving licenses to disabled parking stickers. In London, the other raids uncovered a Second World War German-made Schmeisser sub-machine gun, shotguns and ammunition, 2kg of PE4 military-style plastic explosive and detonators. It was a remarkable operation and went like clockwork - a great many villains ended up with dozens of years of jail time. Afterwards, Commander Penrose sent a letter of commendation to SO3 highlighting the valued contribution made by my specialized team. Commendations all round? Alas not. While SO3 acknowledged receipt of the letter, they never acted on it.

# PSYCHO PETE

We had a crazed armed robber on our hands. According to witnesses, the man, who had hit a variety of locations over a four month period starting in the autumn of 1992, was black, agitated, intimidating and carried a hand gun or shotgun. He occasionally struck with an accomplice.

The Squad identified him as Peter Rulston aka Psycho Pete, who was, to use the technical term "unlawfully at large," in that he had escaped from prison after being sentenced to seven years at the Old Bailey for a variety of crimes. Rulston had previous convictions for rape, manslaughter, assault, robbery and firearms offences. The most worrying aspect about Rulston was that he always fired his weapon during the robbery - and he was becoming more aggressive each time he struck. It was as if he *wanted* to kill somebody.

Rulston had fired his shotgun at a Herne Hill bank's security screen, and almost shot a customer during a struggle in a bank in Richmond. He also shot a postmistress in the arm with a handgun in St John's Hill, and shot at staff in a Post Office in Wimbledon though no one was injured. In April 1993, Rulston shot his accomplice in the leg during the robbery of a Battersea restaurant. The accomplice gave the impression that he was relieved to have been caught. Rulston was, he said, "a nutter."

After this, Rulston shot at a cashier at the National Westminster Bank in Norwood and a counter worker in yet another post office. Again, another pair of miracles, no one was hurt. The Natwest cashier had been extremely lucky in that her aluminium nameplate had deflected the bullet, saving her life. The bullet had gone through the nameplate, penetrated the security screen - two glass screens with a gap in between, designed to stop robbers smashing their way in - before ending up in a ceiling tile just above her seat. At this scene I found a spent ammunition case on the floor on the public side, a bullet fragment on a desktop behind the Cashier No. 4 position, where the would-be victim had been sitting, and a bullet on the floor between the desks behind the Cashier No. 4 position. So it seemed that two bullets had been fired, although witnesses only recalled hearing one loud bang. I took swabs around the bullet holes for traces of firearms residue and had the screen dismantled for evidential purposes, together with the ceiling tiles that had been hit by the bullet.

That week Rulston went on to commit three more armed robberies and, on the third occasion, came face-to-face with a police Vauxhall Astra car driven by a uniform constable. Rulston had no hesitation in opening fire. My examination revealed that four bullets had hit the Astra. One to the front nearside headlamp, a second had gone through a nearside body panel, the third through the nearside passenger door and the fourth through the rear tailgate. I found a bullet fragment lodged in the rubber covering the top anchor of the driver's seat belt - inches from the officer's head. Another miracle.

Despite a huge manhunt, Rulston continued to elude police and the Squad. He was finally arrested in June 1993 when officers ambushed him in the street after a tip-off and he was taken without a shoot-out. The forensic evidence from the discharged firearms linked him to the various scenes as the guns were recovered in his possession. So his crime spree came to an end and this time he was given a decades-long sentence and sent to a top-security prison. We could only be thankful for the miracle that no one had been killed but, sadly, many innocent people received life-changing psychological wounds. The Natwest cashier may have been 'lucky' physically but, psychologically speaking, she was traumatized to the extent that she couldn't speak immediately after the raid, and was still having nightmares at the time of the trial. Too often we express relief with the words "at least no one was hurt," but we forget the mental wounds criminals can cause, wounds that sometimes never heal.

# AN EVERYDAY ADVENTURE

To say my role was demanding was putting it mildly. The crime boom had continued and, with more and more weapons being recovered, I was working ninety-hour weeks. The Squad expected it and, from Commander to newly-recruited Detective Constable, we not only accepted this attitude, we encouraged it. This wasn't a job, it was a way of life and there wasn't a single day when I felt frustrated about having to go to work. Every day was an adventure.

Throughout the summer of 1992 it was business as usual with multiple robbery scenes each and every day, along with several long-running pro-active operations. I also continued to work on the Forensic Evidence Preservation Suit (FEPS) but one evening at 5pm I was interrupted by a phone call from George, the fingerprint officer from the Regional Crime Squad. "There's a big job on tomorrow and I'll need your support."

"No problem, what's the operation?"

"Really sorry Larry, but I've been instructed not to tell you anything else."

I told George not to worry and said I'd be ready. The bigger the op the bigger the chance of a leak, so I always accepted the need-to-know rule. Nonetheless, I decided to check with the Squad's Chief Super. He said he knew nothing about it. "It's not one of ours," he told me, "Otherwise I'd know."

Fortunately, I heard some RCS guys had arrived at the Squad's offices to set up the Operations Room for tomorrow's mission, so stuck my nose in, recognized a couple of faces and, after a quick catch-up, they brought me up to speed. They could barely contain their excitement.

"This is the Big One, Larry," one of the officers said. "Tomorrow, we're hitting a 300-tonne ship that's been used to smuggle drugs into London. It's moored on the Thames, which is where we'll hit it, along with a nearby warehouse where the drugs are being taken to be slaughtered - divided and then sent on for sale elsewhere. We're talking a ton of drugs, worth £200million, with multiple villains across the world involved."

My heart was already racing with excitement when he added: "It's a Customs-led op, so we're just there to help out, but we're also being supported by SO19 and the Special Boat Service."

"SBS, seriously?"

"As I said, it doesn't get much bigger than this."

George really should have told me. I needed to start preparing right now. Questions raced through my mind, the first one being: "Suppose it goes wrong and there's a shoot-out?" The SBS and SO19 would have dozens of firearms between them; a shoot-out could lead to thousands of exhibits. I telephoned the Forensic Laboratory's Ballistics Department and asked them how many Firearms Residue

Kits I could have at short notice. Twenty, was the reply. Well, that would have to do.

My next question was: "If there's a shoot-out, suppose someone is killed?" If so, a specific routine had to be followed. All armed officers would be removed from the scene to another location, not necessarily a police station. They would then write up their contemporaneous notes and surrender all their weapons and ammunition regardless of whether they'd been fired or not. All would become exhibits in the subsequent investigations, carried out by the Independent Police Complaints Commission (IPCC), the military and Customs & Excise.

I'd been at so many shootings since joining the Squad that I'd written guidelines that refined these procedures so they included the taking of firearms residue swabs from all of the officers, even if they hadn't fired their weapon. Another refinement was to give the ballistics guys at the forensic laboratory a heads-up immediately after the incident, so they knew how many firearms to expect, this way speeding up the process, so weapons would be quickly returned to the relevant teams. All of these weapons would have to be securely transported, a job handled by the Special Escort Group (SEG) based at Vauxhall, so I'd need to make sure they were ready as well.

I gave my own SOCO team a simple heads-up, telling them that a high profile drugs raid was on the cards. I ordered them to stay in their office by their phones until they heard otherwise, and to delegate all of tomorrow's scene examinations to the local SO3 officers.

The job was called Operation Emerge and it began with a tip-off from American drug enforcement officers to Scotland Yard six months earlier. It was a huge surveillance operation, with support from the Royal Navy destroyer HMS Cardiff, American Coast Guard vessels, and both the RAF and US air force. They followed the suspect ship, an oil rig support vessel, Fox Trot V, for months as it picked up nearly a tonne of cocaine, dropped into the ocean off Venezuela's coast from light aircraft piloted by the minions of some South American cocaine barons. The vessel was also kept under surveillance by a Royal Navy submarine, supported by an RAF Nimrod surveillance plane, and together they shadowed it on its three-week journey, until it reached British coastal waters and entered the Thames Estuary, eventually mooring near Greenwich in southeast London at 7am on the day before we would strike.

This was the first combined SBS/SO19/RCS operation and the Operations Room at the Yard was already buzzing when I checked in. It was also the first time Britain's special forces had taken part in a high-profile operation in the UK since the SAS stormed the Iranian embassy on May 5, 1980.

My mind was buzzing with the logistics of the op. I had to consider the crew's arrest and where they would be taken. To avoid allegations of forensic contamination, each arrested person would be taken to a separate police station. Then the 300-tonne ship would have to be examined. In addition to drugs evidence, we'd need to examine the bridge and get hold of the Captain's log. Everything would need fingerprinting; never would so much fingerprint powder be used by so few to convict so many.

The vessel was moored up on the south side of the Thames, within sight of the Thames Barrier. The drugs were taken by van to a warehouse in Hope and Anchor Wharf, Deptford, three miles to the west, just south of the Isle of Dogs. SO19 teams were already in place at the warehouse, ready to strike.

Jacqui was on standby at Tower Bridge office and George was with the RCS guys, ready to board the ship once it was under control. The SO19, Customs, SBS and RCS guys all had radios on different frequencies and the sound of chattering provided a constant and excitable background noise. I listened intently with the senior officers, ready to respond with instructions to my team once the hit was over, praying that it would go peacefully.

The atmosphere grew tense. One of the Superintendents, shirtsleeves rolled up, had a twelve-inch wide band of sweat running down his back.

Finally, when everyone was in position, the command was given: "Go! Go! Go!"

The SBS and SO19 officers, their faces blackened to avoid future identification, made their assault crossing the Thames in their inflatable boats and swarmed over the vessel's side using special ladders, Heckler & Koch MP5 submachine guns slung over their backs. At the same time an armoured JCB battered down the doors of the warehouse, followed by armed police and Customs officers. The SBS quickly secured the bridge and SO19 searched the rest of the ship - which turned out to be empty - no sign of crew or drugs.

I ordered Jacqui to go and help George, whom I'd tasked with supervising the extraction of all exhibits from the boat. I would deal with the warehouse. When I rolled up the press were already outside. They'd either been tipped off or, thanks to their scanners, had overheard uniformed police on their unencrypted radios being ordered to the scene.

Six people had been arrested at the warehouse, five Brits and one Spaniard. No shots fired, no injuries. Hundreds of kilos of cocaine were inside. A great result for SO19 and co; now it was down to the forensic team to make sure all the evidence counted. I ordered in officers from the Fingerprint Branch and they immediately set about carrying out an examination of the premises and preserving the drugs for more detailed fingerprint and forensic examination.

I agreed to display an exhibit from the haul for the inevitable press conference, but not before examining the entrance to the warehouse for fingerprints and any other forensic material. This was expected to be the largest ever drugs haul in the UK, so press interest was frenzied. A photograph of me cradling a block of packaged cocaine ended up in all the nationals.

That done, I turned my attention to a white Rover Montego which was parked close to the warehouse and belonged to one of the prisoners. I examined the outside for fingerprints, and then had it craned onto a low loader and removed to Lewisham Police station for more detailed examination.

For integrity, even though the vehicle was locked, I sealed the doors, engine compartment and boot with my signature seals, (labels signed over with my signature), and taped over the opening edges of all compartments. When I recommenced my examination my first step would be to note that the seals were still intact. Defence barristers love to check the integrity of exhibits, so this kind of thinking was essential.

We ended up with one thousand exhibits, another record (for me, at least). The crew of Foxtrot V denied any knowledge of cocaine being on board. Red fluorescent paint had been sprayed over the rubber packaging of the drugs so they would be visible in the sea, and so all of the prisoners' shoes were sent to the Forensic Science Laboratory for comparison with samples of the fluorescent paint taken from the drugs packages.

Over the coming weeks and months I made many trips down to Tilbury docks, where the vessel had been taken. There I examined the various tenders and inflatable craft on the ship for traces of the red fluorescent paint. I was still carrying out my examinations five months after the day of the hit and had a total of sixteen officers supporting me. Fingerprints taken from the vessel Foxtrot V identified all of the crew, despite some crewmembers denying they had ever been on board the vessel, and others were linked to the warehouse. I submitted a report to the SO3 Fingerprint Branch acknowledging and commending the SO3 officers for their professionalism and diligence.

Jacqui and I submitted over fifty exhibits to the Forensic Laboratory, in addition to the seized drugs, to prove the offence of importation of drugs into the United Kingdom. The cocaine, weighing 795kilograms, worth £200million at 1992 prices, was destroyed under the supervision of the Government Chemist and Customs and Excise, at a secret location, somewhere in the Home Counties.

Unfortunately for us, the people arrested that day were acquitted after a long and expensive trial that started in December 1993. Proving they had been 'knowingly concerned in the importation of the drugs,' had been too difficult as no forensic evidence physically linked the men to the drugs, so they could conceivably have been unaware that drugs were on board. Whatever the case, it was clear to us that these men were small fry, and the main players had stayed away from the drugs once they were in the UK.

The investigation didn't stop there of course. George Sansom, 42, the cousin of ex-England football star Kenny Sansom, and Coleman Mulkerrins, 53, were arrested and charged with drugs importation a few months later. Sansom, it was argued, was in charge of marketing the drug in Britain while Mulkerrins was the "money man" who financed the operation. There was evidence of others involved at an even higher level but Mulkerrins and Sansom were definitely near the top. Mulkerrins had been involved in both the purchase of the boat and had travelled to New Orleans to supervise its fitting out for the purpose of smuggling. He'd also been involved in changing huge sums of money at a foreign exchange shop, £1.2m into Swiss Francs, to buy drugs. Sansom was proven to have been involved in the planned distribution of the drugs in the UK.

The first trial failed after the jury, given round-the-clock police protection, was discharged after complaints of "unwarranted attention". The second trial was successful and both men were convicted of being knowingly concerned in the illegal importation of cocaine. They both received 30-year sentences, the longest in UK history for this offence, which was fitting, considering the record haul.

Some months after Operation Emerge, I came face-to-face with Met Commissioner, Sir Robert Mark, in a lift at New Scotland Yard.

"Good morning Sir," I said.

"Have we met before?" he asked, "Your face looks familiar."

"I don't think so sir. Perhaps in another lift? I visit various departments in the Yard quite often."

Sir Robert wasn't satisfied with my reply and left the lift on the fifth floor, where his office was located. As he walked away, I noticed he was carrying the Met Police's Annual Report and my picture, the one from the newspapers where I was holding the drugs, was slapped across the front cover.

# BULLET TO THE HEAD

After big operations like Emerge, we would have one of our team lunches at an Italian in north London, or at a Spanish tapas restaurant in Vauxhall, reminiscent of the local watering hole in the BBC TV Series *Ashes to Ashes*. When I saw the first episode of *Ashes to Ashes*, I thought it was a drama documentary. Along with *Life on Mars*, *Ashes to Ashes* captured the era so well; the characters were just like the people I'd worked alongside. Over the years I'd come to understand and respect my police colleagues (I was more 'police' than 'scientist') and enjoyed good relationships with everyone from the Commander to the foot soldiers. I never swore outside of work but when I was with the lads, I spoke their language, which included the necessary use of expletives, which helped me to help them appreciate the nature of forensics or exhibit integrity.

I was still trying to prevent the break-up of the SOCO Team and expand our role into counter-terrorism work, although now we had two Fingerprint Officers in our team of six. Pete the Fingerprint Officer based at the Barnes SW London office was a team player and able to ask for advice if he wasn't sure of the correct procedure.

I held a unique place for a civilian in that I attended the senior SO8 monthly management meeting, during which covert projects were discussed. As a result I was invited, along with the senior officers, to attend a dinner hosted by Police Commissioner Sir Paul Condon. Sir Paul would be third Commissioner I'd met out of the five that had served since 1971 - the other two were Sir Robert Mark who I met in the Yard lift and Sir Keith Newman, with whom I'd had my photograph taken at a Wandsworth Police Station Open day. I'd also meet Sir Paul again, when he presented me with my twenty-year Good Conduct Certificate - police officers got medals but us civvies were only entitled to a high-quality piece of paper.

After a pleasant evening's feast, speeches were made, which included anecdotes from Assistant Commissioners to yours truly. I ended my speech with piece about the importance of specialist SOCOs supporting specialist squads. This was met with much banging on the table and "Here, here!" I hoped Sir Paul had got my message and it seemed as though he had because I was subsequently invited to a Brains Trust meeting held at the Yard to discuss ways forward for the police. It included all of the heads of the crime fighting departments, Customs, Provincial Forces and MI5, as well as some covert departments. One of the longest debates we had featured the escalation of gun crime, and the availability of guns on the streets - and with good reason.

I was still working on the Forensic Evidence Preservation Suit (FEPS) and had gained the interest of the

Counter-Terrorism section, as they knew only too well that loss of firearms or explosive residue from someone who has handled explosives, or fired a gun, is microscopic in size and quickly falls from skin and clothing. If the suit could minimize this problem following arrest then more convictions were likely, as more evidence would be preserved.

I was eventually granted a patent and the suit was manufactured by a specialist fabrics company in Derby . They liked it so much that tried to break my patent so they could make the suit without me but the person I'd hired to put my patent together had, thank goodness, made it watertight. I also established a new arrest procedure whereby a non-firearms officer would handle and search a suspect before placing them inside the suit while an armed officer(s) controlled the suspect from a short distance. Once in the suit, the suspect would be transported to a police station using a car not associated with armed officers. The suit would then be removed after the suspect had arrived at a police station before being closed and preserved for examination.

The Flying Squad was a powerful outfit and my role as their senior Scenes of Crime Officer gave me an influential voice when talking to other agencies or police forces. To this end, I'd managed to convince the Association of Chief Police Officers (ACPO) that use of the Preservation Suit should be adopted by police forces across the UK, not just the Met.

Soon, I heard that the suit was to be used on the next anti-terrorist covert operation involving MI5 and the

Anti-Terrorist Squad. I awaited is first operational use with nervous excitement. I was also excited as word about the effectiveness of the SOCO was spreading; perhaps I would be able to realize my ambition of a team of dedicated SOCOs that would be active with the Anti-Terrorist Squad, MI5 and beyond.

This was an even busier time than usual as Jacqui went on leave, and I covered her patch. I joined the lads from Tower Bridge on an ambush operation to arrest a couple of persistent armed robbers in southeast London. I was at the briefing for 6am and covered the usual procedures to deal with firearms residue and taking of non-intimate samples - this was shortly before the preservation suit got the go-ahead for its first - and taking non-intimate sampling trial.

Five of us were positioned in an empty first floor flat overlooking Barclays Bank in Blackfen Road, Sidcup, one of three surveillance points. We were lying down on the floor of the lounge, six feet back from the window so the robbers wouldn't be spooked by be-suited men moving around in what was supposed to be an empty property.

A few minutes later, the shout went up. The two criminals had carried out an armed robbery – but not on the bank - on a nearby Security Express custodian, and had escaped before the Squad could stop them with £17,000 contained in a security box. They were fleeing the scene in a red Vauxhall Astra pursued by a Squad gunship, a Vauxhall Senator (top speed 165mph) with four Squad guys on board including Jumbo, an eighteen-stone observer and radio operative in the front passenger seat.

The five of us legged it out of the flat, leapt into two cars and joined the chase.

During the pursuit, one of the robbers leaned out of the front passenger door window and, using a machine gun, rattled off a volley of bullets at the pursuing detectives. Six bullets hit the Senator. One went through the windscreen, whizzed past Jumbo's ear and struck Mickey, a Detective Sergeant, in the head. The driver fought to control the car, which screamed to a halt with a burst tyre and steam jetting from the bonnet.

We shot past at 60mph, still in hot pursuit, as Mickey was being laid on the kerbside.

The robbers were too far ahead and we lost them; we spent the next ten minutes driving at high speed around various council estates. None of the officers in our car were armed. These robbers were armed and had nothing to lose; they'd already shot up a car full of detectives. If we did find them, then what were we going to do?

I was in the back seat and leaned forward to speak to John. "Drop me at the scene, I need to start gathering evidence. Our job's going to get a lot harder, the longer we wait to recover those bullets."

John duly dropped me off back at Blackfen Road, as near as he could to the scene. Chaos reigned. The roads were jammed with traffic; the pavements were full of residents who wanted to see what was going on. The crime scene was spread out over several miles; there was the bank and then the scene of the shooting, with vehicles hit by bullets and an injured police officer, possibly dying, and an on-going pursuit. Where to start?

Co-ordination was the key. Plus I needed to know the moment the robbers were (hopefully) caught. I had a police radio and heard that the robbers had dumped their Astra and had hijacked a green Ford Capri, forcing the woman driver out of the car at gunpoint. Further shots had been fired at uniform police officers who'd interrupted the hijacking, and then the robbers had escaped with the woman into a house. So now we had a siege situation on top of everything else. I called the Reserve Officer at Central Office so they could make sure my SOCO and fingerprint officers were on their way to the local nick where they would await instructions.

My thoughts turned to Mickey, the shot officer. I didn't know it then but this was the first time that a machine gun had been used in mainland Britain against the police. If he dies, I wondered, whom do I select to attend the post mortem? Should it be me? But there was so much to do here and I wanted to make sure it was done right. It seems a strange thing to say, Mickey was a colleague, but I didn't have time to worry, this was the nature of The Job. I also had to brief the local Chief Superintendent when he rolled up a minute later and I requested he send me ten uniform officers to assist in the search of the road to recover shell cases and bullets. That done, my thoughts again returned to Mickey, which were soon interrupted by a call that came to me via the Super's radio. It was Detective Sergeant Ron Stocks, a Laboratory Liaison Officer.

"Looks like you've got your hands full. Just wanted to let you know that if the Squad guy dies I'll do the post mortem for you."

I'm forever grateful to Ron for that offer. I thanked him, adding, "I don't have up to date info on his condition, so can I leave that to you?" Ron said he would take care of it and that left me to concentrate on the scene.

A Traffic Division car pulled up next to me. They had an onboard video and offered to record the scene for me. I said I'd give them the nod to do so once we'd recovered shells and bullets from the road. I then turned my attention to the Vauxhall Senator. It was an unmarked car used on many covert operations, so I covered the number plates with brown paper sacks, so no villain would recognize it. Professional robbers frequently employed spotters to observe and record cars leaving various police stations and locations the Squad was known to use. The night before a blag these spotters would go around the streets looking for surveillance cars. We changed the plates regularly, and they were blocked on the DVLA computer but I couldn't take any chances and made sure the Senator's were covered as soon as possible.

Then I called Central Office on the radio. I arranged for the vehicle to be lifted and removed to a convenient police station to await examination. At that moment, Geoff, the Squad's Super, announced that the two robbers had surrendered and their kidnap victim was unharmed. Officers had also recovered the machine gun along with two Magnum revolvers. The robbers were taken to separate police stations. I tasked Ashley and John, the SOCO from Rigg Approach, to examine them for firearms residue, head hair samples, and to take their clothing and weapons.

Then the tow truck arrived and, once the Senator was on board, I searched the ground underneath for bullet fragments. All clear, I started working the route. The Great British Public joined the great bullet hunt and called me over whenever they'd found bullets and/or shell cases, either in the road, pavement or in their front gardens.

After some additional help from uniform officers who knew how to handle evidence, I was satisfied we had recovered most, if not all of the shells and some of the discharged bullets. I placed the shell cases in polythene exhibit bags, which I spread over a section of pavement with a uniform officer posted to keep an eye on them. I then examined the cars parked in the road, looking for bullet holes and ricochet marks.

A BBC London News reporter, Duncan Kennedy, had turned up. He caught my eye and asked me for information.

"Sorry mate," I told him, "We have a Press Officer for that and I have no doubt they will be here soon."

But, at the same time I looked the reporter in the eye and gestured with my head as I walked off to the left. He was quick to understand and beckoned to his cameraman. They followed me around the corner to the array of plastic exhibit bags spread over the pavement containing dozens of shell cases. He nodded a thank you.

Six hours later I finally gave the traffic guys permission to drive the route of the scene with instructions to exhibit and drop off the video with a statement to the Squad Exhibits Officer who was operating from Lewisham Police station. A debrief took place an hour later, where

I said my piece before logging all the exhibits from the scene into the police system.

It was then we got a call from Squad officers at the hospital. Mickey was going to make it! He'd been so lucky, the bullet had 'creased' his temple, leaving a terrific dent but it hadn't penetrated it.

Mickey wasn't the only lucky one that day. My examination of the Senator revealed that one of the bullets had been heading for Jumbo's chest but had been deflected by the near side windscreen washer nozzle. It had nevertheless only just missed Jumbo's head by a few millimetres. For such a large target, he seemed to be hard to hit.

When I joined the Squad detectives at the local pub that night, I told Jumbo he'd had not one, but two lucky misses that day. He shrugged.

"Life goes on, Larry. Do you want another drink?"

Over twenty shell cases were eventually recovered. My detailed examination of the Vauxhall Senator revealed the radiator had been penetrated three times, the windscreen once and the tyre once. Six bullets. I also recovered the bullet that had hit Mickey from the rear passenger footwell.

The two robbers, both ex-squaddies, received decades-long prison sentences. Four of the guys from the operation received the Queen's Gallantry Medal, including Mickey and Jumbo. The guys at Tower Bridge Squad office held a lunch for Mickey on his eventual return, and wore sticking plasters in the shape of an 'X' on their temple.

# A LIFE-CHANGING MOMENT

B y 1993 I was working on a number of groundbreaking projects. I formulated a new forensic approach to deal with Tiger Kidnappings, which were on the rise in the 1980s and 1990s as bank and cash transit security improved. This method is still in use today so I can't tell you what it involves - remember what Mrs. T said.

The team's fingerprint identification successes had increased significantly during my stewardship. Forensic results, always excellent, had improved and Senior Police Officers from various departments frequently acknowledged our expertise and teamwork. So I could hardly believe it when a report landed on my desk from the Senior Identification Officer, (SIDO) who was in charge of the Fingerprint Checking Team handling our fingerprint exhibits.

The report lambasted all members of the SOCO team, especially me but not the fingerprint guys. It accused us of systematic malpractice in scene examination and the destruction of official documents. Wow! That got my attention.

"Guvnor, fucking read that," I said, putting the file on the Chief Superintendent's desk. "The bastards at

SO3 have started their assault to get the SOCOs off the Squad."

I immediately instigated a grievance procedure under Civil Service rules. Unfortunately it was not a police matter otherwise I would have had the accusers' bollocks within twenty-four hours. I had to wait months until a meeting was held between senior Fingerprint Officers, the Head of Department, SO3, also a Fingerprint Officer, myself, together with a Union representative who was a senior SOCO and the SIDO who wrote the report.

During the discussions, the SIDO insulted me - in front of the senior officers. They told him to calm down after he was unable to verify his allegations. At that point I should have walked out of the meeting and instigated a second grievance procedure and buried him. I was persuaded to stay, however and once the meeting was over, the Head of Department offered me anything I wanted. He didn't want the grievance escalated, telling me: "Let's just keep our dirty washing in house."

It was not my, nor my SOCO team's intention to have the SO3 branch brought into disrepute, but we weren't happy with the unfounded and malicious allegations. The department accepted that the report had no foundation and it was agreed that the following would be placed on the record:

*"Having examined all the papers received from the SO8 Scenes of Crime Officers in relation to the suggested destruction of official documents... Under a grievance procedure I can find no evidence of any form of systematic malpractice in relation to the suggested destruction of official documents...*

*I have every confidence in the honesty and integrity of these officers in support of the police service."*

Sadly, the accusing fingerprint officer was not even reprimanded for his malicious report. The Fingerprint Branch was by this time already schmoozing the Squad's senior management with promises of closer liaison between the two departments if a Fingerprint Officer was put in charge of the forensic team and this, they argued would supposedly increase the number of fingerprint identifications, (our identification statistics were already at an all-time high). This was also around the time that DNA was starting to be used, with brilliant results that suggested DNA had the potential to surpass fingerprint identification as the main evidence at a crime scene. By the time I learned what was afoot, it was already too late for me to do anything. SOCOs had either turned themselves over to the IDO scheme, or had joined other Police forces and, by 1993, only a handful of SOCOs remained in the Met, including the three Squad SOCOs and myself.

Six months later, despite being the longest-serving member of the Squad's Forensic Team, I was informed by SO3 that I would be transferred back to the normal duties of district scene examination. I decided it was time to sound out possible moves that SO3 could not stop if the police supported me. One option was to apply to MI5 as a training officer to their field agents, with particular regard to the presentation of exhibits to the Criminal Justice System.

And then came the life-changing incident that one cannot prepare for. The Accident.

I tripped and tumbled down a flight of stairs, bouncing on my back. It left me with several ruptured discs and unable to walk for any distance due to the pain. The consultant surgeon gave me two options: "Either have the operation on your ruptured discs, and risk a thirty per cent chance of being incontinent, or take the pain." He paused and then added. "Pain never killed anyone."

I was left with a stark choice, possibly destroy my life by becoming incontinent or destroy my life by not doing the job I loved. I was not enthusiastic about district work and as I was now medically signed off I couldn't see any of my contacts regarding a possible "counter-transfer" proposal. You had to do these things face-to-face.

My disappointment was compounded when I received a telephone call at home from the Anti-Terrorist branch. They were about to use my preservation suit on an operation with MI5 the next day. Would I join them to provide support? Just what I had been waiting for, but I was certified as being on sick leave and couldn't just jump up and sign myself off. At the time I could neither sit nor stand in one position for more than five minutes, so sitting in a car up to eight hours would have been impossible. I had to decline the invitation, a heartbreaking moment for me, especially as they decided not to use the suit without me and subsequently, without my presence, the FEPS was never introduced.

Finally, I had to accept the truth of the situation: I simply could not work any longer. The surgeon supported my retirement and, with great sadness, I handed in my notice, aged just 49.

At my retirement bash I was presented with a green Squad jacket, reminiscent of the style presented to the winner of the US Golf Master tournament, a copy of the book *The Flying Squad: A Dramatic Account Charting the First 75 Years of the Real Life Sweeney* by Neil Darbyshire, signed by all my senior Squad colleagues, and an inscribed glass goblet featuring an etching of the swooping Eagle of the Flying Squad. The lads at Tower Bridge lads presented me with an inscribed fountain pen. By the time I finished attending the last of the drinks parties at all the Squads' locals (including Rigg Approach, Barnes and Finchley) I was already in the early stages of depression, a condition that lasted for most of the three years it took me to get back on my feet.

Some time after my retirement, the Squad decided to abandon the use of specialist scene examiners - John, my fellow SOCO at Rigg Approach, moved on to Surrey Police, while Jacqui was transferred to the Detective Training School as an Instructor.

But our legacy remains.

Originally, the senior SOCO Specialist Operations post was mainly administrative but I'd decided to lead by example by supporting my team in the field. Simon, Paul, John, Judy, Jacqui, Ashley and Yvonne were always there for me in return and worked at levels above and beyond the call of duty. When I wanted to introduce improvements, they stood behind me 100% and for this I'm forever grateful. We worked as a team to produce best practice in terms of examination of suspects, scenes, and motor vehicles. I'm also grateful for the support of the Squad's senior management, along with the Regional Crime Squads who also supported the creation of guidelines on the presentation of exhibits to the Criminal Justice system, a huge step forward in the uniformity of evidence gathering, packaging, and continuity and presentation of exhibits to the courts, preventing wily defence barristers from finding tricky ways to help their clients evade justice.

Alas, once a Fingerprint Branch officer was put in charge of the last bastion of SOCOs, the Flying Squad (immediately after my retirement), it was over for the SOCO.

However, time did tell. Today, the SOCO has returned as hundreds of scene examiners have since been recruited who are trained in the basics of scene examination, photography and interpretation and, over time, they attend various advanced courses in both forensic and fingerprint techniques. Each London borough now has a shift system of examiners available to attend crime scenes twenty-four hours a day.

The SOCO scheme was introduced in 1968, and in 1971 when I walked into the Detective Training School in Victoria, London I was a quiet, newly-married young research chemist with a mild north east accent. The accent is gone and that quiet young man has changed beyond all recognition, but I'm delighted to say that, almost 45 years later, Jennifer and I are as happy as ever.

The job changed me, as it does all who make it a career. I have witnessed many horrific scenes that I have had to work up close and personal to. I have spent too much time among the dead: grandparents, parents and newborns. I have seen children who died accidentally at school and people shot in gang wars; I have seen friends and colleagues shot; all kinds of suicides, and have seen the horror of premeditated evil. I have, as a consequence, drunk copious amounts of alcohol and have sworn like my fellow troopers in the never-ending battle against crime and tragedy (although I never swore at home or in the presence of my wife and children).

I learned to fight my corner; in the early days I faced animosity from older police officers suspicious of civilian scientists being allowed to do police work and, in the latter days, I faced political aggression from the Fingerprint Branch who were still unable to accept SOCOs 25 years after their creation.

As a civilian in the police, I learned to think, act and speak like a policeman, but I was not a policeman. As such, I never challenged them but made 'suggestions' when I had a 'better' way of doing things with regard to a crime scene. Over time, my opinion became acknowledged and then respected. By the time I arrived at the Flying Squad, I was able to sit at the senior managers' table and have the confidence (backed up by the authority) to say, still quietly, "Do it this way". By this time I'd learned to make quick, positive and logical decisions, thanks to the many fast-moving, high-pressure operations that had required my direction.

In the 70s I worked five days a week and every other weekend. In the 80s I worked five days a week and every third or fourth weekend. In the 90s I had weekends off but could work in excess of ninety hours a week. Therefore, I was not around much as my two sons, Richard and Robin grew up. When I was there - thanks to the tragedies I'd dealt with that involved children - I was an over-protective father and saw danger in every step.

My early retirement provided me with much more than a silver lining, as I got to spend much more time with my two sons, who were by this time teenagers, and I supported them in their studies of music and law. Today, they run their own music academy.

I have developed some curious hang-ups. I can't cope with my hands being dirty or sticky and wash them frequently throughout the day - I'll even use bottled water if no sinks are close by. I'm impatient but that may be because my brain has been trained to work quickly, an asset at major scenes and rolling pro-active operations, but an unfortunate irritation for others in everyday life. I also have to steer clear of graphic crime TV shows, as these can trigger vigorous nightmare-type experiences which make me unpopular with Jennifer. The nightmares are not flashbacks from scenes I've examined; instead I find myself cornered by images from the TV programme. I sometimes wonder if I have a form of PTSD, in that I spent so many years on high alert that my brain still sometimes switches back into that mode even when there's no reason.

The world of crime has changed almost beyond recognition, as criminals now prefer cyber-crime to putting their actual necks on the line with a bank robbery.

So too has the world of forensic science. Fingerprint comparison, once the principal method of criminal identification has been surpassed by DNA analysis, first used by the UK police in 1988. At the time, because it was a complex, experimental and expensive process, it was rarely used but, by the mid-1990s it had become a staple of police investigations , although it's still subject to problems such as cross-contamination, and even though villains wear gloves and wipe surfaces, they still usually leave hair, or a spec of blood, saliva or sweat at a scene, and we're not far from being able to tell the probable height of the person, as well as the colour of their hair and eyes from DNA samples.

Fingerprints are still used, of course, and with the advent of automated fingerprint recognition, the laborious task of comparing hundreds of sets of prints with a partial mark from a crime scene is today performed by computers. There are even lasers and special reagents that can be used to find prints that have been wiped away, as well as equipment (currently in development) that can analyze a finger mark at a scene to identify traces of explosives, drugs and other materials.

With all this technology I wonder how many rapists, murderers, armed robbers and terrorists I would be able to identify today. How I would love to attend court to give all this evidence!

Today, the Flying Squad still exists, although in much reduced form from the hundred-plus officers and five SOCO's back in the early nineties, when bank robberies hit an all-time high. But every now and again I see a major news item featuring the Flying Squad, from jewellery heists to cash depot robberies, which stirs memories of that uncompromising, feared, respected and brave unit, and I think that the *Hill Street Blues* catchphrase: "Be careful out there!" should be applied to the criminals.

# EPILOGUE: A STING IN THE TALE

olphin Square, a stone's throw from the Thames and a short distance south of the Houses of Parliament, is a block of 1250 luxury private apartments, with many amenities, including restaurant, swimming pool and gym. Built between 1935 and 1937, the development was once home to more than seventy MPs and ten Lords. My first visit took place in 1972 when Harold Wilson, then Leader of the Opposition (Labour) after losing the 1970 election to Edward Heath, called to report a burglary. His door had a five-lever mortise lock on his front door and a quality rim lock, yet there were no signs of forced entry. It's possible to pop a rim lock (Yale-type lock) using a credit card but this technique would never work on a mortise. To gain entry, a burglar has two choices: jemmy the door open or use a set of 'twirlers,' (lock picks). Twirlers were quite bulky in the 1970s, and required luck as well as skill.

Normally burglars would empty drawers on the floor or on a bed in their haste to find saleable items but Mr Wilson's apartment looked immaculate. He said he'd noticed that he'd had an intruder because he always, without exception, closed his desk drawer until he felt it touch the frame. When he went to open it this time however, he immediately noticed that the drawer was a couple of millimetres from the frame.

Was anything missing?

"No!"

Could he have simply not closed it properly?

"No chance!"

I examined the door for finger marks and the door locks for striation marks, performing various forensic tests and repeated the process for the drawer and desk. Nothing. Mr Wilson's allegation had therefore to be recorded thus: "Insufficient evidence to establish a crime had been committed."

In 1972, I was still an inexperienced Scenes of Crime Officer and each day was a huge learning curve for me. One evening, not long after my visit to Harold Wilson's apartment, I found myself in the United Services Club in Piccadilly. There were four of us from Gerald Road CID (Andy, John, Dick, and Graham) and we'd started at 2pm at the Duke of Boots followed by the Star and the Grenadier. John, a temporary detective constable, was ex-military so I assume that's how we ended up this particular establishment and why we felt confident enough to have a go on their snooker table.

Two men were already playing. One was a man in his early sixties, just below average height, dapperly dressed with moustache and greased-back hair. According to John, his tie revealed him to be an ex-paratrooper. His partner was a young man in his twenties wearing a M&S suit who

I could see was like myself, new to whatever game he was in and I'm not talking about snooker.

We exchanged pleasantries and Andy placed a fiver on the snooker table as a challenge, which was readily accepted. There were no introductions, no names exchanged and I started to feel more and more curious about these two men. I noticed that the young man had a small but distinctive mole on the left side of his neck.

Andy and John lost the game, so we bade the men farewell and were given a lift back to the Duke of Boots for last orders by the guys driving the Q Car, who were at the end of their shift.

I forgot all about this encounter until, almost 22 years later, in February 1993, the Commander of the Flying Squad called me into his Office.

"Ah Larry, don't sit down, as I've an assignment for you. Follow me, please."

As we walked he chatted away, mainly about how my SOCO team were doing, showing genuine interest. After a couple of minutes of walking I suddenly realized I was in a part of the Yard I'd never seen before and by this time I'd been anywhere of interest in that building, or so I'd thought.

The Commander knocked on an office door and we walked in.

The office was unremarkable, quite big and with no windows. A large portrait of HRH The Queen was hanging on a wall adjacent to a large mahogany desk, behind which sat a man in his early fifties, wearing a dark pin-striped suit - definitely Saville Row, I thought - and sparklingly clean black leather shoes.

"This is Larry, our senior Scenes of Crime Officer," the Commander said. "He's worked with all the major Squads."

"Thanks for coming Larry," the main said in an Etonian accent. "Are you available this afternoon to visit a premises with one of my colleagues?"

"Yes, no problem."

"Good, could you meet one of my colleagues at 5pm in the basement garage? He'll be at bay 142 and will introduce himself."

We shook hands and as we made ready to leave, the man added, as if in afterthought, "Oh, and you'll need your equipment."

"Of course."

Once we were back in the corridor I had to ask. "That was a bit cloak and dagger Guv. Do you know what it's about?"

"No Larry, I don't. It's need-to-know and you and I clearly don't need to know."

Sure enough, at 5pm in Bay 142, I found a man in his forties, dressed in a dark suit, pale blue shirt and tie, a black raincoat, and black leather shoes. Behind him was a grey Ford Sierra.

He greeted me as I approached.

"Larry?"

"Yes, that's right."

We shook hands but there were no introductions.

"Can I ask what sort of equipment this job requires?" I asked.

"Your usual forensic equipment and fingerprint knowledge, nothing else."

My car was in the next row, so I grabbed my gear and off we went. As we drove up the ramp, I thought this was the kind of job that the Official Secrets Act was written for.

We arrived at a large terraced house in St John's Wood. We'd come a curious route and, as it was dark, I couldn't tell you the address except that the door my guide and driver was knocking on was No. 30.

The door opened.

"This is Larry".

"OK, will give you a shout later".

My driver left and the man in the house said. "We need a forensic examination carried out to find any hairs, fibres, foreign material, or other exhibits you can find."

This officer was a couple of years older than me, approaching fifty. Another Saville Row suit and then I noticed a distinctive mole on the left side of his neck.

"Have we met before?" I asked.

"I can't recall any meeting between us Larry," the man said with a smile.

Fair enough, I thought, remembering exactly when and where we'd met, all those years ago.

"So what's the scenario?"

"There isn't one, just examine each room to see if there's any physical trace evidence; that's what forensics is, right? Don't worry about the outside."

"Beds as well?"

"Yes, everything. And can you point out any objects that will yield fingerprints when you are finished?"

"I think I need a bit more info than that, don't you?"

"Sorry Larry, I can't tell you anything. Just examine the place covering all bases".

There were two bedrooms, a dining room, kitchen and one bathroom. I started in the hallway. The floor was tiled so I swept it and retained the sweepings as Exhibit 1, before pointing out the front door, light switches and ornaments on the hallway table as probable locations for fingerprints.

I examined each room, taking tapings from the chairs and the leather settee in the lounge as well as the carpet, and a control sample of fabric from a corner of the carpet. There were no signs of blood but I decided to test the carpet anyway using a reagent. Clean. Again, I pointed out surfaces that would yield finger marks.

The bedrooms were time-consuming because apart from the usual tapings and the search for blood and fibres, I also screened the bedding for traces of semen using a UV light. After the first bedroom I went back to the lounge and dining room and scanned the carpets and furniture with the UV light just to make sure I hadn't missed the obvious. Nothing. I then pointed out various items in the bathroom that would yield finger marks in addition to all the surfaces that were ideal for fingerprinting in any bathroom due to the shiny finish. I found no weapons of any description or evidence of a gun being fired.

To all intents and purposes the place was clean.

Too clean.

I wondered whether I was there to check on the cleaner, or to teach the cleaner how to clear up.

By the time I'd finished it was 1am and I had over forty exhibits.

I then looked at my 'keeper.'

"Am I making these exhibits mine our yours ?"

"Just leave them for me, I see the exhibit bags are labelled to identify where the exhibit came from, so nothing else is required"

"What about the address?"

"I will take care of that."

"And my contemporaneous notes?"

"You don't need any, your job is done," and with that the doorbell rang and my driver appeared to take me back to the Yard.

I arrived back at the Yard at 1.30am and returned to my car. Despite my keeper's claim that I didn't need to make any contemporaneous notes, I wrote them up anyway, including the date and time, and described the exhibits, the house and the people I'd met. 'It's my back,' I thought to myself, 'And there's nobody to watch it but me.'

And then the memory of Harold Wilson's apartment popped into my mind. Like the house I'd just examined, his home had been too clean. Could it be that I had been called to check on the cleanliness of a Black Operation to examine the home of a person of interest?

Then I thought of something that former Met Police Commissioner Sir Robert Mark had said back in the 1970s: "I protect the Establishment; I am the Establishment."

Four months later, I was asked to do the same thing again, at a different address in the East End, in exactly the same way. And then I wondered, what with the Security Services' increasingly active role on the front line fight against terrorism, if they kept asking for my help with jobs like this, perhaps, one day, there'd be a role for me there?

But that's another story…

# ACKNOWLEDGEMENTS

This book is dedicated to my wife, Jennifer, who not only shared me with The Job but supported me every step of the way.

I'd also like to thank Susi de Lacey for her enthusiasm, assistance and encouragement, and my former colleague, Colin Ambrose, Ret'd Senior SOCO, for assisting with some of the book's technical aspects.

50261047R00246

Made in the USA
Charleston, SC
19 December 2015